PUBLICATION DESIGN

PUBLICATION

Wm. C. Brown Company Publishers

Dubuque, Iowa

DESIGN *Roy Paul Nelson*

JOURNALISM SERIES

Consulting Editor:
Curtis D. MacDougall
Northwestern University

Copyright © 1972
Wm. C. Brown Company Publishers

Library of Congress Card Number: 78-176306
ISBN 0-697-04323-1

Second Printing, 1973

Printed in the United States of America

By Roy Paul Nelson

Publication Design
The Fourth Estate (with John L. Hulteng)
Visits with 30 Magazine Art Directors
The Design of Advertising
Fell's Guide to Commercial Art (with Byron Ferris)
Fell's Guide to the Art of Cartooning

Preface

Publication Design deals with a continuing problem in journalism: how to coordinate art and typography with content. Through text and illustration, the book suggests ways to make pages and spreads in magazines, newspapers, and books attractive and easy to read. As a book of techniques, it directs itself to potential and practicing art directors and designers and to editors who do their own designing.

It also directs itself to journalists in general, trying to build in them an appreciation for good graphic design. While these journalists may not be called upon to actually design and lay out pages, they may have the responsibility for hiring designers and approving their work. A goal of this book—perhaps it is an unrealistic goal—is to help editor and art director work together more harmoniously. Friction exists between the two on many publications: the editor suspects that art and distinctive typography detract from articles and stories; the art director thinks his editor is a visual illiterate.

The bibliographies at the ends of chapters 10 and 11 carry the names of a number of recent books on newspaper makeup and book design. But as the reader browses through these and all the other end-of-chapter bibliographies, he will find only one book dealing specifically with magazine design, and it is more a showcase of beautiful examples than an instruction book. The person wanting help on magazine design has had to rely largely on the many books on the broader subjects of typography and graphic design. This seems strange when you consider that magazines have proliferated in the 1960s and 1970s, and many of their editors have performed without professional design help. So while this book will deal with all the print media, it will concentrate on magazines.

Design is used here in its broadest sense. It means more than the layout of the pages, and it means more than the look of the book. It takes into account the plan and organization of the publication and what the publication is saying. The reader will find this book as concerned with the goals of the editor as with those of the art director.

Publication Design can serve as a textbook or supplemental reading for students of Publication Design and Production, Graphic Design, Graphic Arts, Typography, Magazine Editing, Newspaper Editing, Picture Editing, Book Publishing, Publishing Procedures, Business and Industrial Journalism, and Supervision of School Publications.

—RPN

University of Oregon

Contents

PUBLICATION DESIGN

Chapter 1
Emergence of magazine design

Books produced in fifteenth-century Italy, after movable type was developed by Johann Gutenberg in Germany, are prized today by museums and collectors as art of a high order. Bibliophiles see in these books a design and printing quality not found in latter-day publications.

Their excellence is all the more remarkable when you consider that the men of incunabula had to design their own types, cut them, make their own inks and in some instances their own papers, write their own books and do their own translating of the classics, set their own type, do their own printing, and sell their own product.

Or maybe that explains the excellence. With so proprietary an interest in the product, fifteenth-century artisans gave appearance and readability all necessary attention.

But when the demand for printing grew, printers found it expedient to mechanize. Some men designed and cut types—exclusively. Others set type—exclusively. Others ran presses—exclusively. Others wrote and edited copy, while still others took care of business matters. Specialization set in, and, inevitably, quality deteriorated.

By the time periodicals took their place alongside books as products of the press, page design was all but forgotten. Nobody elected to stay with the product through its various stages to see to it that it had, overall, the beauty and readability of earlier products of the press.

Then came photography and photoengraving—in the nineteenth century. As art was combined with type on the page, the need for coordination of these elements became apparent. Because art, when it was used, tended to dominate the page, the men responsible for fitting type and art together became known, first, as art editors and, later, as art directors.

Stand me now among the stars
by Samuel H. Miller

From the oratorio, "What Is Man?",
sung at the Seventh General Synod,
Boston, Mass., June 29, 1969,
Music by Ron Nelson.

When I consider thy heavens, the work of thy
fingers, the moon and the stars, which thou hast ordained—
What is man, that thou art mindful of him,
And the son of man that thou visitest him?
Thou hast made him a little lower than the angels
And hast crowned him with glory and honor.

Stand me now among the stars,
When my fingers reach.
Through tides of space and hidden fire
To hold the planets in my hand,
To steer new worlds amid the old,
To let my engines roar with the comets,
Stand me now among the stars.

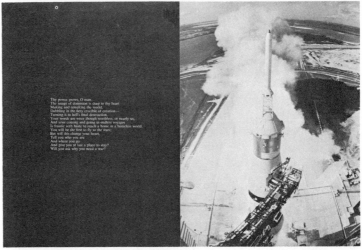

Thy power grows, O man.
The image of dominion is deep in thy heart
Making and remaking the world,
Dabbling in the fiery crucible of creation—
Turning it to hell's final destruction.
Your words are weet though worthless, or nearly so,
And your coming and going in endless voyages
Is frantic with haste to reach a home in a homeless world.
You will be the first to fly to the stars;
But will this change your heart,
Tell you who you are
And where you go
And give you at last a place to stay?
Will you ask why you need a star?

Do not forget, O man, in speed so desperate,
The end and origin so deep in you,
The past which follows like a shadow
Deeper than a shadow.
Built within your flesh
For memory or something deeper still,
So being man, the past is yours,
And you belong to that old beginning,
Oft forgotten but never lost, from which you rose
And to which you must return.
The ancient fend is in your bones;
The tempter rises in your heart;
The god you cannot find and wish to avoid
Will find you out;
And once again Eden's early strife
Will play itself beneath the wider skies
Where stars are apples in the sky.

What is man?
Dust of the earth, marked with God's sign,
Made for dominion, tangled and tortured,
Free but lost in the way!
Crowned with glory and honor,
Mingling the saint and the sinner,
Reshaping the earth but forever the same!
What is man? Driven by dreams;
What is man? Driven by hope;
What is man? Hungry for faith;
What is man? Lonely with doubt,
Crowned with glory and honor,
Mingling the saint and the sinner,
Free but lost in the way.

United Church Herald *art director Raymond Waites, Jr., was able to devote five spreads to a section from an oratorio, and here is how he made use of his space. For most spreads he devoted one page to copy (reversed on black) and one page to art. Note how art comes up strong at the end. No color; all black and white.*

The first magazine art director

No one can say who functioned as the first art editor or art director of a periodical. One of the first in this country, certainly, was Charles Parsons of the Harper & Brothers organization (now Harper & Row), publishers of books and magazines. It was Parsons who conceived the idea of gathering together a group of illustrators and schooling them in the needs of a publishing concern, and working with other artists on the outside as need for art increased at certain times of the year. He became a director of art.

Himself an illustrator of note, Parsons joined the staff at Harper's in 1863, serving twenty-six years. He directed artists for both the book- and magazine-publishing divisions of the company. Among his staffers were Winslow Homer, Thomas Nast, Edwin A. Abbey, and W. A. Rogers. Of Parsons, Rogers wrote: "Thanks to the clear vision and good common sense of wise old Charles Parsons, every man who came to Franklin Square [where the firm had offices]—and it was the Mecca of illustrators in those days—was encouraged to be true to his own ideas, to develop his own style."[1]

So great was Parsons' influence on commercial art of the late nineteenth century that artists referred to his department as "The Franklin Square School." As many as eight artists worked full time. Free-lancers, including Frederic Remington and Howard Pyle, took on special assignments.

By the 1880s, Parsons was able to pay free-lancers an average of $75 per illustration. For some works, he paid $150 or more.

Nearly all the illustrations had to be hand engraved on wood. It was after Parsons resigned in 1889 that photoengraving became a reality and illustration—including photos—became a vital part of most magazines. *Harper's Weekly* and *Harper's Magazine* were no longer alone as vehicles for illustrations. Every publication could run them.

Still, no one apparently thought to coordinate art with type to achieve real design in magazines.

The pioneering fashion magazines

The magazines that, as a group, pioneered in good design were, understandably, the fashion books—especially *Harper's Bazaar*.[2]

It was in 1913, after it had been purchased by William Randolph Hearst, that Erté, a designer for the theater, joined the staff. An illustrator in the manner of Aubrey Beardsley, Erté introduced an entirely new visual sensibility to the magazine.[3]

In the early 1930s a Russian-born designer, Alexey Brodovitch, became the art director. He sought to give the magazine what *Print* magazine called "a musical feeling, a rhythm resulting from the interaction of space and time—he wanted the magazine to read like a sheet of music. He and [Editor] Carmel Snow would dance around the pages spread

1. Quoted by Eugene Exman in *The House of Harper*, Harper & Row, Publishers, New York, 1967, p. 107.
2. Some of what follows in this chapter and some of chapter 2 appeared in a different form in the author's *Visits with 30 Magazine Art Directors*, published by the Education Committee of the Magazine Publishers Association, New York. Copyright 1969 by the Magazine Publishers Association. Reprinted by permission.
3. See "Harper's Bazaar at 100," *Print*, September–October 1967, pp. 42–49.

before them on the floor, trying to pick up the rhythm."

Brodovitch introduced to magazines the use of large blocks of white. For freshness, he used accomplished artists and photographers for kinds of work they had not tried before. At *Harper's Bazaar* he got Cartier-Bresson, Dali, Man Ray, and Richard Avedon to do fashions.

According to *Print*, Brodovitch "kept apprentices at his side much like an Old World master painter." One of his students, the photographer Irving Penn, has said: "All photographers are students of Brodovitch, whether they know it or not." Allen Hurlburt, director of design for Cowles Communications, has added: "This also applies to graphic designers." Brodovitch remained as art director for *Harper's Bazaar* until 1958.

Another leader in magazine design was Dr. M. F. Agha, who became art director of *Vanity Fair* in 1929. Hurlburt has said this of Dr. Agha: "He entered areas of editorial judgment long denied to artists and created a magazine that brought typography, illustration, photography, and page design into a cohesion that has rarely been equalled. After exposure to the severe test of more than thirty of the fastest changing years in history, the pages of *Vanity Fair* remain surprisingly fresh and exciting."[4] Hurlburt gives much credit, too, to Editor Frank Crowninshield for his "rare discernment and good taste."

Unfortunately, *Vanity Fair* became a Depression victim; but Dr. Agha continued his association with the Condé Nast organization until 1942 as art director of *Vogue* and *House and Garden*. Many of today's top designers trained under Dr. Agha.

Changes in the 1930s

Still, the well-designed magazine was an exception. Well into the 1930s, most American magazines fitted themselves together, newspaper-style; when there was a column that didn't quite reach the bottom of the page, the editor simply threw in a filler. If a visually oriented man was around, his job was primarily to buy illustrations, especially for the cover, and maybe to retouch photographs.

Two early-1930s books on magazine editing gave scant attention to art direction. John Bakeless in *Magazine Making* (Viking Press, New York, 1931) carried a six-page appendix on "Methods of Lay-Out." In it Bakeless discussed briefly a travel magazine that used "the daring device of running a picture across all of one page and part of another." The book itself mentioned "art editor" twice and recommended at least one

4. Quoted from *Magazines: USA*, the American Institute of Graphic Arts, New York, 1965. See Cleveland Amory and Frederic Bradlee (Editors), *Vanity Fair: A Cavalcade of the 1920s and 1930s*, Viking Press, New York, 1970.

such man for "a large, illustrated periodical." Bakeless said that magazines using no pictures "obviously do not require an art editor."

Lenox R. Lohr in *Magazine Publishing* (Williams & Wilkins Company, Baltimore, 1932) devoted a chapter to illustrations and another to "Mechanics of Editing," but in them he gave only six pages to "Make-Up of an Issue."

One of the first non-fashion magazines to be fully designed was *Fortune,* introduced in February 1930 at a bold one dollar per copy. The designer was T. M. Cleland, who later set the format for the experimental newspaper *PM.* And *Esquire,* when it started in 1933, started right out with an art director. But he was a cartoonist, John Groth, who filled a good part of the first issue with his own cartoons.

Several designers from the Bauhaus in Germany, fleeing Hitler, arrived in America in the early 1930s and influenced not only magazines but also advertising design. The Bauhaus emphasis was on the functional in design. The look was one of order and precision.

Among native Americans, Paul Rand, with *Apparel Arts,* and Bradbury Thompson, with *Mademoiselle* and several other magazines, were standouts as magazine designers.

And in the past thirty years

In the 1940s Alexey Brodovitch designed a magazine that, with breathtaking beauty, showed other art directors what a well-designed magazine could be. Called *Portfolio,* it lasted three issues. That it was "ahead of its time" is probably an appropriate appraisal. In the late 1940s and early 1950s *Flair* (Louis-Marie Eude and later Hershel Bramson, art directors), although not universally admired by other art directors, encouraged format experimentation. It also was short-lived. In the early 1960s *Show,* with Henry Wolf as art director, shook up magazine design thinking. Allen Hurlburt observed: "[Wolf's] imaginative cover ideas and the precise simplicity of his pages have begun to influence a new generation of designers."

Stimulated by these thrusts, the well-established magazines began paying more attention to design. Allen Hurlburt took over as *Look's* art director in 1953 and gradually built the magazine, from a design standpoint, into one of the most admired in America. After the mid-1950s and "Togetherness," Herbert Mayes, the new editor of *McCall's,* let his art director, Otto Storch, have a free hand: what Storch did with types and pictures prompted all magazines to make themselves more exciting visually. Prodded by what Arthur Paul was doing in design with the upstart *Playboy, Esquire* redesigned itself. For a time Henry Wolf helped out.

A one-page feature from Fleet Owner *(Bud Clarke, art editor). The right edge of the first line of the title lines up with the right edge of the photo; the left edge of the last word in the title lines up with the left edge of the photo. Paragraphing is accomplished by means of small boxes, which relate to the boxed photo. In all, a strongly unified page. (With permission from* Fleet Owner. *Copyright 1970 by McGraw-Hill, Inc. All rights reserved.)*

Allen Hurlburt has noted a change in the art director's function with the coming of television. Before TV, the function of the art director, in an agency or on a magazine, was simply "arranging things that were handed him." With story boards for TV, the art director provided ideas, and the copywriter filled in with words. The art director became more important. As his status improved in advertising agencies, it improved on magazines.

One of the important influences on magazine design in the 1960s in America was Push Pin Studios, New York. (A founder of Push Pin, Milton Glaser, is currently design director of *New York*.) The organization was described by a magazine for the book trade as "one of the pioneering forces in developing an imaginative contemporary style that has had a major influence on the direction of current visual communications on an international scale."[5] The same magazine quoted Jerome Snyder, art director of *Scientific American*, as saying that if imitation or plagiarism is any indication of flattery, Push Pin "is by far the most flattered group in contemporary graphics."[6] "The growing reputation has allowed Push Pin the luxury of a healthy snobbishness in their acceptance of assignments, and potential clients have been conditioned into calling on Push Pin only when they were ready to accept the excellence of their work without too many suggestions for 'improvement'," Henry Wolf writes in the Foreword to *The Push Pin Style*.[7]

Also wielding important influence on magazine design in the 1960s were two magazines in Europe, *Tuyonne* and *Twen*, art-directed by Willie Fleckhaus. Art directors on American magazines drew considerable inspiration from these and several other European magazines, including some published in Great Britain. It may be true that European art direction has lagged behind American art direction where advertising is concerned, but in the case of magazine art direction, it could be argued that Europe has been more innovative than America.

Magazines of the 1970s

In the 1960s magazine design had been dazzling and spectacular, but it seemed *fitted on* rather than incorporated into the content. *Print* called the look "stupifyingly shallow." In the 1970s, magazines seemed to enter a new era: the emphasis was on content.

Communication Arts and *Print* in 1970 both put out

---

5. "Louvre Holds Retrospective of Push Pin Studios' Graphics," *Publishers' Weekly*, April 13, 1970, p. 70.
6. *Ibid.*, p. 72.
7. Published by Communication Arts, Palo Alto, Calif., 1970.

special issues on magazine design. Both were critical of what they had seen in the 1960s. The magazine industry, they agreed, was in a bad way because it had not adjusted to the times—not in content, not in design. (*Communication Arts* was even disturbed about methods of auditing circulation and campaigns to get readers to resubscribe.)

Both agreed that flashy graphics often covered up for lack of any really meaningful content. Nor were the graphics of a kind to delight the eye.

The chief problems were those of slickness and sameness. *Print* said major magazines look alike because their art directors play musical chairs, moving from magazine to magazine, "spreading their best ideas and perpetuating their worst mistakes." Dugald Stermer, ex-art director for *Ramparts*, was quoted as saying, "This makes magazines very inbred, almost incestuous."

The hope of the 1970s seemed to lie with specialized publications.

". . . The magazines that are doing well (and a surprising number are doing very well indeed) are the ones that don't try to be all things to all people—that have well defined subject matter along with a well defined audience," said the editors of *Print*.[8]

In an interview conducted by Dick Coyne for *Communication Arts*, Henry Wolf described magazine design in this way: "There hasn't been anything really new in the past twenty years. Most of the magazines are very professional, very slick, and you can hardly tell which one you're looking at."

Allen Hurlburt was somewhat encouraged by what he saw in lesser publications. "There is something that started with the underground press and then got picked up in *Rolling Stone* and now it's being demonstrated in *Rags*. This kind of brutalist, rough paper, rough printing, roughly expresssed thing is as close as you can get to a trend in the physical appearance of magazines. Is this only happening because those magazines can't afford anything else? Do they dream of the day when they will be slick?"

Richard Hess, of Hess and/or Antupit, answered: "Unfortunately, too many of them do. And the terrible thing is that, when they round off the rough edges, all of that vitality seems to leak out."[9]

Writing in *Print*, Samuel Antupit also liked *Rolling Stone* ("It is designed and written by people it aims at. . . . The format is large and the design is loose."). The only other magazine he praised was *Harper's*. He noted its "gimmick-less layout,

8. "Magazines After McLuhan," *Print*, July/August 1970, p. 19.
9. "Magazines," *Communication Arts*, vol. 12, no. 4, 1970, p. 27.

Specialized magazines

Part of the impetus for better publication design today comes
from small magazines, especially the new ones. Their editors,
realizing that their readers are accustomed to exciting visuals
from sources other than magazines, attempt to make their
magazines just as exciting to look at as the new films, the new
products, the new paintings. These editors don't have to buck
tradition. They serve homogeneous audiences. They have less
to lose.

One specialized magazine that has proven to be a trend
setter is *Psychology Today*. In an early issue (January 1968)
Nicolas H. Charney, editor and publisher, credited the magazine's "lively new look in graphic design" to its then art
director, Donald K. Wright. "We think he was born with that

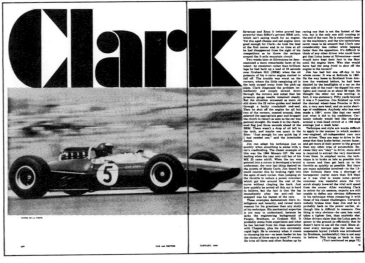

bemused and faraway look. . . . He has an incredible mental
file of graphic oddities. . . . And he is an unbudgeable perfec-
tionist in seeking the precise scene to illustrate every article."
By the time the magazine was eight issues old, the art director
had (1) tranquilized rabbits to make them better models for
the photographer, (2) traveled to Mexico to find some chessmen
for special faces, (3) packed in to the desert, climbed mountains,
traveled 100 miles along the railroad tracks "to find the necessary open land for just one photograph."

*A still contemporary layout
from a 1966 issue of* Car and
Driver *(Gene Butera, art director). The title, "Jim Clark," in
heavy, stenciled letters, starts
on one page and continues on
the next two pages, carrying
the reader with it. The top of
the x-height of the title on the
inside two pages aligns with the
tops of the columns of text.
The article begins in one size
type, then—newspaper style—
breaks down into two columns
set in a smaller size.*

10. Samuel N. Antupit, "Understanding Magazines," *Print*, July/August
1970, p. 23.

Company magazines

It is possible to make a generalization about another category: the house organs—or company magazines. Some of the very best graphic design is found in this group—and some of the very worst. In one respect, these magazines are an art director's dream. They carry no advertising around which editorial matter must wrap. The design theme can run through without interruption. That it does not do so in many house organs can be laid to the fact that their budgets preclude hiring an art director; they remain undesigned. And many others are designed in outside shops, inhibiting thorough integration of design and editorial matter.

Trade journals

Of all magazine groups, the trade journals—or businesspapers, as they prefer being called—are probably the least design conscious. Excepting those going to physicians, architects, and similiar professional groups, these magazines—especially the smaller ones—are "laid out" by editors rather than designed by art directors. These editors are newspaper-oriented in their choice of typefaces, arrangement of headlines, and use of photographs. Exceptions include McGraw-Hill's *Fleet Owner*.

"For many years publishers have used the words 'trade journals' as an excuse for poor taste and bad design," observes Bud Clarke, art editor of *Fleet Owner*.

The art editor or art director of these publications was either using the position as a stepping stone to consumer books or semi-retirement. And in many cases the editor wore two hats. . . . [The position of] art director was an unnecessary expense.

Now, however, times are changing. Our readers have more demands placed upon their "free" time, i.e., TV. The reading they do must be selective, interesting, and suited to their particular way of life.

This basically is why there is a small, but rapidly growing interest in design for the specialized reader. Many designers and art directors today feel that trade publications are a rewarding end in themselves rather than the means. Budgets and, of course, salaries are growing along with this interest, and a new era of good taste and design is emerging.[11]

11. Letter to the author from Bud Clarke, Aug. 17, 1970.

Suggested further reading

CHAPPELL, WARREN, *A Short History of the Printed Word*, Alfred A. Knopf, Inc., New York, 1970.

FEREBEE, ANN, *A History of Design*, Van Nostrand Reinhold Company, New York, 1970. (Covers Victorian, Art Nouveau, and Modern styles.)

HAMILTON, EDWARD A., *Graphic Design for the Computer Age: Visual Communication for All Media*, Van Nostrand Reinhold Company, New York, 1970. (By the art director of Time-Life Books.)

KIELL, NORMAN, ed., *Psychiatry and Psychology in the Visual Arts and Aesthetics: A Bibliography*, The University of Wisconsin Press, Madison, Wis., 1965.

MULLER-BROCKMANN, JOSEF, *The Development of Commercial Art*, Hastings House, Publishers, New York, 1968.

NELSON, ROY PAUL, and FERRIS, BYRON, *Fell's Guide to Commercial Art*, Frederick Fell, Inc., New York, 1966.

NIECE, ROBERT CLEMENS, *Art in Commerce and Industry*, Wm. C. Brown Company Publishers, Dubuque, Iowa, 1968.

REED, WALT, ed., *The Illustrator in America, 1900—1960's*, Reinhold Publishing Corporation, New York, 1967.

SOCIETY OF INDUSTRIAL ARTISTS AND DESIGNERS, *Designers in Britain: A Review of Graphic and Industrial Design*, Universe Books, New York, 1964.

WEISS, E. B., *The Communications Revolution*, Advertising Age, Chicago, 1967.

The Push Pin Style, Communication Arts Magazine, Palo Alto, Calif., 1970.

Art Direction, New York. (Monthly)

Communication Arts, Palo Alto, Calif. (Bi-monthly)

Print, New York. (Bi-monthly)

Chapter 2
The magazine art director

Bob Graf, editor of *Portrait* magazine published by General Telephone Company of California, has said: "[Magazines] are not just read, they are in a sense beheld; they are enjoyed beyond the power of the information they contain to cause enjoyment, and when they finally are discarded, it is with a sort of reluctance, as there is when you reach the end of a good book." If that is true, the art directors of these publications deserve much of the credit.

This chapter, based in part on the author's interviews with 30 magazine art directors on magazines in New York, Washington, San Francisco, Oakland, and Los Angeles, explores the role of art directors on American magazines. Whether the reader of this book designs his own magazine or employs an art director to do it for him, he needs to better understand and appreciate that role.

By any other name

As art directors have risen on magazine mastheads—in some cases to a spot just below that of the editor—they have become vaguely dissatisfied with their titles. No one has yet come up with a title that fully describes the art director's several functions: to buy and edit illustrations and photographs, choose typefaces, make production decisions, and design and lay out the magazine. Titles in use include *art editor, designer, design editor, design director, design consultant, type director, production editor, picture editor*. *Art director* remains as the most common title.

But *art director* does not connote concern with type and design. *Art editor*, the preferred title of the 1930s and 1940s, is worse: it brings to mind a person who runs a section of the magazine devoted to a discussion of painting and other of the fine arts. The old terms no longer seem adequate, especially now that some art directors are making editorial and management decisions.

Perhaps a magazine should have two chief editors: a *verbal editor* and a *visual editor*. Maybe *editorial director* and *design director*, used on some magazines, represent the best combination of titles.

Some art directors are flirting with the term "communicator." And not necessarily "visual communicator." The word "visual" in some art directors' circles is outmoded. On some magazines, the job is more than "visual." Art directors are interested in bringing *all* the senses into play—not just the sense of sight. The *feel* of the paper, for instance, is part of it.

Illustrating the trend: the National Society of Art Directors (representing advertising as well as editorial art directors) in 1967 decided to change its name to the National Society of Communicating Arts. Noting the change, *Printers' Ink* (which itself changed to *Marketing/Communications*) on August 11, 1967, observed: "The emergence of a new breed of creative generalist would be hard to document, at this point, but you have to think like a da Vinci before you can become one."

One for every magazine

Ideally, every magazine should have an art director. If he is not employed full time, he can be employed part time. If he isn't part of the magazine's own staff, he can be a free-lancer or a designer attached to a design studio.

James W. O'Bryan, art director of *National Review*, runs a design studio in the building and treats the magazine as one client, although a very special one.

William Delorme handles *Los Angeles* from his studio miles away from the magazine's editorial offices. The magazine takes 70 percent of his "working" time. He spends the other 30 percent on other graphic design assignments and on fine arts painting. "I put 'working' in quotes . . . because at least three weeks out of the month my time is my own. . . . The magazine work can be done at home in the evenings or on weekends. One week out of the month is practically round-the-clock labor on the magazine in order to meet printing deadlines." He visits the magazine for editorial conferences and to present his rough ideas and finished layouts. He sees photographers and illustrators in his studio.

Many company magazines are designed in this way, if not by studio designers, then by advertising agency art directors. But what about the small magazine that can't afford this help? What if the editor doesn't want to—or can't—do his own designing?

Samuel Antupit has said that if a magazine cannot afford an art director, it cannot afford to publish. That seems a little acrimonious. Bernard Quint suggests that an imaginative printer can do a lot for a magazine. Perhaps more than other magazines, the small magazine should hunt out such a printer and pay a little more for printing, if necessary. Quint feels that too many small publications are printed by printers who cut corners, making already dull periodicals even duller.

And if a magazine cannot afford an art director, it should at least hire a designer temporarily to set a simple, standard format that an editor can follow.

Certainly if a designer is not available, the editor should avoid unusual typography, trick photography, and complicated layouts. Some of the best-designed magazines are the simplest.

The art director's background

Schools do not offer adequate training programs for magazine art directors. The art schools—the commercial schools—are mostly advertising-oriented. The fine arts schools seem mostly interested in developing painters. The journalism schools by and large still think in terms of newspaper makeup.

So art directors come to magazines by circuitous routes. In the early history of magazine art direction, when the job involved primarily the purchasing of art work, they came largely from the ranks of illustrators. Even when type direction became a more important part of the job, the illustrator's background served him well. A good illustrator is as interested in the design of his painting as in the draftsmanship. The feel for design can be transferred from the canvas board to the printed page.

But today art directors increasingly come to magazines with backgrounds other than in illustration. They come with a more thorough knowledge of typography than their predecessors. Many neither draw nor paint. A few feel that a background in illustration would prejudice them in their art buying.

Advertising agency art direction provides a major training ground for magazine art directors. Art directors today move freely from agency to magazine jobs. This is surprising when you consider the unlikelihood of an advertising copywriter moving into a magazine editorial slot.

On small magazines, art directors may even find themselves assigned the job of designing ads for small firms who don't have their ads prepared by or placed through advertising agencies.

But the two jobs—magazine art direction and advertising art direction—are quite different. The magazine art director sees his mistakes in one issue, works to correct them in the next. He continues to polish a lasting product. His improvements are cumulative. The advertising designer, on the other hand, deals essentially with one-shots. And he has clients as well as readers to please. Henry Wolf in 1965 told why magazine work had it over advertising work:

> In a time when most activities are dictated by ulterior motives, designing a magazine provides a happy, if outmoded, thrill: to do something for its own sake and run out on a limb with it, waving.[1]

The art director's nature

Society has always regarded the artist with some suspicion. Even the art director—an artist gone businesslike—has a reputation for being "different." A *National Observer* article about art directors (Nov. 6, 1967) has Jo Foxworth, vice-president and creative director for Calkins & Holden advertising agency, saying this: "I know a $20,000-a-year art director who gleefully ragpicks his way through every secondhand clothing store on the Lower East Side, hunting for such treasures as pants with buttons instead of zippers and Army shirts from World War I. The other day when I had occasion to visit his agency, I couldn't tell what he had worn to work that day, because he was sitting cross-legged on his window sill, totally cocooned in an old Indian blanket that looked like a leftover from Custer's last stand. He said he was cold. And I'm sure he was; he was sitting on the air-conditioning outlet."

But there is probably less of the bizarre among magazine art directors than among advertising agency art directors. On magazines, routine is more pronounced, deadlines more regular.

Magazine art directors seem to have an aversion to group activity and meetings and hence avoid joining the art directors' clubs, which are dominated by the people in advertising. New York does have a Society of Publication Art Directors, but none of the art directors interviewed for this chapter mentioned it; some had never heard of it. At the end of the 1960s, however, the Society appeared to be more firmly established. More than 1,300 entries were submitted in its 1969 awards contest for good magazine design.

Nor do art directors have much interest in the social sciences and the tools available to them to measure the effectiveness of magazine design. Design is too much a matter of personal preference. Art directors do not want dictation from their editors, and certainly they don't want dictation from their readers.

Beyond page layout

Magazine art directors, like other journalists, have taken sides

---

1. But by 1967, settled into an advertising job, Wolf had changed his mind about magazines.

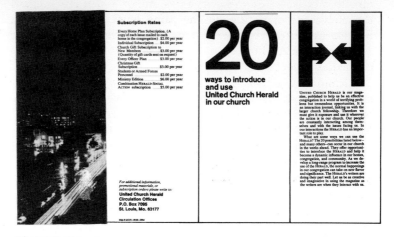

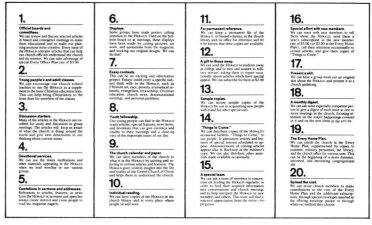

The art director of a small magazine doubles as a promotional art director. Both sides of a Raymond Waites-designed three-fold, eight-panel folder are shown here. The panel with the heading, "20 ways to introduce and use United Church Herald in our church," serves as the cover when the folder is folded down to fit into a No. 10 envelope. The side with the cover was printed in black and a second color: red.

in the struggle for social, economic, and political changes. The art director for *National Review*, James W. O'Bryan, worked free at first because he shared the philosophy of the *Review's* ultra-conservative publisher, William F. Buckley, Jr. Dugald Stermer played the important role he did on *Ramparts* because he believed in the leftist causes of that magazine. For the cover of one of its issues—in 1967—Stermer arranged for a photograph of four hands holding up burning draft cards. One of the hands was Stermer's. "If you're looking for an editorial in the usual place this month," said the magazine, "forget it. It's on the cover." The partners at Hess and/or Antupit, besides designing magazines and advertising and corporate pieces, handle a number of causes gratis or for low fees.

One thing becomes clear as you talk to art directors: they no longer are content merely to lay out pages. They argue— and the logic here is inescapable—that for a magazine to be effective both verbally and visually, its art director must be involved in the planning as well as the production stages. Art directors on some of the magazines, major and minor, regard themselves as operating on the same level as their editors. Some art directors say that if they didn't have a say about the policy their magazines adopt and the articles and stories their magazines accept, they would resign.

Richard Gangel, art director of *Sports Illustrated*, is part of a triumvirate which decides policy. He sees his role as primarily journalistic. Dugald Stermer, when he was art director of *Ramparts,* said he wouldn't be content to be "just an art director." He estimated that 80 percent of his time on the magazine was spent on editorial matters, including fund raising. Kenneth Stuart, art editor of *Reader's Digest,* checks articles before they are digested and suggests that certain sections be left in because they are illustrateable. Samuel Antupit on *Esquire* took an active role in accepting or rejecting manuscripts for publication.

Life with free-lancers

Among his other jobs, the art director acts as an art broker. It is up to him to find the right illustrator or photographer for every cover, article, and story. In most cases, he must deal with talent outside the organization.

The art director often finds the photographer more difficult than the illustrator to deal with. One reason may be that the art director does not recognize the photographer as an artist, and the photographer resents it. The art director is much more likely to edit the product of the photographer. He will crop a photo to fit the available space. He will even have it retouched. An illustration is different.

Mike Salisbury, art director of *West,* Sunday magazine of the Los Angeles *Times,* thinks photos are easy to edit and often exercises his right to edit them. But he thinks illustrations shouldn't be changed. Nor does he request an illustrator to make changes once he's submitted the work.

If the illustrator is sufficiently dependable, the art director does not even ask to see roughs first. Frank Kilker, former art editor of *The Saturday Evening Post,* tells the story of his acceptance of an illustration from a regular contributor, painted to fit a large area set aside for it in one of the layouts. But clearly, the illustration was not up to that artist's standard. Rather than throw it out, Kilker revamped the layout to make the illustration occupy a smaller space in the spread.

When an art director assigns a job to an illustrator, he often specifies a size and shape to fit an already existing layout. Seldom does the illustrator play a role in the selection of the typeface for the story title or in the placement of the title and body type on the page with his illustration. But of course art directors work differently with each of the various illustrators. An illustrator like Al Parker might well design the page or pages on which his illustration appears and incorporate the title into his painting. In vol. 2, no. 4, issue 8 (1967) of the quarterly *Lithopinion*, Parker tried his hand at redesigning the covers of eight leading magazines. Herbert R. Mayes, the magazine editor, evaluated the experimental covers: "When I had my first glimpse of these covers, my reaction was that my old and dear friend Al Parker had gone completely off his nut. At the end of two hours, my reaction was that my young-thinking friend Al Parker had done something that, in the years ahead, may knock the stuffings out of the traditional approach."

Life with the editor

It is understandable that the relationship between the editor and his art director is sometimes strained. The one is word-oriented, the other visual-oriented, and the two orientations are not necessarily compatible. The editor may actually consider display typography and pictures an *intrusion* on the text. Or the editor may expect the impossible of his art director, asking him to fit a particular story and set of photos together in too tight a space. The art director, on the other hand, may be more interested in showing off his tricks with type than in making his magazine readable. Or he may resort to the tired ways of laying out his pages while his editor is trying to move his magazine in some new direction.

The editor may think that his art director looks upon the job as one of solving design problems rather than of putting out a magazine to serve readers. He may put his art director in a class with the writer for *Architecture/West* who, in an article on the population explosion, wrote that if the present 2 percent per year increase continues, in 650 years "there will be merely one foot of space per person—a situation presenting unusual design problems." (*The New Yorker* picked up the quote and ran it under a "Department of Understatement" heading.)

Ideally, the editor and his art director should work as equal or near-equal members of a team, with the art director not only designing the magazine but also helping to make the decisions on editorial policy and content.

Art directors seem unimpressed by, if not hostile to, editors who have design backgrounds. Samuel Antupit thinks such editors, because their knowledge of design is likely to be superficial, are harder to work with than editors who know nothing about design and admit it. Editors who know design know only design clichés, he says.

Herb Lubalin agrees. Lubalin is an art director who will not take dictates from the editor on graphic matters. But neither does he interfere with strictly editorial decisions. Some of Lubalin's best work—and it's been masterful—has been done

for the rather sleazy publications of Ralph Ginzburg: *Eros,*
Fact, Avant Garde. He said once that "maybe the graphic excellence will rub off on editorial." He likes working with Ginzburg
because Ginzburg gives him a free hand to do what he likes.

Lubalin doesn't think editors, even on smaller magazines,
should do their own designing. "They are bad enough as
editors."

The art director and the writer

When free-lance writers submit articles for publication in small
magazines they often submit photographs, too. The photographs may be of only routine quality. It is up to the art director
to pick those that are usable and perhaps to ask that others be
retaken. Sometimes the art director can improve the composition of the photographs by cropping them. Sometimes he can
turn the photographs over to illustrators to use as guides for
paintings or drawings.

But free-lance writers almost never have anything to do with
the way their articles are laid out. Perhaps magazines should

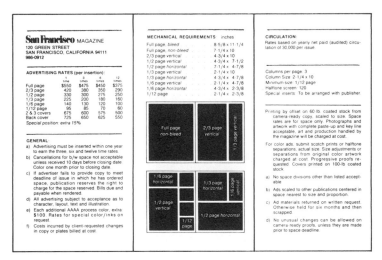

*Inside panels of San Francisco's
1969 rate card designed by art
director Dan Marr. Note his
helpful diagrams of ad sizes:
full page, ⅔ page, ⅓ page-
vertical, etc.*

make more of an effort to cooperate with writers on design
matters. In gathering examples of page design to be included in
this book, this author found it necessary to write to another
author to get reprint permission, even though the article would
be reproduced in a size too small to read. It was a routine
matter. But this is the note that came back: "I hope you don't
think me a prig, but I must refuse your request. Each to his own
taste—I happen to think the layout for my article . . . was an
abomination. Title (not mine), blurb, pictures and layout all
worked together to violate the theme of my article. I cannot

separate the layout from its purpose, and its purpose clearly was at odds with the text it supposedly was working with."

Some of the office stationery and a business card designed by United Church Herald's art director, Raymond Waites, Jr. Waites has coordinated the design of the stationery, forms, and papers of the office to the design of the magazine itself. Note that the business card is vertical rather than horizontal. The reverse side contains addresses, phone numbers, and other appropriate information. The reproduction does not show that part of the printing is in a second color: red.

When the art director takes half a loaf

On some magazines, the art director does not control the appearance of all the pages. James W. O'Bryan, for instance, does only the cover and the more important spreads for *National Review.*

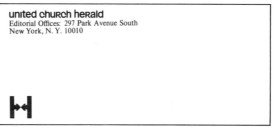

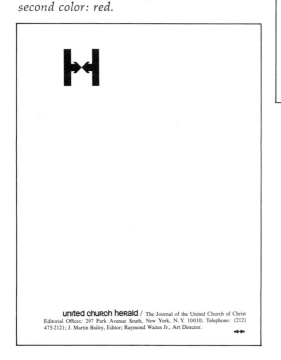

Recent art directors at *Esquire* have not done the covers: George Lois, an advertising art director and agency executive, does them. At *Newsweek*, art director Fred Lowry does not control the cover or the inside color section.

When he was at *True*, Norman P. Schoenfeld left back-of-the-book makeup to the back shop, a practice common among magazines. In a way, you could say the whole of *The New Yorker* is put together in this way.

When a magazine sees the need for a thorough revamping of its format, it is likely to call in an outsider to confer with its

We regret that your manuscript does not fit the HERALD's present production requirements and are therefore returning it to you.

Thank you for submitting it to us; we will welcome the opportunity to review other pieces of your writing from time to time.

The Editors

united church herald / The Journal of the United Church of Christ. Editorial Offices: 297 Park Avenue South, New York, N.Y. 10010 →←

The front cover and the inside of a 6 x 3¼ folder (the fold is at the top) that serves as the rejection slip for United Church Herald.

art director. Herb Lubalin twice in the 1960s came to the rescue of *The Saturday Evening Post* with ideas for revamping, but that was not enough to save the magazine.[2]

Raymond Waites, Jr., the innovative art director of the *United Church Herald,* finds it necessary to include in his publication Polaroid shots taken by near amateurs, yet manages to keep the pages attractive.

That he does not oversee *all* the pages; that he gives up control of the most important page of all, the cover; that he is willing to accept art and photography he knows to be inferior; that when redesign is considered it is some outsider who gets to remake the magazine—all this is rough on an art director's ego. That he is willing to live with these conditions is a tribute to his devotion to his magazine. And maybe it means that, like most of us, he's concerned about job security.

2. What Lubalin—and Henry Wolf, who worked with him—would like to have seen for the *Post:* a *Vogue*-size format, with side stitching; a return to *The Saturday Evening Post* full logo, but in a doctored Bookman face; heavier paper stock.

Tenure for the art director

All too many magazine art directors lack a feeling of job security. Between the time the author conducted his research into the role of art directors on American magazines and published his report with the Magazine Publishers Association, a two-year period, at least seven of the thirty art directors he interviewed had moved. *Art Direction* in an October 1969 editorial noted "a flurry of job changes by ADs of top consumer magazines" giving the magazine art director "all the stability and dignity of a major league baseball manager."

Some of the changes obviously were forced by top management people looking for scapegoats for dwindling circulations and loss of advertising revenue. But *Art Direction* admitted part of the problem lay with the art directors themselves. It recognized few great art directors compared to the late 1950s and early 1960s. It concluded that perhaps the top talent had been siphoned off into the film industry and TV.

"Today's magazines—with few exceptions—seem less exciting in content and appearance," *Art Direction* said.

Size of the art staff

On most magazines the art director is not so much a director as a doer. He is a one-man department.

On large magazines, the art director employs several assistants. When he was at *Life*, Bernard Quint had a staff of about twenty, not counting the picture editors. That *Life* comes out weekly makes so large an art staff necessary. Several are there to carry out the rough sketches of the art director, others to do keylines and assembly, others to handle production matters. *Look*, the biweekly, had about fifteen. The big monthlies operate with smaller staffs. Herb Bleiweiss, *Ladies' Home Journal*, has four assistants, but he uses them in a way different from most art directors: he lets each assistant handle all the details for a single article or story. It makes for unity within a feature, but it means the magazine lacks some unity overall.

Samuel Antupit, when he was at *Esquire*, had two assistants and a secretary. In his opinion, "the smaller the staff the better." (These figures do not include artists and designers in the advertising and promotion departments.)

The art director as illustrator

The smaller the magazine, the more likely the art director is to do his own illustration. Raymond Waites, Jr., does many of the illustrations for his magazine. Dugald Stermer did some illustrations for *Ramparts* while he was art director, causing

Norman Rockwell to remark: "I didn't know he was a painter as well as an art editor. Boy, he has it both ways." In 1971 Stermer did cover paintings for *Time*.

And for those who cannot draw, there is the camera. It was natural that the art director, working closely with the photographer, should take up the tool himself and do his own shooting. Perhaps the photographer missed a deadline. Perhaps the art director realized he had a better feel for proportion than the photographer had. Otto Storch became so intrigued with the camera that he gave up his job at *McCall's* to go into film work. The startling photo of a woman's thighs on the February, 1970, cover of *Harper's* was taken by that former magazine art director Henry Wolf.

Some art directors arrived on magazines by way of careers as illustrators. Kenneth Stuart, former art editor of *The Saturday Evening Post*, now art editor of *Reader's Digest*, is one. But Stuart as art editor did not employ Stuart as illustrator. Those who use their own art in magazines have some misgivings about it; but for some magazines, there is no budget for outside work. The art directors do what they must do.

But most art directors can't draw or paint well enough for publication. Samuel Antupit certainly does not consider himself an illustrator. "And I'm afraid to learn. I might be tempted to pick out people who did my kind of illustrating," he says.

Some art directors don't even design. They do only what their titles suggest: they direct. They feel their time is better spent working out solutions than actually executing them.

The art director as inventor

The best of the art directors develop a mechanical aptitude as well as a design sense. Sometimes the effect the art director wants can't be had with ordinary photographs of ordinary props.

For the first issue of the now-defunct *Careers Today*, published by *Psychology Today*, art director Don Wright, to illustrate "The University Womb," cut a womb-shaped hole in a piece of plywood; put supports under the plywood to bring it up from the floor; nailed sheets of clear mylar around the hole to form a well; filled the well with water; put a nude, sandled male in the well; and photographed the setup from the top.

Readers interested in how art directors get the effects they do will be interested in seeing *Advertising Techniques*, a monthly that usually carries one feature on special effects. Though these effects are achieved by advertising rather than magazine art directors, the techniques used can be applied to magazine design problems.

The influence of advertising

Magazine art directors take some inspiration, too, from their colleagues in advertising art direction. Henry Wolf, who left magazine art direction to become a principal in an advertising agency, thinks the best design these days can be found in the ads. Peter Palazzo, who designed *New York* when it was part of the New York *Herald Tribune,* thinks advertising has the best possibilities for graphic excellence.

Bernard Quint, formerly art director for *Life* and *McCall's,* thinks advertising design has had too much effect on magazine design. "The use of design for its own sake has increased in contemporary magazines in direct ratio to the lack of content."

When he was art editor of *The Saturday Evening Post,* Frank Kilker reported that whether or not an art director was acceptable to the advertising fraternity weighed heavily in the consideration of the editor who was about to hire him.

Most art directors interviewed for this chapter felt that advertising was setting the trends; magazine design was following. Herb Bleiweiss, of *Ladies' Home Journal,* thought otherwise. Mike Salisbury, of *West,* suggested that the trend-setting function moves back and forth between advertising and magazines, and that magazines would once again be in the forefront.

One thing all agreed on: advertising art directors are better paid. But in the opinion of Roger Waterman, former art director of *Kaiser News* and now art director of *Chevron USA,* advertising art directors are under more pressure and so *should* be better paid.

Attitudes toward magazine design

Art directors are quick to defend certain magazines that appear to have no design. They consider *The New Yorker,* for instance, handsome enough, although it doesn't even have an art director. Its visual excitement comes partly from its cartoons and spot drawings but mostly from the beautiful advertising it carries.

Art directors like a magazine to be unpretentious. A magazine, they feel, should be what it must be, and nothing more. The clean, no-nonsense, almost monotonous look of *Scientific American* is much admired by Herb Lubalin, who says of the magazine: "It makes no pretense at great design. But its design really works!"

The younger art directors are particularly outspoken about the necessity for honesty in design. One of them, Charles Rosner, whose experience has been mostly in design for social causes, has even criticized Herb Lubalin for work that is "over designed."[3]

3. Vance Johnson, "Charles Rosner," *Communication Arts,* vol. 12, no. 4, 1970, p. 75.

Major art directors are especially critical of trade journals and, among general circulation magazines, the publications of Time, Inc. Jerome Snyder, speaking at the University of Oregon, invited students to compare *Life* with *Paris Match*. *Paris Match*, he said, is what *Life* could be. (A dissenter is Mike Salisbury, art director of *West*, who greatly admired *Life* when Bernard Quint was art director. "I sent him a fan letter once," he told this author.)

Henry Wolf says, "Mass magazines today don't take time for aesthetics. Instead of real design they offer typographic gags. . . ." Remembering the 1950s as the golden age of magazine design, he adds, "There is less freedom now on magazines."

Samuel Antupit thinks magazines are hurt today by "screaming graphics," used by people who have nothing to say. Design should be clean and uncluttered. Pages should have the fewest possible distracting elements. And that includes illustrations used solely to break up columns of gray type.

"It bugs hell out of me to see a cartoon in the middle of a serious article in *Harper's*," he told *Newsweek*.[4]

If a magazine is beautiful, says Antupit, you can bet that either the magazine has no content or the magazine is about to die. "If meaningful photography, art and design are ever to become a part of American magazines," he has written,

the editors must reorient themselves. I do not know a single editor of any national magazine who does not view artwork either with genial contempt or as a threat.[5]

"Our magazines are over-designed and under-art directed," he observes.

Antupit draws a distinction between a designer and an art director.

An art director, to distinguish him from a designer, must concern himself with converting the verbal into the visual by exploring and controlling the use of photography, drawing, painting and typography within a magazine. By developing these elements he becomes a visual editor, interpreting and expressing the message of the magazine in visual terms. A designer is an arranger. He makes beautiful (if he's good) layouts which incorporate these elements. A designer's ultimate criteria, unfortunately, are the looks, not the meaning. A good art director may intentionally give the editor an ugly page if it best represents and expresses the material.[6]

Type preferences

The various art styles—the realistic, the stylized, the psyche-

4. "Magazine Doctor," *Newsweek*, Dec. 2, 1968, p. 56.
5. Samuel N. Antupit, "Laid Out and Laid Waste: On the Visual Violation of American Magazines," *The Antioch Review*, Spring 1969, p. 59.
6. *Ibid.*, p. 62.

delic, etc.—all find a place in American magazines. Some art directors prefer one style over another, but art directors are not united on what style is best.

They can better agree on what type styles are best. On almost every art director's list of beautiful and readable types is Times Roman, the face designed by Stanley Morison for the *Times* of London in the early 1930s and now generally available everywhere. It would be interesting to conduct a survey on the most used body type among the well-designed magazines; Times Roman would surely be at or near the top.

And almost all art directors appreciate the beauty of the newer sans serifs or gothics. There is disagreement over the readability of these in large blocks, but for article and story titles, the faces are greatly admired, provided the settings are tightly spaced.

One gets the impression, too, that art directors as a rule prefer the old style romans to the moderns.

Art directors, of course, see great differences between types that ordinary editors or laymen would miss. *Life* in the front of the book used to make extensive use of a face that looked a lot like Ultra Bodoni Italic—but call it that and art director Bernard Quint would have thrown you out of his office. The type was Normande, and indeed, on close inspection, one sees subtle differences between the two.

For all that, art directors are not very good on names of faces. This is especially true now that so many of the types are ordered in photolettering under new names. James W. O'Bryan was once asked what face he used for the logo for *National Review*, and he had to look it up. Turned out to be Albertus Titling.

The exercise of taste

When a new art director takes over a magazine, he immediately makes changes. What to the casual reader would seem unimportant might greatly disturb an art director: length of ruled lines, choice of body type, the logo, placement of captions, etc. "A change of editor or art director is reflected instantly in . . . [a magazine's] pages," Henry Wolf points out. "A magazine is still largely the extension of an individual idea, a peculiar personal vision."

While they would be slow to admit it, art directors in their choice of type and art and in their arrangement of these elements on a page lean heavily on what is fashionable. For a time the Bauhaus-inspired sans serifs are "in"; then the Swiss-inspired sans serifs. Everybody bleeds photographs for a time; then suddenly, everybody wants generous white margins around pictures. Letterspacing is thought to "open up" the typography, making it more pleasant to read; then close fitting of letters takes hold, to make it possible for the reader to grasp whole words rather than individual letters. For a time, all space divisions are planned so they'll be unequal; then spaces are divided equally, and new magazines come out in a square format rather than a golden proportion size. For a few years, the look is austere, simple, straight; then swash caps and column rules and gingerbread prevail. It is the rare art director who can resist adapting current art trends to his design: witness the psychedelic look on magazine pages at the end of the 1960s. A few art directors break away, rediscover old styles, come up with unused ones; and they become the leaders. In a few months, others are following.

"Let us . . . not delude ourselves that we are lastingly right," cautions Henry Wolf.

Once in a while an art director decides to go with the banal, the obvious, the square, or the discarded. An illustrator has passed his prime, his style outmoded. Very well, bring him back. He's the kind of an illustrator who would never have appeared in that magazine even when he was on top. But that makes him all the more appealing now. His shock value is worth a lot to the art director.

Or the art director picks one of the typefaces that, even when it was first released, was dismissed as gauche by discerning designers. He uses it now, smugly, cynically even.

A little of this goes a long way. The trouble with some magazines today is that their art directors, caught up in the revolutionary mood of the country, are breaking all the rules of typography and design. They insist on doing their own thing. Some of their experiments succeed, and less self-indulgent art directors probably will incorporate them into magazines of the future. But most of the experiments fail. They fail because the experimenters do not recognize *readability* as the one overriding requirement of magazine design.

Design is everything (almost)

A friend of the author's—a graphic designer—once set out to buy an electric razor for his wife. He went from store to store to check out each brand, and none suited him. He didn't try out the razors. He just looked at them.

He found one that pleased him—except for one thing: it had a little star fastened onto the face of it. "Do you have one without this star?" he asked the clerk. "The star spoils the design." Unfortunately, in this brand, they all came with stars; and the store lost a sale.

This man once went into a grocery store to make some routine purchases. On his rounds he spotted a package of seasoning. He didn't need the product, but with great delight he picked it off the shelf. He mentioned the exquisite beauty of the package—its clean color and crisp design—to the checker. She smiled indulgently. Here was some kind of a nut.

This is a man who buys his car not by looking under the hood but by stepping back and observing its lines. He is not alone in this. Herb Lubalin in 1967 told the author he drove a Mustang, not because he thought the car performed particularly well, but because, at the time, it was one of the few cars which was acceptable to him in its design.

Bob Pliskin, an art director and vice-president at Benton & Bowles, the advertising agency, says ". . . art directors always judge books by their covers. It's the one infallible way to tell a good book from a bad one. Appearances, after all, color our entire culture. Even ordinary non-visual people select homes, doctors, wives, and most . . . packaged products on appearances alone. . . ."[7]

But is the art director's preoccupation with the details of appearance worth it? Sometimes the art director wonders. George Lois, the *Esquire* cover artist, observes with some sadness that people don't really appreciate good looks in print. They have been trained to read, not see. Lois expresses the feeling of many art directors when he says, "I have got to live in a world of blind people."

7. *Art Direction*, January 1967, p. 39.

Suggested further reading

NELSON, ROY PAUL, *Visits with 30 Magazine Art Directors*, Magazine Publishers Association, New York, 1969.

Chapter 3
Formula and format

So much for the preliminaries.

This chapter and the chapters that follow will get to fundamentals: how to make a given magazine attractive and, more than that, readable. But before the designer can accomplish these objectives, he must first understand and appreciate the nature of his magazine.

The magazine's formula

Every magazine has its unique mixture of articles and stories. We call this its *formula*.

Most editors do not put their formulas down in words, but they and their staff members have a general understanding of what kind of material the magazine should run.

A prime consideration is: what is the purpose of the magazine? Does the magazine, like *Life* or *Iron Age*, exist to make money? Does it, like *The New Republic* or *National Review*, exist to spread ideas? Does it, like *Ford Times* or *Friends*, exist to do a public relations job? Does it, like *The Rotarian* or *Junior League Magazine*, exist to serve members of an organization?

Keeping the purpose in mind, the editor of any magazine works out a formula that best serves his intended audience. Or, if he's opinionated enough for it, or idealistic enough, he works out a formula that pleases him and hopes his audience will like it, too.

The bigger the magazine is to be and the more that is invested in it, the more likely the editor is to rely on opinion research of his intended audience when he works out his formula. The object is to win as many readers as possible within the area the magazine has staked out for itself.

Even magazines that operate in the same area have subtle differences that distinguish their formulas from one another.

Life places heavier emphasis on the sciences than *Look*, which was more interested in the social sciences. *Harper's* is more politically oriented than *The Atlantic*; *The Atlantic* is stronger in literature.

The New Yorker has worked out a formula that puts it into a unique category: humor mixed with social consciousness; great reporting done in a casual and sometimes rambling style; stories that have no endings; and, of course, the best gag cartoons anywhere. *New York*, a new magazine some people have compared to *The New Yorker*, really has quite a different formula: a merging of the so-called "new journalism" with helpful advice on how to survive in Manhattan.

Reader's Digest is another magazine with a unique formula: dogmatism, conservatism, optimism—and simplistic solutions to complicated problems. It is among the most consistent of magazines. Its formula has not changed basically since it was started in the early 1920s, nor, with the largest circulation of any magazine in the world, is it likely to.

The Number 2 magazine in any field is the one most likely to change its formula. When *Playboy* outstripped *Esquire* in the mid- to late-fifties, *Esquire* dropped the nudes and turned to more serious matters. When the women's magazines were locked in a death struggle in the mid-1950s, *McCall's*, second to *Ladies' Home Journal*, tried to spread out to include the entire family, calling itself a magazine of "Togetherness." The formula didn't work, and today *McCall's* and *Ladies' Home Journal* are very close again in formula, with *McCall's* perhaps the more cerebral. That *McCall's* now leads *Ladies' Home Journal* in circulation has been attributed to some of its imaginative art direction following the days of "Togetherness."

The formula stays pretty much the same from issue to issue. If a magazine feels it is losing its audience or if it wants to reach out for a new audience, it changes its formula. Sometimes the change is gradual. Sometimes—especially if the magazine is desperate—the change is sudden.

The magazine's format

When a magazine changes its formula it also usually changes its *format*. The format is the *looks* of the publication: its size, its shape, its arrangement of copy and pictures on the page. Format includes design.

Sometimes a magazine changes its format, or at least its design, without changing its formula.

Settling on a format

Ruari McLean makes two major points in *Magazine Design* (Oxford University Press, 1969). One is that it is more important to be noticeable than to be clean and dignified. The other is that it doesn't matter what the magazine looks like if its contents are not worth printing in the first place.

The second point seems obvious enough. The first point is arguable. It all depends on what kind of a magazine you are putting out and what kind of an audience you are serving.

Some magazines are best suited to visual excitement and novelty. Others are best suited to visual order.

Which means that magazine design boils down to two main schools, both with respected followings. The visually exciting magazines are represented, among others, by *McCall's* and the now-defunct *Look,* both pioneers in that kind of design. The highly ordered magazines are presented by *Sports Illustrated* and *Scientific American.* This does not mean that a magazine needs to belong exclusively to one school or the other. *Sports Illustrated,* for instance, within its ordered format, has much excitement in art and photography. It does mean that a magazine should be mostly one, or mostly the other. (More about this in chapter 5.)

The first thing an editor and art director must decide, then, is What kind of a look am I after? The purpose of the magazine should have something to do with the kind of look he settles for.

A magazine published to make a profit must lure and hold the reader with visually exciting pages. Illustrations are a must. These days such a magazine almost has to use color.

A magazine published to disseminate ideas can exist with a more austere format as, for example, *Foreign Affairs.* Its readers already believe; they don't have to be pampered. Such magazines generally will settle for a coarse, sometimes cheaper paper stock and pages unrelieved by illustrations.

A magazine published to do a public relations job needs a glossy appearance, if it is to go to outsiders; if it is an internal publication, it can be more homey.

A magazine published to serve members of an organization must watch closely what it spends. If the members of the organization pay fees to belong, they are not likely to appreciate getting an overly pretentious publication. The author once served as editor/art director of a magazine for members of a tight-fisted trade organization; his biggest challenge was to make the magazine look good without making it look expensive.

But purpose is only one factor in deciding format. Policy is another. Two magazines have as their policy the spreading of ideas: the one is leftist and activist; the other is moderately Republican. Will the same format serve both? Possibly. But if the tone of the articles is different, it seems reasonable to expect a difference, too, in the setting in which these articles are presented. Are there angry, vitriolic typefaces available for

Joe Bianco, editor of Northwest, *newspaper magazine of* The Oregonian, *has accepted the fact that his letterpress operation can't produce quality process color work. Yet he wants color on his covers. So he settles for bold, flat colors and a poster format. This example shows that the poster approach to covers can result in design of memorable quality. The artist: E. Bruce Dauner.*

headlines? There are. And what about artwork: are some drawing styles more militant than others? See the work that appeared in the 1930s in *New Masses*.[1]

In an interview in *Alma Mater* (April-June 1969), William Hamilton Jones, editor of the *Yale Alumni Magazine*, explains how he designs his magazine to make it appropriate to the university that publishes it. He makes two observations about Yale: (1) it is the second oldest American university and (2) it is exciting, creative, and innovative.

I . . . [want] to capture in the design this kind of tension between the old and the new, the traditional and the innovative. The way we have ended up doing it, for the most part, is using a very traditional typeface, Garamond, and doing some very untraditional things with it, like using a ragged setting and using white space in a way that it's not often used in magazines.

While opinion research may dictate in part a magazine's formula, it has little to do with deciding a magazine's format. Format is still largely a matter of personal preference, taste, and intuition; and that's what makes format so challenging a topic.

Anything goes

Conditions beyond the control of the designer may dictate the choice of format. When a strike in 1964 made a regular magazine impossible for Vail-Ballou Press, Inc., Binghamton, N.Y., a printing and manufacturing firm for the book trade, it brought out its house organ in galley proof form as an emergency measure. The "publication" was 5" x 21", single column. The format seemed particularly appropriate for this particular company. The circulation, after all, was only 600.

Editor L. Jeanette Clarke said at the time: "No company should feel that if it can't have a breath-taking, expensive magazine, newsletter or tabloid it should have none at all. To a large extent employees are captive readers." She said that because her readers are curious, they don't have to be lured by fancy trimmings.

Another strange format was introduced by *Datebook*, a teenyboppers' magazine, now defunct. To create the effect of two magazines in one, *Datebook* carried a front cover at both ends. The teen-age reader worked her way through half the magazine, came to an upside-down page, closed the magazine and turned to the other cover, and worked her way through that half.

Format innovation was one of the selling points of *Flair* when it was being published in the early 1950s. The editors

1. A source is Joseph North, ed., *New Masses: An Anthology of the Rebel Thirties*, International Publishers, New York, 1969.

constantly titillated readers with die-cut covers, inserts of sizes different from the page size, sections inside the book printed on unusual paper stocks, and so on. These practices live on in other magazines, but the editor who resorts to them is advised to check first with the post office, where regulations change frequently on what is allowed under second-class and bulk-rate mailing permits.

What design can do

Perhaps it was their impecuniosity. Perhaps it was the fact that their progressivism existed only in the political arena. (When it comes to design, the most radical of editors seem often to be the most reactionary.) At any rate, the history of journalism records the names of a number of editors who were able to build and hold audiences for publications that, from a design standpoint, had the grace of a row of neon signs or, at best, had no design at all. One remembers Lyle Stuart's *Expose* and *Independent* and George Seldes's *In Fact*. One thinks of I. F. Stone's newsletter.

As Professor Curtis D. MacDougall of Northwestern University has observed: "Strong editorial material can overcome bad design. On the other hand, bad design can't kill good contents."

But why give editorial matter the additional burden of bad design? The job of communicating is already difficult enough. Readers won't recognize bad design necessarily as bad design; they just won't be comfortable with it.

Good design, by itself, can't make a publication useful or important, but combined with well-conceived, well-reasoned, and well-written content, it can help.

Design and personality

How a publication looks should not be dictated by taste alone but by a knowledge of the personalities of typefaces and an understanding of how, when they are combined with other elements on a page, they affect the mood and "color" of the page.

Here are some moods an editor might want and some suggestions on how his art director can achieve them:

1. *Dignity.* Use old roman typefaces, centered headings and art, generous amounts of white space, medium-size photos or paintings, or drawings made to resemble woodcuts.

2. *Power.* Use bold sans serif typefaces, boldface body copy, flush-left headings, large, black photos or drawings made with lithographic crayons.

3. *Grace.* Use italic with swash caps or script types, light-face body copy with unjustified (ragged edge) right-hand mar-

gins, carefully composed photographs or wash drawings, an uncrowded look.

4. *Excitement.* Use a mixture of typefaces, color, close cropping of pictures, an unbalanced and crowded page.

5. *Precision.* Use the newer sans serifs or a slab serif for headings and body copy, sharp-focus photos or tight line drawings, horizontal or vertical ruled lines, highly organized design based on a grid system.

These suggestions are offered only as a starting point. Obviously, an experienced art director would find other ways to establish a correct mood. He could, in fact, take a type or a design approach associated with one mood and apply it successfully to another. For instance, in the hands of a good art director, old roman type, with its built-in dignity and grace, could be enlisted to establish a mood of excitement or even power.

Restyling

This book has already made the point that the publication undertaking a revision of format and design is usually a publication worried about dwindling circulation. But not always. The New York *Times* recently updated the design of its Sunday magazine and the book review and other of its Sunday sections, notably "The Week In Review," and it made these changes while yet a leading newspaper. It was a sign of progressive spirit on the paper rather than one of desperation. When another leading newspaper, the Louisville *Courier-Journal* and its sister publication, the Louisville *Times,* changed to a better looking six-column format, *Columbia Journalism Review* (Fall 1965) commented: "Abrupt changes are common among teetering publications; it is a bold act for a prosperous organization to attempt improvements on an already successful format."

Feeling the need of a change in format, the editor and art director may find, on getting into it, that the old way of doing things wasn't so bad after all. A case in point is *Advertising Age.* Many readers, including this author, have felt the magazine has needed a face-lifting. Its editors apparently felt the same way.

In 1966 they called in John Peter to consider changing the looks of the magazine. At first, Peter offered a multiplicity of suggestions for changes. "But the more he and our editors discussed the matter, the more they all agreed that only a minimum of change should be made—that basically, the typographic dress we've been using for 15 years or more was still pretty sound," the magazine said in a 1967 statement. A weekly, the magazine is really a news magazine; and so it wants a newspaper look.

Peter did do these things:

He eliminated column rules.

He modernized the logo, using a condensed Clarendon, a better looking slab serif type than the more standard slab serif the magazine had been using.

He modernized (read that: *simplified*) the standing heads.

In 1971 *Advertising Age* made another modest change by substituting a modern sans serif for the slab serif it had been using for its heads.

Christianity and Crisis is another magazine that thought it needed a complete change, and then decided against it. The magazine gave full freedom to two designers to make major changes. The changes they recommended were trivial. They came up with a new logo and a new masthead, and that's about all. One of the designers, Robert Newman, was quoted in the May 15, 1967, issue: "While all avenues were open, we decided not to change it very much. We concluded that the magazine is what it seems to be, which is rare and a virtue in typographic design."

Most art directors change the looks of their magazines gradually, even when they feel changes are long overdue; even when they feel that the changes must be substantial. In other words, they *educate* their audiences to good design, slowly, surely, patiently. In many cases the problem of visual illiteracy is not so much the reader's as the editor's, and the education begins there.

Only when a magazine desperately needs to change its image should it undertake sudden change. Consider *The Saturday Evening Post*. The last sudden change, just before it died, may have been necessary, but a few years earlier, in 1962, a sudden change left readers gasping. Long-time followers were irate, hurt, or at least puzzled; the new ones didn't come running, as the *Post* had hoped.

The secret is to hold on to old readers with familiar typographic landmarks while luring new readers with innovation.

When restyling, it is a good idea, even if the magazine has a good art director, to bring in an outside designer for consultation purposes. In many cases, the outsider can see things the art director, too close to the job, cannot see. In some cases, the outsider does the complete restyling job. The permanent art director follows through with the outsider's suggestions.

The art director finds restyling time a good time to reconsider all current design and production practices. Can he save money for his magazine by changing or dropping some of the practices? For instance: are initial letters at the beginnings of articles necessary to the design of the magazine? If their value is marginal, they should be abandoned. They do add to typesetting costs.

Are bleeds necessary?

And what about page size? Would a slight change there save paper or mailing costs?

The fading American newspaper format

Chapter 10 describes the move made by some newspapers away from the traditional 8-column newspaper format to a 6-column format with more of a magazine look: more white space, bigger pictures, a horizontal look. Some papers are changing from the full-size newspaper page to a page about half that size: the tabloid format.

At the same time, magazines that have appeared in tabloid format are going to a smaller format; they are trying to look more like magazines. This is especially true of internal house organs. While changing their looks they are deemphasizing short news items in favor of better-developed features.

This is good. Most of these publications come out monthly or even less frequently, so it is not only impractical, but impossible for their stories to be timely. A news style does not become these publications.

The change from tabloid to magazine format dramatizes the change of policy.

James Russell, editor of *Bulletin*, published by the Central Hudson Gas & Electric Corp., is glad he changed. He says the tabloid is a jigsaw puzzle, requiring the editor to wait until all copy and pictures are together before starting his layout. ". . . And how does one know just when enough copy is on hand for a particular issue?" Russell changed from the newspaper format to a 9 x 12 magazine, and now goes in heavily for features.[2]

But house organ editors who change find some disadvantages in magazine pages. They get better display, yes, but it comes by increasing the amount of white space, leaving less room for stories. And the magazine, in contrast to the newspaper, has a tendency to look a little more like propaganda from management.

Magazine page sizes

Magazines come in three basic sizes:
1. *Life*-size, roughly $10\frac{1}{2}$ x 13.
2. *Time*-size, roughly $8\frac{1}{2}$ x 11.
3. *Reader's Digest*-size, roughly $5\frac{1}{2}$ x $7\frac{1}{2}$.

By far the most popular size is $8\frac{1}{2}$ x 11. Most house organs, trade journals, and many slicks come in this size.

2. See James Russell, "The Tabloid is a Pain in the Neck," *Editor's Notebook*, September–October 1967, pp. 4, 5.

These three sizes aren't the only ones. *Small World*, published by Volkswagen, comes in an appropriately small 6 x 9 size. *GF News*, published by General Foods, comes in—or has come in—a 7½ x 9½ size. *IFFer*, published by International Flavors & Fragrances, Inc., is 7 x 10. *UI News*, published by United Illuminating Co., is 9 x 12. *Famous Photographers Magazine* is 8½ x 13. Some house organs, especially for internal audiences, come in newspaper tabloid format (roughly 11 x 17).

Magazines almost always choose a page size with a width-depth ratio that approximates the "golden mean," or roughly 3:5 (the author in this book will always mention width first). And the page almost always is vertical. (A magazine not dependent upon advertising should consider the novelty and even the design advantages of a 5:3 page. Opened out, the magazine would be unusually horizontal.)

A few magazines in recent years, along with some books—particularly art books—have gone for a square format. *Avant Garde*, an 11 x 11 publication, is one. But because it uses a standard-cut paper stock, there is some waste. The magazine uses the leftover odd-size sheets for its direct mail advertising campaigns.

It is possible to order paper specially cut to fit any size, thus eliminating waste.

Whatever size page a magazine adopts, if it contains advertising, it should provide column widths and lengths that are compatible with other magazines in the field. An advertising agency doesn't like to custom design each ad for every magazine scheduled to run it. The reason *Media/Scope* went to an oversize format in the late 1960s was probably to make it easier for the advertiser who would buy *Advertising Age* to also buy equivalent space in *Media/Scope* without need for redesigning. Unfortunately, the change in size was not enough to save *Media/Scope*.

In late 1970 *Ladies' Home Journal* took a chance when it decided to stay with its large format.[3] *McCall's* had announced it was going to the smaller size of *Cosmopolitan*, *Good Housekeeping*, *Family Circle*, and *Woman's Day*. It meant agencies would have to prepare special plates for *LHJ*. It also meant the magazine couldn't take advantage of lower postal rates.

Lithopinion, the graphic arts and public affairs quarterly of Local One, Amalgamated Lithographers of America, changes format from issue to issue to "illuminate the versatility of lithography by example." Vol. 1, No. 4 (1966), for example, was 7 x 12, with one column of copy per page set off with wide margins of white. On the other hand, about the *only thing* that stays the same for *Kaiser News* is the page size: 8½ x 11. It

3. " 'Journal' to Keep Large Page Size," *Advertising Age*, Oct. 26, 1970, p. 61.

constantly changes design, frequency of publication, and printers. "What we are striving for is continuity through change," says Editor Don Fabun.[4]

The page size, of course, seriously affects the design. Most art directors feel that a *Life*-size book is easier to design than a *Time*-size book. Certainly a *Life* or *Time* page is easier to design than a *Reader's Digest* page. Ralph Hudgins, art director of *Westward* (5½ x 7½), finds his pages rather difficult to work with, but he says that he gets satisfaction in coming up with effective layouts within the limitations of the format. His pages are sometimes crammed, but there is an excitement about them.

An advantage of the *Digest* size is that it is close to book format, and readers have more of a tendency to save the magazine. Portability, too, is an important consideration. The *Digest* size was adopted by magazines originally, of course, to fit the pocket.

The grid

For any kind of a format some kind of a grid is almost mandatory. A grid, made up of vertical and horizontal lines, sets the limits of printing areas. It is usually a printed two-page spread with lines ruled in to show the edges of the pages, edges on the outside of the pages to indicate bleeds, the place for folios, and columns for body copy. The columns are often prepared with a series of ruled lines, one for the bottom of each line of type.

The art director draws up a master grid in India ink, and the printer runs enough of them, in a light blue or gray ink, to last a year or two. The printed grids can be used for both rough layouts and finished pasteups.

For a more formal looking publication, with highly organized pages, a more detailed grid is called for. It is calibrated not only in columns and lines for copy but also in areas for pictures and headings. Areas for pictures are marked off in dotted lines to distinguish them from type areas.

One grid system involves the dividing of the pages into squares, which in the design can be gathered into quarters, thirds, or halves of pages. Under this system, all headings rest on a line in the grid, and all photos and columns of copy occupy one or more squares.

Width of the columns

How wide should a column of type be?

4. Don Fabun, "Dedicated to Human Questions," *DA: The Paper Quarterly for the Graphic Arts*, Second Quarter, 1970, p. 8.

Well, any width, really. Just remember: the wider the column, the bigger the type should be.

An oft-stated rule for length of line is 1½ alphabets of lowercase letters, or 39 characters. The rule is too restrictive. George A. Stevenson in *Graphic Arts Encyclopedia* (McGraw-Hill, 1968) lays down the 39-character rule and in a column of type which is itself more than 60 characters wide!

A column can be a little less than 39 characters wide, as in a newspaper, or even more than 60, as in some books. It depends to some extent on the age of the reader. It depends also on the mood the magazine is trying to create.

If the magazine wants to create a mood of urgency, narrow, 39-character columns are best. Narrow columns with column rules say "News!" Wider columns suggest dignity and stability.

There is no reason why a magazine can't have some narrow-column pages and some wide-column pages. A *Time*-size magazine, for instance, can run two columns per page for part of the book, and three columns per page for the remainder.

Body copy is easier to read, ordinarily, when it is leaded one or two points. Leading depends upon the typeface used. Types with large x-heights need more leading than types with small x-heights. (More about this in chapter 6.)

The lineup of magazine pages

The magazine designer arranges his articles and stories a little like a baseball manager arranges his batting lineup. In baseball, the lineup has traditionally started off with a man who gets singles consistently. The second one up is a good bunter; the third one another consistent hitter, but one who more often gets extra-base hits; the fourth one a home-run king; and so on.

The lead-off article in a magazine may not be the blockbuster; it may be a more routine kind of an article. The second piece might be entertaining. The third piece might be cerebral. And so on. The editor—and his art director—strive for change of pace from feature to feature.

When magazine articles and stories are not arranged by kind in the magazine proper, the arranging is usually done in the table of contents at the front of the book. There all the articles are grouped together; all the short stories are grouped together; all the regular departments or columns are grouped together. Some magazines even carry a separate table of contents of advertisements listed alphabetically at the back of the book.

Editors—and advertisers—know that most readers read magazines front to back, but others—especially the browsers—read them from back to front. So far as advertisers are concerned, the best display impact is found in the first part of the magazine on right-hand pages; the best impact for the last part of the magazine, especially if it is side-stitched, is found on the left-hand pages. Most advertisers consider the first part of the magazine more important than the last half, and right-hand pages for them are highly desirable. They often accompany their insertion orders with the note: "Up-front, right-hand placement urgently requested." They don't always get it.

Convinced that many readers work through the magazine from back to front, some editors start editorials or articles on a back page and continue them on preceding pages. *U.S. News and World Report*, when it runs a long editorial by David Lawrence, does this. So does one of the hunting and fishing magazines. *Esquire* follows a maddening practice of starting articles or stories in the middle or back part of the book and continuing them on pages near the front.

Some of *The New Yorker's* best articles start in the last half of the magazine.

But articles and stories in most magazines begin in the first half of the book. Most editors and art directors, given a choice, would prefer a spread (two facing pages) for each opening, but this is not always possible. When they start a feature on just the right-hand page, they favor giving a rather gray appearance to the tail end of the article before it. This assures the new opening more impact.

Page numbering

The reader will thank his art director for leaving room on every page for page numbers. The art director will make exceptions only for full-page bleed photos or advertisements. Even then, the reader would prefer the numbers. Right-hand pages are always odd-numbered, of course; left-hand pages are even-numbered.

When the art director has a last-minute signature to insert and the other pages are already printed with numbers, he can number the insert pages with letters. For instance: if the last numbered page in the signature before the new one is 48, the first page of the new signature would be 48a, the next page 48b, and so on. You see this numbering system used in the slicks.

Some magazines, embarrassed because of the thinness of the issues and not wanting the reader to realize they are only 24- or 36- or 48-page magazines, start numbering the pages from the first issue of the year and carry through the numbering until the last issue of the year. The reader can pick up an issue in July, for instance, and find himself at the beginning of the issue with, say, page 172. Some of the opinion magazines use this system. They might argue that they do it because the issues are part of a volume, and such numbering is an aid to the researcher.

Page numbering for some magazines starts on the cover and

for other magazines on the first right-hand page after the cover. It is the embarrassingly thin magazine that considers its cover Page 1.

A magazine's thickness

Most magazines let the amount of advertising dictate the number of pages of any particular issue. The more ads the magazine gets, the more pages it runs. Its thickest issues are in late fall, before Christmas. Its thinnest issues are right after the first of the year and in the middle of the summer. The ratio of ad space to editorial space, ideally, runs 70:30. For some magazines, it runs closer to 50:50 or even 40:60. When the ratio gets that low, the magazine is in trouble.

A few magazines, *Newsweek* among them, offer readers the same amount of editorial matter issue after issue. Only the amount of advertising changes. A magazine as departmentalized as *Newsweek* almost has to operate like that.

Magazines that do not contain advertising often run the same number of pages issue after issue. House organs fall into this category. And, because they contain so little advertising, so do opinion magazines.

The number of pages for most magazines runs to 32—two 16-page signatures. A signature is a collection of pages printed on one large sheet of paper. After the printing, the sheet is folded down to page size and trimmed. Signatures come in multiples of four, or eight, or sixteen, or thirty-two, depending upon the size of the page and the size of the press used to print the magazine.

If a magazine has a cover on a heavier stock—a separate cover—that's another four-page signature. Wrap it around two 16-page signatures and you have a 36-page magazine.

The back of the book

Every editor and art director is concerned about the back of the book and how to make it as attractive as the front.

Jan V. White, a magazine design consultant, notes that the "compulsion to make columnar matter have the same exciting flavor as feature matter seems irresistible . . . even though it is like shooting at hummingbirds with howitzers." He says:

> Mr. Editor, you work too hard. You believe the same approaches will solve all problems, dissimilar though the problems be. Thus you force yourself to apply to minor items in fractional pages the same journalistic flair appropriate to major feature stories, and you get frustrated when you don't succeed.[5]

5. Jan V. White, "Theory of the Dinner Jackets," *Better Editing*, Winter 1967, p. 19.

So White recommends pigeonholing back-of-the-book items to make them easy for the reader to find. Organize the material into "simple patterns easily discerned. And in the front and back of the book it is even more essential . . . to make . . . editorial matter stand away from the ads."[6]

Those # ! % & ads!

One problem the art director of most magazines faces will probably never be solved. That is the problem of ads and their intrusion into the editorial portion of the magazine. Advertisers do not have enough confidence in their ads to let them stand on their own merit. They do not want them buried in a sea of advertising. They insist that, instead, their ads be placed next to "reading matter" so that readers who otherwise would ignore the ads will wander into them, if only by mistake.

This means that only a few pages in each magazine are free of advertising. These are the pages the designer concentrates on. Here he has room to innovate. Here he applies the principles of design to solve visual problems. The other areas to be designed are nothing more than bands of white separating and breaking up the ads. On some magazines, ads are allowed to float in the middle of the pages. There is not much the designer can do to enliven such pages. If the art director were to succeed, he would detract from the advertising.

William Fadiman in an essay in "Phoenix Nest," a column in the *Saturday Review* for Feb. 22, 1969, shows what it's like to begin a short story in a magazine and follow it through the ads. From his first paragraph:

Halfway up the steps . . . established since 1848 . . . he stopped to think of her . . . rugged endurance, dependable performance, and low operating costs. He finally knocked at the door determined to . . . ask for it by name. She opened the door slowly . . . and could not help admiring his manly form . . . built of mahogony and reinforced at the corners.

It was amusing comment on the design of American magazines made all the more striking by *Saturday Review* itself which, unintentionally, stuck a full-page ad in the middle of it, with this result: "Darling, he interrupted with a . . . Color Slide Art Lecture in Your Home for $1."

Floating ads, as *The Saturday Evening Post* used to run, and checkerboard ads, as *Esquire* has run (see the Lord Buxton belt ad on pages 105 and 106 of the December, 1968, issue), and other odd shapes or placement make back-of-the-book design even more difficult. But magazines in general have shied away from the step-up half pyramid of ads that newspapers put on

6. *Ibid.*, p. 20.

their inside pages. At least designers of back-of-the-book material have rectangles to work with.

It is important for art directors to make editorial matter look different from advertising matter. This is why most magazines let the advertisers have all the display—the art, the color, the big type—on the back pages and content themselves with solid, gray type broken up by quiet subheadings and column headings. This is why publications run the slug line, "An Advertisement," over any ad designed to look like an editorial page. The reader deserves the warning.

Magazine binding

By definition, a magazine is a bound publication of eight or more pages issued on a regular basis more often than once a year. Not all publications are bound. Newspapers consist of unbound sheets of paper folded and wrapped loosely around other folded sheets. Sometimes a newspaper carries a single sheet, printed on both sides, slipped inside one of the four-page "signatures."

At the least pretentious level a publication may consist of a single folded sheet of four pages. Or it may consist of a single sheet, unfolded, printed on both sides. Or it may consist of several sheets held together by a staple in one corner or by a couple of staples at the side.

There are several kinds of bindings, but only two really work for most magazines—saddle stapling (let's call it saddle stitching) and side stapling (let's call it side stitching).

The big advantage of saddle stitching is that the magazine opens up easily and lies flat on the table or desk. Readers can tear out pages they want to save.

And a saddle-stitched magazine may be easier to design. For instance, you can more easily run pictures and type across the gutter. When *Harper's* went from side stitching to saddle stitching, it said, in its announcement, it was doing it for design reasons. *The Atlantic* soon followed with a saddle-stitched format.

Side stitching, on the other hand, makes for a more permanent binding. It suggests to the reader: this magazine ought to be kept. If the editor wants to make it easy for his reader to tear out articles, he can have the pages perforated. Side stitching is especially recommended for magazines of many pages. Any reader can testify that the December issues of magazines like *Playboy*, *The New Yorker*, and *Sunset*, swollen with advertising, soon come apart in their hands.

After World War II *Reader's Digest* experimented with perfect binding—binding without staples—and today the *Digest* and several other major magazines are bound in this way.

It took printers long enough to admit that offset lithography deserved admittance to the ranks of printing processes, to take its place with letterpress and gravure. Printers are not likely to further open the gates to grant admittance to the various duplicating processes.

Duplicating, in contrast to printing, produces only a few hundred copies per master. And even though the quality is inferior to printing, the product of the duplicator may be just as important to readers, and it may command just as much respect.

Chief among the duplicating processes, so far as publications are concerned, are spirit duplicating and mimeographing. In spirit duplicating, also called fluid duplicating, the image is typed or drawn on a master backed by an aniline-dye carbon sheet. A deposit of dye is transferred to the back of the master, which is used to do the printing. In mimeographing, a stencil permits ink to pass from a cylinder to the paper. Although it is possible to make stencils electronically for a mimeograph machine, both spirit duplicators and mimeograph machines reproduce successfully only typewritten copy and simple line drawings.

The publication thus produced can be simple, clean, and easy to read. And that is design enough. Editors make a mistake when they try to dress duplicated publications to make them appear to be printed.

Here are some suggestions for duplicated publications:

1. Forget those electronically produced stencils with their imitation halftones. Such halftones can never be as good as halftones made by regular printing processes. Settle instead for clean, crisp line drawings traced directly onto the masters.

2. Forget justification of the right-hand margins of body copy. An ordinary typewriter does not have the subtleties of spacing necessary; the copy ends up with large, uneven spaces between words. There is nothing wrong with an unjustified right-hand margin. If it is good enough for art directors with access to Linotype machines, it ought to be good enough for editors of duplicated publications. Besides, by not justifying the lines the editor saves the extra typing necessary to figure justification.

3. Decrease the number of columns per page. If you have three columns per 8½ x 11 page, go to two. Typewriter type is too large, even in elite, for narrow columns. Such type looks better in a two- or even a one-column format. Besides, you can avoid considerable hyphenation.

4. Type the headlines in all caps rather than letter them by hand. Your page will look neater. And don't feel that you have

The newsletter is the simplest and least expensive of the formats. No photos or drawings are needed to make it inviting, provided the designer uses enough white space and plans carefully the placing of his headings. The front page sets the style. Note that for this one the news items are blocked off into two-column rectangular units. The format works for either a printed or a duplicated piece. (Designed by the author.)

to run the headlines all the way across the column. Leave plenty of white space above, below, and at the right.

5. Avoid newspaper layout practices. Avoid ruled lines, boxes, and other typographic dingbats and strive for a clean, simple page. It is better to give your publication the quiet, self-confidence of a newsletter than the awkward, self-conscious look of a publication out of its visual class.

There is a process that lies somewhere between duplicating and printing, but closer to printing, called Multilith. If yours is a duplicated publication, you should investigate its possibilities, for it can reproduce photographs and art and print in color just as its big brother—offset lithography—can.

Suggested further reading

ANDERSON, WALTER G., ed., *The Industrial Communications Handbook*, American Association of Industrial Editors, Buffalo, N.Y., 1968.

FERGUSON, ROWENA, *Editing the Small Magazine*, Columbia University Press, New York, 1963. (Paperback)

PETERSON, THEODORE, *Magazines in the Twentieth Century*, University of Illinois Press, Urbana, 1964. (Second Edition)

ROOT, ROBERT, *Modern Magazine Editing*, Wm. C. Brown Company Publishers, Dubuque, Iowa, 1966.

SHAHN, BEN, *The Shape of Content*, Vintage Books, New York, 1960. (Based on a series of lectures given at Harvard)

WOLSELEY, ROLAND, *Understanding Magazines*, Iowa State University Press, Ames, Iowa, 1965.

The Company Publication, S. D. Warren Company, Boston, Mass., n.d. (16-page booklet)

Producing the Company Publication, S. D. Warren Company, Boston, Mass., n.d. (16-page booklet)

Better Editing, American Business Press, Inc., New York. (Quarterly)

IABC Notebook, International Association of Business Communicators, Akron, Ohio. (Monthly)

Chapter 4
Production

"You don't simply read *Aspen* . . . ," said one of its early promotion pieces, "you hear it, hang it, feel it, fly it, sniff it, play with it." *Aspen* was "the magazine in a box," a collection of odds and ends that portended the end to magazines as we had known them: the simple flat, two-dimensional storehouses of printed information, opinion, entertainment, and advertisements.

In the 1960s Marshall McLuhan forecast the demise of magazines, but McLuhan has lately had second thoughts. For the magazine is far from dead—especially the one that narrows its content to appeal to a select audience.

And despite some widely heralded improvements in technology—even in printing technology—the actual job of producing magazines will remain pretty much unchanged.

This chapter deals with production: the activity necessary after the editor has done his editing and the art director has laid out the pages. Defined broadly enough "production" includes the laying out of the pages (but not the actual designing of the magazine).

The art director needs a knowledge of production in order to (1) get the effects he wants and (2) cut down on costs. Most magazines have a production director or editor who acts as a sort of middleman between the art director and the printer.

The main consideration in production is printing.

Gutenberg and before

Johann Gutenberg in Germany did not invent printing; the Chinese beat him to it. He did not invent movable type; the Koreans beat him to that. But, unaware of what Koreans had done, Gutenberg worked out his own system and introduced it to the Western world. He designed his types, taking as his model the black, close-fitting, angular calligraphy of the lowlands; carved them; punched them into metal to make molds; and cast them. The characters could be stored in individual compartments and used over and over again. Until then, printing had to be done from wood blocks into which characters were carved, in relief. Once used, the characters served no further purpose.

Before printing of any kind, there were the scribes, working alone, who copied manuscripts by hand. When many copies were needed, a group of scribes would sit together in a semicircle around a reader. The scribes wrote while the reader dictated. This produced several copies of a manuscript at a time. This was Middle Ages mass production.

Printing processes

The printing process Gutenberg used is still very much alive. We call it *letterpress:* printing from a raised surface. It is the process used by most daily newspapers and many big national magazines.

Other processes are *offset lithography* (printing from a flat surface) and *gravure* (printing from tiny wells incised in a metal plate). Offset is the almost universal printing process for company magazines; gravure is the process for the big-circulation picture magazines (not including *Life,* which is letterpress).

Many magazines use more than one printing process for a single issue. *Esquire,* for instance, is part letterpress, part gravure. The letterpress signatures are reserved for late-arriving ads. Former art director Samuel Antupit preferred gravure for the illustrations, but he found that type in the gravure sections had a tendency to come out darker than he anticipated. The reader notices the difference when he makes the transition from a letterpress signature to a gravure signature.

National Review is offset but its cover is usually letterpress. Many small magazines use the opposite arrangement. Their art directors feel that offset is better—and cheaper—than letterpress for short press runs of color and art, hence they use it for their covers.

Some printers insist that the newer processes can't match letterpress for quality, especially if a coated paper stock is used. In letterpress, halftones can be beautifully crisp, type can be remarkably defined.

A disadvantage of letterpress is the high cost of photo-engraving. If a magazine is heavy on art and the press run is small, it is likely to find that offset lithography is a more appropriate printing process. So far as small magazines are concerned, letterpress is competitive only when pages are made up mostly of type.

The type most often used in letterpress printing is set by one of the "hot type" composition systems: foundry (the system Gutenberg used), Ludlow (used primarily for headlines), Linotype and Intertype systems (used for body copy), and Monotype (used for high-quality letterpress printing). All of these systems can be used for offset lithography, too, after a first "printing" is made (after a repro proof is pulled), but offset lithography has the additional advantage over letterpress of being able to use any of the "cold type" composition systems besides: hand lettering, hand "setting" of paper type, typewriter composition, photolettering, and phototypesetting. Before cold type composition can be used in letterpress, it must first be converted to a photoengraving.

Many art directors prefer offset lithography to letterpress because with offset lithography they have firm control over the precise placement of each element on the page. In letterpress, the printer uses the art director's *rough sketch* or *rough pasteup* only as a guide. In offset the printer takes the art director's *finished pasteup* (also called *camera-ready copy*, or

Early in the term of his Publication Design and Production course at the University of Illinois, Prof. Glenn Hanson distributes copies of manuscripts and asks students to copyfit them and incorporate them into page design. This is a first effort by student Ralph Sullivan: a spread involving five photos. The student writes notes in the margins to indicate his preferences in type styles and sizes. This is a rough layout. For a more comprehensive layout, he would be expected to omit the black outlines around the gray rectangles and, using the drawing tools available to him, make the rectangles actually look like photographs.

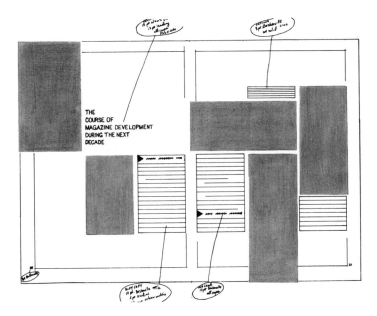

the mechanical) and actually photographs it. (Everything in offset is photographed, including the type.)

But this means that someone on the magazine—the art director himself, his assistant, or the production man—has to do a finished pasteup: a tedious, demanding, time-consuming job. (Gravure requires a finished pasteup, too.)

What the magazine turns over to the printer is what the printer prints, exactly—crooked lines and columns, uneven impressions on the repros, smudges, and all. It is safe to say that the editor of an offset magazine has more production headaches than the editor of a letterpress magazine.

It is, of course, possible to make an arrangement with the printer so that he will make up the magazine on the stone, as he would a letterpress magazine, and make repro proofs of each full page. That, then, is "camera-ready" copy, but the job costs more. It also means that the editor and his art director give up some of their control on spacing.

Art, provided it is actual size and does not require screening, can be pasted into place with the repros. So far as the printer is concerned, it is all line art anyway.

A study of offset magazines, especially the smaller house organs, suggests that editors do not know how to take advantage of the flexibility of the process. They either treat their magazines as though they were produced by letterpress, and as a result their magazines look stilted—or they overreact: tilting pictures, cutting them into strange shapes, drawing unnecessary lines around them, fitting crude cartoons onto the page, and in general making their magazines look like the work of amateurs.

Getting along with the printer

Understanding the printing processes will keep the art director from asking the impossible of his printer. It will also open his eyes to printing's possibilities.

But Alfred Lowry, art director of *Newsweek*, thinks there is such a thing as knowing *too much* about printing. If you think an effect can't be had, you won't ask for it.

Every art director should know at least enough about printing and production to be able to converse intelligently with his printer.

On any magazine, the printer and art director must reconcile differences resulting from a pragmatic approach to the job on the one hand and a visionary's approach on the other. Frequent consultation is necessary.

If the printer and the editor and his staff sit down and reason with each other, explain to each other their needs and limitations, and talk frankly about costs, and if each side is willing to compromise, the relationship between editor and printer can be pleasant enough. Too many editors (and art directors) arrive at some arbitrary effect or size and hold out for it, despite the fact that with slight modification, the time involved in production (and hence the cost) could be greatly reduced.

Printers are like anybody else: they don't like to try something new if they think it will take more time or effort.

Ideally, printing offices and editorial offices should be in the same city, but for reasons of economy, publications tend to let

The opener—a right-hand page —of a major article in Buildings. *The article itself begins on the following page in the publication. The art is a line reproduction of a photograph. Art director John E. Sirotiak uses a solid black foreground as a place to display his title, done in reverse letters.*

out contracts to printers in other parts of the country. For instance, many of the magazines edited on both the East and West Coasts are printed in the Middle West.

In seeking out a printer it is important to find one interested in innovation. Settling for the printer who comes in with the lowest bid may not be the most economical way of publishing a magazine.

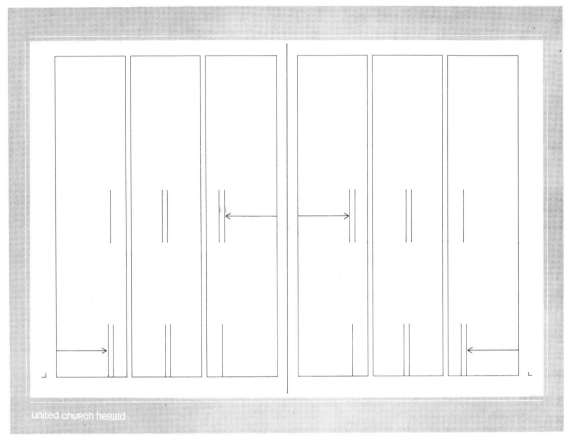

united church herald

The layout sheet or grid for United Church Herald *spreads. Art director Raymond Waites, Jr., has designed the sheet to accommodate either a three- or four-column format. The tiny marks at the bottom left and right are for page numbers. The white lines in the grayed area are the edges for bleed pictures. This sheet can be used for both the rough layout and the paste-up. Some magazines design their layout sheets to show number of lines per column.*

Every printer has his strengths and idiosyncrasies. Every printer has his preferred ways for the editor to mark and prepare copy. An unhurried discussion at the start and frequent conferrals with the printer over the year will do much to ease production problems on the magazine.

Printing's own revolution

Carroll Streeter of *Farm Journal* sees the day when his magazine will custom build each copy to fit the special needs of each subscriber: what that subscriber wants will be recorded on electronic tape, and a computerized bindery will pick up only materials that interest him.

Less dramatic changes in format have taken place already. Printing and typesetting technology has brought great fidelity to the printed page, better color, more flexibility. Some of the newest magazines are coming out in a square rather than in the usual rectangular format. Gatefold covers and center foldouts and booklets bound within magazines are commonplace. *Venture* used three-dimensional color photographs on its covers. *Aspen* put itself in a box. *American Heritage* has wrapped itself in hard covers. *Evergreen Review* was making plans in 1971 to come out as a "video magazine" to take advantage of the video cassette and cartridge market.

In a 1966 article[1] *Newsweek* pointed to experiments in the graphic arts that attempted to

1. put 100,000 pages on one photosensitive crystal,

2. develop a lensless photographic system for three-dimensional home TV, and

3. develop a no-contact, no-pressure printing technique that could "print a message on a pizza and put a trademark on a raw egg yolk."

Newsweek saw these developments as part of a new industry that threatened what was then a ten-billion-dollar communications industry.

The new technology was made necessary, *Newsweek* said, by rising costs of traditional printing processes and by the increased amount of information that had to be recorded. The cost of composition was particularly prohibitive. By 1966 some fifty U.S. dailies had gone to computer composition. Computers produced tape that was fed into linecasting machines, quadrupling the speed of setting.

And computer editing was at hand. That was a system whereby copy was first typed into a computer, which hyphenated it, justified it, and fitted it into a layout. The layout was presented to the editor as a TV image. The editor used an electronic pointer and a keyboard to rewrite and rearrange the material.

The system moved to actual type after the editing was done, thereby eliminating any resetting. And if offset lithography was the printing process, hot type composition was eliminated altogether. Under the system, pages could be transmitted instantaneously via facsimile to regional printing plants.

Charles W. Lake, Jr., president of R. R. Donnelley & Sons Company, one of the nation's great printers of magazines, admitted that

a lot of revolutionary methods for putting images on paper have been coming off the drawing boards, and our research and develop-

---

1. "Good-by to Gutenberg," *Newsweek*, Jan. 24, 1966, pp. 85–87.

ment people are constantly evaluating every new approach. Some day, perhaps, one of these new processes will find its application in the magazine field, but it's going to take a long time and tremendous investments before any of the presently conceived new approaches can reach the quality, speed and economy of today's basic printing processes.[2]

In 1970 *Life* began using an Editorial Layout Display System (ELDS) as reported in 1970 by *Publishers' Weekly*.[3] ELDS is a 7,000-pound electromechanical optical system with a screen, a table-top instrument panel, and some powerful transistorized equipment. Using projectors and computers, it "edits, records and prints layouts on demand."[4] It gives the art director immediate visualization of various layout ideas, in full color and in actual size.

It works this way: the art director mounts all elements in the layout on 35 mm slides and slips them into the machine. The machine holds ninety-nine of them, plus a basic library of typefaces and a layout grid.

Using the instrument panel, the art director can call any combination of elements into position, enlarge any of them, crop any of them—and work anywhere on the spread. *Publishers' Weekly* says operators can be trained to use the machine in about two hours.

Irwin Glusker, art director at *Life*, sees many advantages, including "happy accidents" that occur while the machine is being manipulated.

It's all rather breathtaking to contemplate. Still, the beauty of the printed page, even with all this sophisticated equipment, stems as always from the good taste and sound judgment of the art director.

Choosing paper

Four considerations should guide the editor and art director in their choice of paper for a magazine.

1. *The look of the paper.* How does its brightness, color, and texture match the mood of the magazine? Offset papers as chosen by editors of magazines are usually washday white, but they don't have to be. An off-white or even a light cream-colored stock has a richer appearance.

If the magazine is chiefly a picture book, whiteness of the paper *is* important. You want as much contrast as possible between the ink and the paper.

---

2. In a talk to the Magazine Publishers Association Conference on Color, New York, Nov. 18, 1965.
3. "Art Direction Enters New Age As LIFE Begins Layout by Machine," *Publishers' Weekly*, July 6, 1970, pp. 28, 29.
4. *Ibid.*, p. 28.

A magazine seldom publishes on colored stock, but for special issues or for special sections, a colored stock is arresting. It is cheaper than using a second color in printing, but with pure white gone, the art director faces a problem in giving his photographs their best display.

As for texture, glossy or smooth papers best display photographs; coarse paper best displays type.

Some editors and art directors change stock from issue to issue and even use more than one stock in a single issue.

Some editors like a paper stock with a noticeable pattern in it: like a stipple. The editor should remember that the texture stays constant as the size of the sheet increases or decreases. The pattern may look innocuous enough on a large-size sheet, but when the sheet is cut down to page size, it may be too intrusive. Such a pattern would be better in a *Life*-size magazine than in a *Reader's Digest*-size magazine. Better to avoid it altogether.

2. *The feel of the paper.* Does the editor want a rough feel or a smooth one, a soft feel or a hard one (a paper can be both rough and soft, or smooth and hard), a thick sheet or a thin one?

Interesting thing about roughness: it can carry the feel of cheapness, as in the paper that was used by the old pulp magazines, or the feel of quality, as in an Alfred A. Knopf book printed on antique paper. The feel of the paper does tell the reader something about quality.

On the matter of thickness: an editor may prefer a thicker sheet so that his magazine will appear heftier. The name for such a sheet: high bulk paper. A 60-pound sheet in one paper may be thicker than a 60-pound sheet in another simply because the one has been bulked.[5]

Most people like the feel of coated or polished stock, and that may be reason enough for the editor to choose it—if he can afford it.

3. *The suitability of the paper.* Is the paper heavy enough to stand the strain of continued use? Ordinarily, the editor chooses for his cover a stock that is heavier than for the inside pages.

Is the paper permanent? A newspaper, quickly discarded, can go with newsprint. A scholarly quarterly, which will be bound and used for years by researchers, needs a longer lasting stock.

Is the paper suitable for the printing process? Papers manufactured for letterpress equipment will not work for offset.

---

5. A paper's pound designation is determined by taking 500 sheets in the manufacturer's basic size—25 x 38 for book papers—and weighing them.

Offset needs a paper stock that can adapt to the dampness of the process and that will not cause lint problems. Letterpress needs a paper stock that isn't too crisp. This does not mean that the various textures, smooth and rough, aren't available in both letterpress and offset stock.

What typefaces will be used? Old style romans call for an antique stock, modern romans a glossy or polished stock. But most papers offered for magazine printing are versatile enough so that, within reason, any type can be used.

Does the editor need a paper with high opacity, or can he settle for one that is more transparent? If photographs are a consideration, or if masses of dark inks will be used, he'll have to have an opaque paper.

For good reproduction of photographs magazines should use at least a 40-pound stock, but to fight rising costs, some have gone to lighter papers. To save postage, *Life* in 1970 was using 34-pound stock. "Every time postage goes up, the quality of paper and reproduction goes down," says Clay Felker, editor of *New York*, speaking of magazines in general.[6]

4. *The cost of the paper.* It always boils down to this, doesn't it? Paper cost represents a major production cost to a magazine, which uses so much of it. The Magazine Publishers Association estimates that for a small magazine, paper represents 18 percent of operating costs; for a large magazine, 30 percent. The cost of the paper itself is only part of it. The cost of mailing comes into the picture, too. The heavier the paper, the more it will cost to mail copies of the magazine. A slight reduction in paper weight can mean thousands of dollars difference over a period of a year in mailing costs. If an editor is choosing between two papers, he should have his printer make up dummies of each to take to the post office for a consultation.

A magazine doesn't have to use high-quality paper to look well designed. First, *Rolling Stone* proved that; then, *Rags*. Using newsprint, *Rags* in 1970 was able to print and mail copies at less than 10 cents each.[7]

The Economist, published in London, uses a Bible paper, at least for its U.S. edition, presumably to cut postage costs but perhaps for prestige reasons, too.

The publication using the most unusual stock in the late 1960s was a daily newspaper in Italy, *Giornale di Pavia*, with its bright color photographs printed on polyethylene. You could read this paper in the pouring rain, and when you were

6. Quoted by Charles R. Reynolds, Jr., "Magazines: Dead or Alive (Part II)," *Infinity*, December 1969, p. 21.
7. Cummings Walker, "Rags," *Communication Arts*, vol. 12, no. 4, 1970, p. 63.

through you could shake it out, fold it up like a handkerchief, and put it in your pocket.

Color in magazines

From the time it was possible, color in printing has played an important role in the growth of many general circulation and specialized magazines. The magazine world's initial interest in color was spurred in the 1960s with the coming of color to television and with the coming in the late 1950s of Hi-Fi and later SpectaColor to newspapers.

Newspapers were fighting back with color. But with their better paper stock and less hurried production deadlines, magazines clearly had it over newspapers. And magazines, because they contracted for their printing, had more than one process to choose from.

"There are no bad processes for color printing today," Charles W. Lake, Jr., the printing executive, told a Magazine Publishers Association conference on color in 1965. "We got rid of the early crude processes many years ago. The past few years have seen significant improvements in each of the three basic color printing processes for magazines." He added:

Perhaps the most important overall development has been a blending of the capabilities of letterpress, gravure and offset. There was a day when each of the processes produced a far different result. But what may have been an advantage for one of the processes a few years back likely represents far less of a distinct superiority today. And the dividing lines keep getting finer and finer. All of which further emphasizes the need for a very careful value analysis of all the processes, even if you have considered every available process in the past.

For smaller magazines wishing to use color, the obvious choice was offset, especially when lots of art was also a consideration. Offset for some of them made run-of-book full color a possibility.

But cost was always—and still is—a factor. A second color throughout can increase the printing bill for a magazine by 25 percent. Full-color can double that. So the art director should know what he's doing when he uses color. Otherwise, he should leave experimenting to others. The best advice one can give regarding color is this: Build a file of the uses of color by others. Study that file. And profit from the mistakes and successes it shows.

One thing the art director should remember about color: when you see it in isolation, it looks one way, when you see it next to another color, it takes on a different look. Another thing: it looks one way on antique or uncoated stock, another way on coated stock.

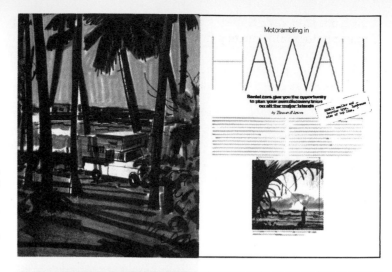

Roger Waterman's full-color comprehensive rough layout of a spread for Chevron USA *(top) along with the two pages as they actually appeared in the magazine. The typed note pasted down at an angle on the right-hand page is a reminder to the designer to make some adjustments: "HAWAII" is to be smaller and in heavier type. And "Motorambling in" is to be bigger. The reproduction does not show it clearly, but the smaller photo is marked to be recropped and lifted slightly on the page. Note the finished look of this rough. Most magazines do not require so high a degree of finish. Waterman, the art director, is associated with Kaiser Graphic Arts, Oakland, a firm that designs a number of magazines and treats editors as advertising agencies treat clients: royally.*

If the art director cannot afford color on a regular basis he can use it on occasion, as when he puts out a special issue or special section. The use of color then helps him say "special."

Because of costs, color in some magazines has been more the tool of the advertising than of the editorial department. The hue and placement of color may be dependent upon decisions made by the advertising department in response to insertion order specifications from advertisers. The editorial department gets a free ride, provided it uses color only on pages in signatures carrying color advertisements.

But editors and their art directors these days are demanding more of a say about where and when to use color.

Not that editors are wholly sold on color. Some feel that the additional money spent on plates and color printing could be better spent on additional black-and-white pages for the magazine. Nor are all artists sold on color. Henri Cartier-

Bresson, who with Robert Capa and others founded the Magnum photographic agency in 1947, told *Time* (Feb. 15, 1971): "I don't like color. By the time it goes through the printer, the inks, and the paper, it has nothing to do with the emotion you had when you shot it. Black and white is a transcription of that emotion, an abstraction of it." Irving Penn, another great photographer, has said: "I don't think I have ever seen a really great color photograph." Penn's reservations about color stem from his belief in photography as an *art* form. He once told David Deutsch, vice-president and executive art director for McCann-Erickson, that photography in its purest form must deviate from realism. And color is realism.

William Hamilton Jones, the alumni magazine editor quoted elsewhere in this book, has strong reservations about color. "My own feeling about a second color is that it's usually a waste of time and money to use it."

He says people don't use a second color imaginatively. "They use it in a way that's repetitious. You know, your headline is already bigger than any other type on the page. And if you put it in red besides, you really aren't serving any useful function." Or people use a second color as a tint block behind a picture or as a duotone. "It's a cheap way to call attention to your photograph. . . . It doesn't serve any positive function."

Jones adds:

. . . We have to compete for people's time with all the mass magazines. And if we're going to get into color, we're going to have to compete with *Life* and *Look* and *Playboy* and all the people who use color beautifully. It seems to me that we're much better off using our resources to do what we can do well. And I think using really good photography in black and white is a change of pace for people.[8]

One of the problems is that the editor and art director do not plan an issue of the magazine for color. When color becomes available in one of the signatures, the art director hastily finds some way to use it. Color is *added* to a page or merely *substituted for black*. It is not integrated as part of the design. Hence the many titles in color, blurbs in color blocks, photos in duotone. In some instances, line artwork is added to a page simply to make use of the color. John Peter of John Peter Associates, Inc., magazine consulting firm, calls this the "we-got-it-why-not-use-it" approach to color, an approach that leads to results "that are usually regretted by the time the issue is off the press." He advises: "When in doubt about using color, stay with black and white."[9]

8. William Hamilton Jones in an untitled interview, *Alma Mater*, April–June 1969, pp. 68, 69.
9. John Peter, "Second Color," *Better Editing*, Spring 1968, pp. 9, 10.

Spot color

What William Hamilton Jones means by *second color* is *spot* or *flat color*: color laid in pure, solid form somewhere on the page as an area of emphasis. It is a "second" color because it is used in association with black or some other color. It involves an additional press run (or a press capable of printing two colors at once).

Some ways the art director can use a second color:

1. *For type.* Color is better for display sizes than for body sizes. When used for type, the color should be on the dark side. A bright red is all right. Yellow does not work. Sometimes it is a good idea to run only one word in a title in color to give it emphasis.

If the art director reverses a title (runs it in white) in a dark area, say in a black part of a photograph, he can run color in the reversed area, in which case the color can be a light color, like yellow.

2. *For photographs.* The best way to print a black-and-white photograph is in black ink on white paper. When you print a photograph in a color, say green, you diminish the tonal scale; the lighter the color, the less scale you have, and the less detailed your photograph will be. If the art director must print his photograph in a color, he should choose one that is close to black, like dark brown, dark blue, or dark green. If he should want the photograph merely as a decorative element or as a backdrop for copy printed over it, then he can print it in a light color.

If he wants the complete tonal value plus the mood of color, he can print the photograph twice, once in the color and once in black. This requires two plates printed so that the dots of the black plate register just to the side of the dots in the color plate. We call this kind of halftone a duotone. (Example: you might want to use a brown duotone when you have an old-time photograph to reproduce.) The art director can also run a black-and-white wash drawing as a duotone. And he can apply the color used in the duotone as ordinary spot color elsewhere on the page or signature.

It is possible to take an ordinary black-and-white photo and *posterize* it for a run in black and one or more spot colors. The printer shoots it for line reproduction, dropping out the middle tones. He gives it more exposure for the color plate, less for black. In the printing, the black covers only some of the area printed in color.

It is also possible to print part of a photograph in black, part in a second color. If the art director has a mug shot, for instance, he can run it as a silhouette, dropping out the background; and in that white area he can print his second color, so making a regular rectangle of the photograph. He can also reverse a circle, arrow, or number on a photograph, if one of these is needed, and fill it in in color.

3. *For line art.* A drawing can be printed in the second color, or it can be printed in black with second color used to fill in certain areas.

Second color has special value in charts, graphs, maps, and tables. The color clarifies and emphasizes.

4. *For lines, boxes, and blocks.* Lines in black or in color, horizontal or vertical, help organize and departmentalize a page. Putting a box around a word in a title, or a section of an article, makes it stand out. Or the art director can use a box to completely surround an article or story.

A block of color can be in a solid or a tint version of that color. Over these blocks the art director can run titles, body copy, or even photographs. If the blocks are dark enough, he can reverse type in them. A *photograph with a tint block* is different from a *duotone* in that the dot pattern in the former is even and consistent. The photograph with a tint block doesn't have as much contrast as the duotone. It looks as if it were printed on a colored paper stock.

Spot color can involve more than a second color. It can involve all the colors, as in the Sunday comic sections of newspapers. What's needed then are separate pieces of art for each of the primary colors plus black, separate plates, and multiple printings. The art in two-, three-, or four-color spot color work in most cases requires line reproduction.

Process color

A much more expensive form of color is *process color*, necessary when the magazine has full-color paintings or photographs to reproduce. In four-color spot color, the magazine supplies separate art (called *overlays*) for each of the four plates. In process color it supplies only the one piece of art; the printer (or photoengraver) must separate the colors photographically, through use of filters, and painstakingly reconstruct them for the four negatives used to make the four plates.

For best printing results for color photographs (and the art director should refer to them as *color* photographs rather than *colored* photographs; the latter suggests color is added after the picture is taken, as in the tinting of photographs) the art director should supply his printer with transparencies. He shouldn't use color prints unless he has to. They do not reproduce as well, and the printer charges more when he has to use them.

In working with transparencies, the art director should use the same kind of transparency viewer at every step of the reproduction process. It is necessary that everyone who makes a judgment about the transparency make it using the same kind of viewer. To expand this advice a little: the art director should inspect transparencies, color prints, artwork, proofs, and press sheets under identical lighting conditions in order to maintain control of the work, especially color quality. (Printers urge that one man—preferably a production chief—have full authority on production quality control for both the editorial and advertising sides. Printers find it frustrating to get instructions from one person and final okays from another. One often does not agree with the other.)

The art director should not ask his printer to enlarge more than five times the original negative. A 2¼ x 2¼ camera is better for color than a 35 mm, so far as picture reproduction is concerned. A 4 x 5 or an 8 x 10 is best, but of course such cameras are too cumbersome for most publications work.

Coated, or at least a calendered, stock is best for reproducing color photos and probably black and white photos, too, especially if the printing process used is letterpress. If the magazine's process is offset, the smoothness of the stock is not so important a factor in photo reproduction.

Laying out the pages

Whether he provides camera-ready copy or merely rough layouts or pasteups, the editor or his art director will have to work out the arrangement of articles, stories, and features on the various pages of his magazine, issue after issue. We call this arrangement the *dummy*. In the next chapter we will go into design considerations of the dummy; in this chapter we shall consider only the mechanics.

The problem, of course, is to fit all the items, editorial and advertising, together, so they will look good and read easily. It is impossible to tell someone who has not done it before exactly how he should do it; fitting a magazine together is something one does by feel. No two persons do it exactly the same way. There is a good deal of trial and error to the procedure, even for professionals. The designer will try one thing, discard it, and try another. When he sees the proofs he still will not be satisfied, and he'll adjust them, even at that late date.

Almost every magazine has a two-page layout sheet, or grid, on which the editor or his art director does his layouts. These sheets can be used for both the rough dummy and the finished pasteup.

The art director can either draw in, roughly, the titles and art, or he can paste into place, also roughly, the galleys and photoprints of the art. If he uses galleys, they will be a second set, marked with numbers to show the printer from what galley forms the various articles and stories were taken. The first set is used for proofreading.

The ads are already blocked in. What's left is what a newspaper would call the "news hole," what we'll call the "editorial hole." The editorial hole consists of a number of beautifully blank spreads ready for the art director's artistry.

The main chore lies with the several major items that start in the front half of the book. The editor has set aside a certain number of pages for each item. By previous decision, some items will occupy several pages, some will have one or two. Some items are to begin on a right-hand page, some on a left. The art director often starts with this already given.

He has a choice of three basic approaches:

1. *Start from the front.* He figures out where he wants his opening art, and how big, and where he wants his title and blurb, takes what space he needs for such display, and trails the article column by column through the remaining space. If he runs over, he asks the editor to cut. If he's under, he increases the size of the art in front or adds art to the body.

2. *Start from the back.* Assuming the editor does not use fillers, the art director starts with the tail end of an article and works forward, allowing for subheads, if that is the magazine's style. The design at first is only tentative; if galleys are used they are fastened down with small dabs of rubber cement. The amount of space between where the feature is supposed to begin and where the first paragraph happens to land is the

Mike Salisbury, art director for West, *originally had full color to work with for both pages, but production changes permitted him color only for the right-hand page. No matter. He rearranged things and came up with a particularly well ordered spread. The art is by James McMullan of Visible Studio Inc., New York.*

amount of space available for title, blurb, and art. If it's not very much, the art director may use it all right there at the opening. If it is considerable, he will move part of the article forward and put additional art into the space thus opened up.

3. *Work backward and forward from the middle.* This results in a better designed feature, usually, and, more than the other two approaches, requires coordination between editor and art director. The art director is as concerned with the looks of the back half of the article as with the opening spread. Some

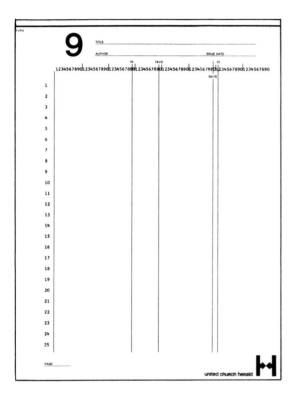

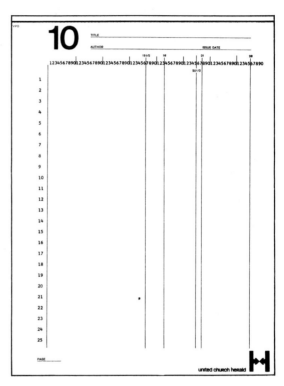

Typing sheets for use by United Church Herald *in preparing its copy for the typesetter. One is for copy that will be set in 9-point type, the other for copy that will be set in 10-point. The typist chooses the vertical line at the right that represents the correct column width and ends each line of her typing as close to that line as possible. The numbers going down the side at the left quickly show the editor how many lines the copy will take when it is set in type, greatly simplifying his copy-fitting problems.*

art directors run their big art near the middle rather than at the beginning.

The art director best estimates how much space the title type will take by actually lettering it. He indicates body copy by boxes or by a series of parallel lines. How does he know exactly how many lines of type the article will take? He uses one of several copyfitting systems[10] or, better, he asks his editor to have all manuscripts typed at preset widths on calibrated copy paper. (See illustration on this page.) On most magazines a little editing at the proof stage is necessary for a perfect fit.

Some editors and art directors, recognizing that such last-

10. See Glenn Hanson's excellent book, *How to Take the Fits Out of Copyfitting,* The Mul-T-Rul Company, Fort Morgan, Colo., 1967.

minute editing is a disservice to the writer and possibly the reader, have gone in for pages whose columns do not necessarily line up at the top or bottom.

Company magazines designed by advertising agencies or design studios and some other magazines require much more finished dummies or layouts—"comprehensive roughs" or "comps," in the language of advertising. The art directors treat their editors as though they were clients. A comp leaves little to the imagination; design that doesn't work can be corrected before type is set and pictures are taken. But comps take time and designers who do them command high fees. Comps are out of reach of most magazine editors.

Instead of using a preprinted grid sheet, the designer doing a comp or even a carefully drawn rough layout is likely to use tissue or tracing paper. For many, many years the drawing and lettering were done in pencil and chalks; now felt-tip pens and markers are the preferred medium. These come in a wide variety of colors and in various shades of gray, both warm and cool.

If the magazine is printed by offset or gravure, the art director carries his layout to a higher level: the pasteup. Using rubber cement or a waxing process, the art director—or a pasteup man under his direction—fastens everything into place: reproduction proofs of titles and text and any actual-size line art. Line art that is to be reduced and photographs and paintings are submitted to the printer separately.

Wrapping it up

The production phase ends with the magazine's being readied for distribution to the reader.

The magazine that goes to the reader via the mails often goes in a wrapper of some kind: a paper sleeve, an envelope, even a box.

A sleeve can fully cover the face of the magazine, as for *Esquire*. Or it can cover part of it, as in the case of *The Christian Century*, a thin weekly that is folded once lengthways, with the binding, before it is slipped into the sleeve.

The *Journal of Marketing, Advertising & Sales Promotion,* and *True,* mailed flat, all go out in transparent full wrappers, which protect the magazines from the rain and also allow the subscribers to recognize the magazines at once when they arrive. The *Harvard Medical Alumni Bulletin* wraps itself in a kraft paper cover—extra cover—which is saddle stitched on. It carries the address label and can be torn off when the magazine is received.

Too often the wrapper is overlooked by the art director. He should be as concerned about its design—about its form and typography—as he is about the magazine itself. The wrapper is the reader's first contact with each issue as it arrives.

Suggested further reading

ARNOLD, EDMUND C., *Ink on Paper: A Handbook of the Graphic Arts,* Harper & Row, Publishers, New York, 1963.

ALLEN, EDWARD M., *Harper's Dictionary of the Graphic Arts,* Harper & Row, Publishers, New York, 1964.

BIRREN, FABER, *Color: A Survey in Words and Pictures,* University Books, Inc., New Hyde Park, N.Y., 1963.

BRUNNER, FELIX, *Handbook of Graphic Reproduction Processes,* Hastings House, Publishers, New York, 1962.

CARDAMONE, TOM, *Advertising Agency and Studio Skills: A Guide to the Preparation of Art and Mechanicals for Reproduction,* Watson-Guptill Publications, New York, 1970. (Revised Edition)

COGOLI, JOHN E., *Photo-Offset Fundamentals,* McKnight & McKnight Publishing Company, Bloomington, Ill., 1967. (Second Edition)

CROY, PETER, *Graphic Design and Reproduction Techniques,* Hastings House, Publishers, New York, 1967.

CURWEN, HAROLD (Revised by Charles Mayo), *Graphic Reproduction in Printing,* Dover Publications, Inc., New York, 1963.

GARDINER, A. W., *Typewriting and Office Duplicating Processes,* Hastings House, Publishers, New York, 1968.

GARLAND, KEN, *Graphics Handbook,* Reinhold Publishing Corporation, New York, 1966.

HATTERY, LOWELL H., AND BUSH, GEORGE P., eds., *Automation and Electronics in Publishing,* Spartan Books, Inc., New York, 1965.

HUTCHINS, MICHAEL, *Typographics: A Designer's Handbook of Printing Techniques,* Van Nostrand Reinhold Company, New York, 1969.

KENT, RUTH, *The Language of Journalism,* Kent State University Press, Kent, Ohio, 1970.

KRAMPEN, MARTIN, AND SEITZ, PETER, *Design and Planning 2: Computers in Design and Communication,* Hastings House, Publishers, New York, 1967.

LAWSON, L. E., *Offset Lithography,* Vista Books, London, 1963.

LEWIS, JOHN, *The Anatomy of Printing: The Influence of Art and History on Its Design,* Watson-Guptill Publications, New York, 1970.

MAURELLO, S. RALPH, *How to Do Pasteups and Mechanicals,* Tudor Publishing Company, New York, 1960.

MELCHER, DANIEL, AND LARRICK, NANCY, *Printing and Promotion Handbook: How to Plan, Produce and Use Printing,* McGraw-Hill Book Company, 1966. (Third Edition)

MERTLE, J. S., AND MONSEN, G. L., *Photomechanics and Printing,* Mertle Publishing Co., Chicago, 1957.

REED, ROBERT FINDLEY, *What the Lithographer Should Know About Paper,* Graphic Arts Technical Foundation, Inc., Pittsburgh, Pa., 1966.

RENNER, PAUL, *Color, Order and Harmony,* Reinhold Publishing Corporation, New York, 1965.

SILVER, GERALD A., *Modern Graphic Arts Paste-up,* American Technical Society, Chicago, 1966.

SLOAN, PATRICIA, *Color: Basic Principles and New Directions,* Reinhold Publishing Corporation, New York, 1968.

STEVENSON, GEORGE A., *Graphic Arts Encyclopedia,* McGraw-Hill Book Company, New York, 1968.

STONE, BERNARD, AND ECKSTEIN, ARTHUR, *Preparing Art for Printing,* Van Nostrand Reinhold Company, New York, 1965.

Strauss, Victor, *The Printing Industry: An Introduction To Its Many Branches, Processes and Products,* R. R. Bowker Company, New York, 1967.

Turnbull, Arthur T., and Baird, Russell N., *The Graphics of Communication,* Holt, Rinehart & Winston, Inc., New York, 1968. (Second Edition)

Yule, John A. C., *Principles of Color Reproduction,* John Wiley & Sons, New York, 1967.

Pocket Pal: A Graphic Arts Digest for Printers and Advertising Production Managers, International Paper Co., New York.

The Fundamentals of Photoengraving, American Photoengravers Association, Chicago, 1966.

Print Media Production Data, Standard Rate & Data Service, Inc., Skokie, Ill. (Quarterly)

Chapter 5
The approach to design

No two magazine designers work alike. Their art is not that systematic.

Designers come to magazines from different backgrounds. Some are ex-illustrators. Some are typographers. Some are editorial people doubling up on duties. Some get their experience with advertising agencies; some are more oriented to the fine arts. Most are neat and orderly, but some are as undisciplined as the most unkempt of the free-lancers they buy from. They have their good days and their bad. A few get along splendidly with their editors; they have mastered the art of compromise.

Compromise is important because design is largely a matter of reconciling editorial needs with visual needs, statement with white space, type with art. A series of compromises helps unify the magazine.

Unity is one of the universal principles of design.

There are at least five others.

We shall deal now with those principles, especially as they apply to magazines.

The principles of magazine design

1. *Balance.* We start with the principle most respected by those who are unsure of themselves in the area of graphic design. The most obvious of the principles—and the least important—it states, simply, that what is put on the left half of the page must "weigh" as much as what is put on the right half of the page. Or: what is put on one page of a spread must "weigh" as much as what is put on the facing page.

The designer who is overconscientious about this principle can take the easy way out: he can *center* everything: the heading, the photo, the text matter. If a spread is involved, he can run the heading across the gutter so half is on each side. He puts a picture on the left page and a picture of equal size across from it on the right page. If he runs two columns of copy under one picture, he runs two columns of copy under the other. The balance is bisymmetric.

For some articles, for some magazines, that solution may be a good one. Usually it is not.

The designer, with a little more effort, can achieve balance that is asymmetric and therefore more interesting. He puts a big picture on one page near the gutter and manages to balance it with a smaller picture at the outside of the other page. It is the principle of balance involved when a father and son use a teeter-totter; the heavier father sits close to the fulcrum; the son sits way out on the end.

The balance becomes more complicated as graphic elements are added. We shall not take the space here to consider the possibilities. Balance comes naturally enough as the designer moves his elements around and pulls white space into concentrated masses. He "feels" the balance; and his intuition is all that is needed. Not confident, he may hold his design up to a mirror and check it in its reverse flow; this will quickly dramatize any lack of balance.

The designer, then, works with optical weights. He knows from experience that big items weigh more than little ones, dark more than light, color more than black and white, unusual shapes more than usual shapes. He knows, too, that a concentration of white space, because it is unusual, can itself be "heavy."

2. *Proportion*. Good proportion comes about less naturally. The beginning designer is inclined to put equal space between the heading and the picture and the picture and the copy, and the copy and the edge of the page. His margins are monotonously the same.

Better proportion comes from Nature. The circumference of the tree trunk supersedes the circumference of the branch. The distance between the tip of the finger and the first joint is different from the distance between the first joint and the second joint.

We have the inspiration of Nature in the "golden section" or ("golden mean") of the fine arts. It provides that the lesser dimension in a plane figure is to the greater as the greater is to the sum of both; or, the dimensions are in a 0.616 to 1.000 ratio. Roughly 3 to 5. We base page size—of typing sheets, of books, of magazines—on this ratio. We find the ratio more interesting, less tiresome, less obvious than a simple 1 to 1. We avoid 2 to 1, 3 to 1, and 4 to 2 ratios, because they are merely variations of 1 to 1. They divide into equal portions. We avoid cutting pages into halves or quarters. We avoid running pictures that are perfectly square because the ratio of width to depth is *1 to 1*.

In most well-designed magazines, the pages are rectangular, the pictures are rectangular (vertical and/or horizontal), and distances between elements are only subtly related.

But with the varying proportions, the designer maintains consistent spacing throughout the book where elements are *meant* to be equal, as in the separation of subheads from the body of the article and captions from their pictures.

The page margin is narrowest between inside edge of copy and gutter, wider between top of copy and top of page, wider

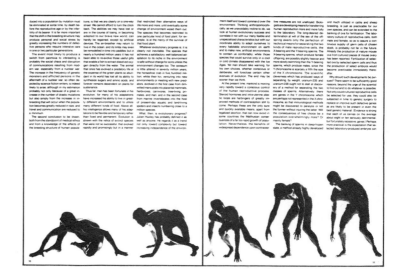

still between outside edge of copy and outside edge of page, and widest between bottom of copy and bottom of page. (This book uses a different margin arrangement for style reasons and to save the reader from having to fight the gutter to read the long columns of copy.)

Total picture area takes up more space than non-picture area; or it takes up less space. The ratio is never *1 to 1*.

3. *Sequence.* First things first. The designer does not leave to chance the order in which the reader takes in the items on a page or spread. He knows the reader ordinarily starts at the top left of a page or spread and works his way to the bottom right. Arranging the elements so they read from left to right

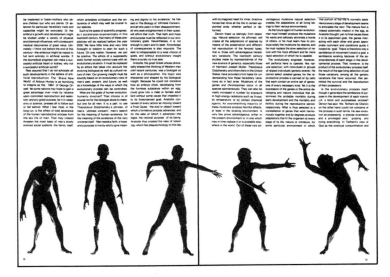

University Review, published by the State University of New York, is easily one of the best-designed alumni magazines in the country. For this August 1969 issue, designer Richard Danne reuses on the cover a portion of some inside art to create a tie-in of the cover with a lead article. The cover is in dark blue and light green. The inside pages are in stark black and white. The bottom of the copy block area remains constant while the art goes through an evolution right before the readers' eyes. Photographer was Herman Bachmann.

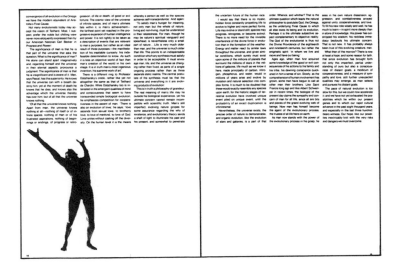

All the principles of design described in this chapter are incorporated by Don Menell, assistant art director of Look, in this single page. It is the opening page of a two-page article that starts on a right-hand page and ends on the (next) left-hand page. Menell combines roman display type with sans serif body type, adds column rules, and carefully fits the type around the illustration. The illustration ties in beautifully with the title, carrying the reader down into the article and dividing the page pleasingly. Note that the hand both holds a pill and forms into the symbol for "okay." The ring on the finger, faintly seen, is a nice added touch. (Reproduced by courtesy of the editors. From the June 30, 1970, issue of Look *magazine. Copyright 1970 by Cowles Communications, Inc.)*

No medication is foolproof, but taken with your doctor's advice…

THE PILL IS SAFE

ONLY ONE birth-control measure is safer or more effective than the pill—total sexual abstinence. And that has never been too popular a choice. Any other method—rhythm, diaphragm, condom, foam, intra-uterine device (IUD)—is either less effective or not as safe as the ubiquitous tablet more than eight million women swallow daily.

Unfortunately, the pill's benefits have been blackened, and its evils—real and imagined—have been magnified at the recent Senate subcommittee hearings chaired by Sen. Gaylord Nelson (D., Wis.). Contrary to newspaper and television reports, the hearings did not uncover new dangers in the pill but merely repeated old stories that the public had heard before and that had already been carefully weighed by responsible medical authorities.

So sensational were the charges, however, that a public-opinion poll suggests that more than a million women have been too frightened to continue using the oral contraceptive, although 87 out of 100 women said they previously were satisfied with it. Planned or not, the anti-pill hysteria has panicked these women into making—on their own—a complicated medical decision that demands a physician's guidance.

Dire predictions of death from blood clots and cancer frightened the women away. While the blood-clot danger is statistically small but real, the cancer scare is neither statistical nor real; it is simply conjectural.

Two years ago, a British survey showed that death from blood

Since 1956, Dr. Tyler has played a major role in developing and testing the pill. An associate clinical professor of obstetrics and gynecology at UCLA, he is also medical director of the Family Planning Centers of Greater Los Angeles.

BY EDWARD T. TYLER, M.D., WITH ROLAND H. BERG

clots occurred nearly seven times more often among pill-users than among similar-aged women not on the pill. A smaller United States survey found that the risk was about four times greater. Seven or four, even the smaller number is significant and must not be ignored. Any woman taking the pill should be aware that there is the danger of blood clots.

Although the risk is real, it is equally important for every woman to know what the added danger actually means. The British study revealed that three women out of every 100,000 taking the pill died from blood clots. The toll involved was no greater than that among women who are killed while riding in cars or crossing the street. Certainly, such accidental deaths are deplorable, but no one suggests that the risk is so great women should stop riding in automobiles.

It is even more significant that pregnancy entails harsh risks of its own. Actually, the chance of death associated with pregnancy is 17 times greater than with pill-taking. Thus, the million or more women who reportedly abandoned the pill in fear because of the hearings may find their lives in greater jeopardy should they become pregnant as a consequence.

Although the blood-clot problem is relatively recent, hints of it appeared eight years ago. As an editorial consultant to the Journal of the American Medical Association, I recommended in 1962 that the Journal publish a report by a clinician linking the occurrence of blood clots with oral contracep-

tives. The Journal did so, and also asked me to write an editorial calling for definitive research on the how and why of the relationship.

To this date, no definitive research has been done. One reason may be the near-impossible task of evaluating the pill's role, when the basic mechanism of blood clotting is largely a mystery to scientists. Another is the unresolved argument over who should foot the bill for the research. Is it the drug companies' responsibility, because they stand to profit from the sale of oral contraceptives? Or should it be the Government's concern because, with eight million users, the pill has become a public-health problem?

During the Washington hearings, several witnesses advocated that women switch from the pill to one of the many intrauterine devices available. (One witness who was the pill's severest critic is the developer of an IUD that is now being manufactured and sold.) An IUD is a piece of plastic or metal (a coil, spiral, loop, etc.) that is inserted by a physician into a woman's uterus and left there. How it prevents pregnancy, no one knows.

With oral contraceptives, however, there are no doubts. The pill prevents conception by tricking the body into believing it is already pregnant. The pill accomplishes this with its two chemical ingredients that mimic the action of the female sex hormones—estrogen and progestogen.

One pill—the sequential type—consists of a synthetic estrogen tablet taken daily for two weeks, followed for one week by a daily tablet containing both synthetic hormones. The other—the combination type—contains both hormones in a single tablet that is taken daily for three weeks.

As each menstrual cycle rolls around, the pills' cumulative ef-
continued

LOOK 6-30-70 65

and from top to bottom is easy enough; but it limits design flexibility.

The reader also has a tendency to move from big items to smaller items, from black to white, from color to noncolor, from unusual shape to usual shape. The designer finds it possible, then, to begin his design *anywhere*, directing the reader to the left, the right, the top, the bottom—in a circular motion, diagonally, whatever way he wishes. Diminishing visual impact does the job.

The designer directs the reader, too, through the use of lines, real or implied, which carry the eye as tracks carry a train. The pictures themselves have direction or facing; as surely as if they were arrows, they point the way. This is why designers always arrange a major mug shot so that the subject looks into the text.

The designer tries to arrange photographs so that an edge or a force from one photograph flows into an adjoining one. The curve of an arm, for instance, if carried over to the next paragraph would merge into the roll of a hill. This happens without regard to what may be the outer dimensions of the photographs; one photograph might be considerably larger than the other and not aligned with it.

Or: taking a line from within the picture—say the edge of a building—the designer extends it (without actually drawing it) and fits against it another item—say a block of copy. Or: taking the hard edge of a picture and extending it, he fits another picture against it somewhere across the page.

And do not discount the possibility of actually *numbering* the pictures. If chronological order is all-important, as for a step-by-step illustrated article on how to build a guest house, the designer may not find a better way for handling sequence.

Developing sequence from spread to spread is also part of the assignment. Which leads to another principle.

4. *Unity.* The typeface must look as if it were designed to fit the style of the illustration. It must fit the mood of the piece. The overall effect of the spread, of the entire article or story, of the entire magazine must be one of unity, of harmony. The pieces, the pages belong together.

Ideally, all typefaces in a magazine come from the same family. Ideally, all art is furnished by the same artist or photographer.

Heavy rules or borders call for boldface sans serifs. Bold sans serifs call for line drawings with plenty of solid blacks.

Thick and thin rules call for modern romans. Modern romans call for well-ordered photographs, or clean line drawings, arranged in severe horizontal and vertical patterns.

And pattern concerns the designer. Stepping back, the designer contemplates the overall effect. No longer looking for individual trees, he surveys the forest. Does it all seem to fit together?

The pattern may be loose, tight, bulky, smooth, rugged, soft, loud, dark, light, hard, straight, rolling, changing, any number of things—but the pattern is unmistakably there.

The designer takes a major step toward unity when he pushes his white space to the outside edges of his spreads. This teams photographs with other elements so that they work together. When large amounts of white space seep into the center, there is an explosion, sending the elements off in all directions. White space on the outside edges should be there in unequal concentrations, in conformance with the principle of pleasing proportion.

5. *Simplicity.* Here we come to a design principle not so universal as the others. Graphic design accommodates to trends in fashion, architecture, the fine arts, the political climate, culture in general. What strikes us as a good magazine page now might not strike us that way ten years from now, or even next year. At times in the history of the graphic arts, a clut-

tered, busy, crowded page, overly decorated, has impressed designers if not readers. Even today, such a page is good, under certain conditions, simply because it is different from others. The principle of contrast—contrast with other designs—gives the page respectability.

But the main thrust of design today is toward simplicity. The reader simply does not have time to browse and hunt.

So the magazine designer gives him as few elements per page or spread as he can. Instead of many small pictures—two or three large ones. Instead of three columns to the page, two or one. Instead of multi-decked headings, a single title. Instead of a three-line title, a title in a single line.

Even when the designer has a half dozen or more photographs to work into the design, he can organize them into one mass, butting them together so they make either a true rectangle or a square.

Some designers organize all the elements so that they will form three basic areas of unequal size separated from each other by unequal distances.

6. *Contrast.* Put negatively, the principle is Contrast. Put positively, it is Emphasis. Either way, something on the page

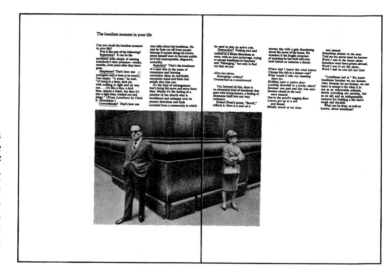

A delightful United Church Herald *spread that carries these lessons: You can get plenty of display for a title without going to a large type size. A photo across a gutter can help immeasurably to hold a spread together. White space works best when it is concentrated in large areas.*

or on the spread stands out from all else. What stands out is probably the most important item on the page. It is probably the item the reader sees first.

The designer achieves contrast or gives an item emphasis by making it bigger than anything else there—blacker, more colorful, or more unusually shaped. Or he gets it by causing all other items to point to the item or by putting it in a different setting, giving it different texture, or otherwise making it seem out of place.

This is important: only *one* item—or one cluster of items—dominates. When the designer gives graphic emphasis to several items, they all compete for attention, frustrating the reader, causing him to bring down his gavel and declare an adjournment.

The principles in perspective

Two men seated together on a plane trip enter into a discussion about the pollution problem. One says to the other: "I-I-I th-th-thi, I-I think . . . we, we, we ought to, uh, . . . I think we ought to c-c-clean up the air and w-w-w-water." And the other one answers: "That's easy enough for you to say!"

And so are these principles. If they sound glib, that's because they are. Designing a magazine is not so simple as all that.

Nor do practicing designers pay a great deal of attention to these principles. Perhaps they could not state them if asked. Certainly they would not give them exactly as they are given here.

Still it is a worthwhile list to contemplate. The amateur designer, or the editor who has the design job by default, especially, should give the principles his attention.

They represent a starting point.

It may have occurred to you that the principles are self-contradictory. How can you have unity, for instance, when you insist on setting up one item to contrast with others? And doesn't use of unequal space divisions break up the sequence?

The challenge in the list lies in knowing when to stress one principle, when to stress another. Obviously they can't all be applied in equal measure. When one does not seem appropriate, the designer should not hesitate to abandon it.

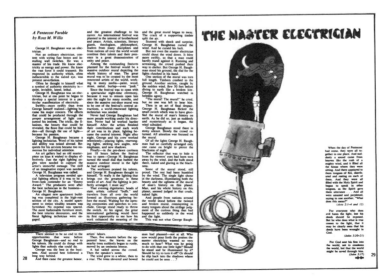

An article complete on this spread. The background in a second color (yellow) and a stretched out wash drawing help unite the two pages. Art director Raymond Waites, Jr., did his own illustration.

Design clichés

In what may be misguided enthusiasm for one or the other of the design principles, or because of his lack of knowledge of what good design is, the amateur designer makes a number of mistakes, and makes them consistently. Perhaps he has seen a design solution, liked it, and used it himself in a new situation even if it didn't fit the problem. It probably has been used to death. Or, if his background was in the newspaper business, he may have brought with him the tired typography of that branch of publishing.

Writers have their "tired but happy"s and "last but not least"s; designers have these:

1. *Picture cutouts.* The amateur designer seems to think that pictures displayed in regular rectangle or square shapes bore the reader. They may. But only because the pictures themselves are boring. Cutting them into circles or triangles or stars or whatever will not make them better pictures. If the pictures are good to begin with, such cutting will stunt their impact, ruin their composition, and demoralize the photographer who took them.

2. *Tilts.* Closely related to Cliché No. 1 is the practice of putting a picture or a headline on a diagonal. Presumably, the designer feels this will make it stand out from others. It will, but at the expense of causing the reader irritation.

The introduction of the diagonal suggests movement. The picture is falling. The reader gets caught up in this phenomenon at the expense of giving his full attention to what the picture actually says. Readability suffers.

More defensible—but just barely—is the practice of putting the entire contents of the spread on a single or on parallel diagonals. The designer should have a good reason for doing this—a reason better than "to be different."

3. *Vertical typography.* The designer has a deep vertical space left over and a title to fit in. So he runs it with the letters on top of each other in succession down the page. The title is unreadable; and the designer has probably run it in type larger than necessary.

He would save white space and make his title more readable —make it stand out better—by decreasing its size and running it in usual left-to-right form at a strategic spot near the article's beginning.

4. *Mortises.* Seeing an expanse of picture that is all sky or all foreground, some designers, prompted perhaps by a lack of space elsewhere, cut out a block and put type there. The block may be completely surrounded by photograph, or it may be at an edge or corner. Wherever the mortise is located, it usually hurts the composition of the picture and cheapens the page.

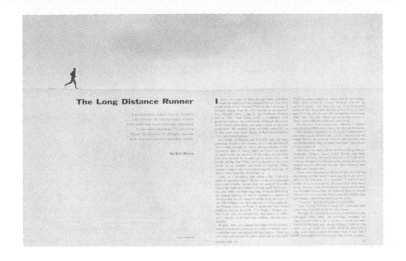

This two-spread, four-page article from Old Oregon, *an alumni magazine, is held together by a single photograph, full bleed on all pages. The designer, Stan Bettis, who took the picture, uses part of it for one spread, part for another. He runs the photo in a light tone so he can surprint the title and body copy. Note how the runner and the title move the reader to the initial letter that begins the article. The horizon line in the photo carries the reader from the first spread to the second.*

The mortise is slightly more defensible when another photograph rather than type is placed into the cut-out portion of the original photograph, providing for a picture within a picture. *Look* used this technique effectively.

5. *Overlaps.* The designer runs his type—usually for a heading—partly in the white space next to a photograph and partly in the photograph itself. As it passes from white space to photograph, the type can remain black (surprint). Or, as it makes the crossing, it can change to white letters (reverse printing).

The designer resorts to this cliché for two reasons: (1) to save space (perhaps the heading is too wide for the space allotted to it) and (2) to draw type and picture together (the principle of unity). But he saves space at the expense of a visual interruption where the type crosses over. And he unifies type and photo at the expense of photo clarity and beauty.

6. Tint blocks. This is the most defensible of the design clichés. Perhaps the designer has no art, and so he brings in a rectangle of gray and reverses or surprints some type on it. Or possibly a second color is available to him on that page, so he runs a sidebar or caption in it, or even superimposes a picture over it.

Often, however, in retrospect after the magazine is printed, the designer can see that the tint blocks cheapened or cluttered the page.

7. Boxes. Newspapers developed them; magazines, especially some of the trade journals, picked them up. For a crammed eight-column newspaper page, a boxed feature makes sense. It provides typographic relief. But for a magazine, unencumbered by column rules and more receptive to white space, the box is an unnecessary crutch—a too-easy solution to the problem of emphasis. It is an overly-familiar device to segregate features on a page.

The list of clichés could be expanded. For instance, it would be easy to make a case against all reverses and surprints. Designers too often resort to these—at some expense to readability.

Occasionally, a venturesome designer, sure of himself, goes slumming among the clichés, picks one out, and lends his dignity to it. In good hands, even a cliché can please.

But after all is said and done, all things considered, it goes without saying that you should avoid clichés like the plague.

Two basic approaches

A magazine designer takes one of two basic approaches to magazine design. The first approach goes like this: Each picture, each caption, each title, each block of copy falls into a consistent pattern to unify the book. The book is orderly. The reader feels secure. He knows what to expect.

The second approach provides great variety, page after page. The reader prepares himself for a series of surprises. The art director worries about unity, but only within a given article or story. He believes that the nature of the article or story should dictate the choice of typeface and illustration.

A magazine may have elements of both approaches, but one approach should predominate. One may be more appropriate than the other for a given magazine, but properly handled, either approach can work, regardless of magazine content.

1. The ordered approach. Herb Lubalin has called *Scientific American* "the best designed magazine in America." One of several magazines Lubalin designs, *The New Leader,* is easily the handsomest of the opinion journals. *Sports Illustrated* impresses many art directors as a magazine of great beauty. The magazines have this in common: they are highly organized, almost predictable in their approach to design. Each uses a single typeface for all major titles. Each makes limited use of ruled lines to set off some of the type, but otherwise, each avoids typographic frills. The art directors frame their pictures nicely in white. They avoid crowding. A look of quiet luxury results. More important, readers can get through their articles, look at their pictures, unhampered by visual pyrotechnics.

Don't be misled by the simplicity of the look. The subtle relationship of spaces is not easy to duplicate. Still, of the two basic approaches, this one is the approach that should be used by the editor-without-an-art-director. Ideally he should call in a consulting art director and have him set up a format, choose the types, and draw up a set of instructions and diagrams on how to handle special features and standing departments. This is essentially what Samuel Antupit, former art director of *Esquire*, did for *The New York Review of Books*.

Two other magazines stand out as unique examples of the ordered approach. *The New Republic* from 1959 to 1967 was about as ordered as any magazine can get, and handsome for it. Noel Martin, brought in as a consultant for a complete format redesign, chose a roman typeface, Palatino, designed in 1950 by Hermann Zapf. Looking very contemporary, Palatino nevertheless draws its inspiration from the early Venetian types. It suggests a happy blend of tradition and progress. Martin used it not only for main titles but for subtitles, credit lines, body copy, the logo—everything. He permitted typographic variety only through varying the sizes and combining uprights with italics. The editors never varied Martin's simple two-column pattern until someone there, unfortunately, decided to jazz up the magazine with boldface versions of the type (most type designs lose their beauty when their strokes are thickened) and with an angular script that for some column headings was run on a diagonal.

The New Yorker's design is so ordered as to be nonexistent. A cartoonist back in the early 1920s, when it was founded, designed its display face, and the magazine has never changed it. It uses a few spot drawings and, of course, those celebrated gag cartoons to provide occasional graphic oases, but otherwise its "designer" simply pours the editorial material into the holes left over by the advertising. There is no opening display for any of the articles or stories. The advertisers love it, because it makes their insertions, always well designed anyway, striking by comparison.

2. *The diversified approach.* Whereas the ordered approach virtually guarantees reasonably good design, even for magazines with limited resources, the diversified approach works

A right-hand page opener from Fleet Owner. *The concentration of white at the left helps separate editorial from advertising. Note how art editor Bud Clarke uses art to break up his two-part title. Note too how he uses art to lead the reader to the article's beginning. The original was in black and green. (With permission from* Fleet Owner. *Copyright 1970 by McGraw-Hill, Inc. All rights reserved.)*

only when directed by a professional designer. Its success depends to a considerable extent on violations of traditional principles of design.

In the diversified approach, the designer may arrange elements to create a large void on one side of a page. He purposely disturbs the reader in order to focus his attention on an article which deals, let us say, with student unrest. Out goes balance.

Or the designer uses square- rather than rectangular-shaped photographs. His reason may be that for this particular set of photographs, cropping to squares brings out the best composition. Or he chooses a permanent square page format, as Herb Lubalin did for *Avant Garde,* to make the magazine stand out from all others. Out goes standard proportion.

Or the designer doesn't care in which direction the reader goes. The designer scrambles the pictures because there is no correct order. The effect need not be cumulative for the article: it is no how-to-do-it. Out goes sequence.

Or the designer wants to show the complicated strategy of a single football play, as *Esquire* did in September 1968. In this case Samuel Antupit ran a chart showing all players on both sides, officials and coaches, fans in the stands, the press corps, the stadium and scoreboard, with labels and captions and directional lines and boxes fighting for attention with the article itself and its title. Out goes simplicity.

Or the designer is dealing with an article that makes five or six main points, equally important. No one item should stand out. So the designer decides on a series of equal-size pictures. Out goes contrast.

And yet in each case the designer maintains a semblance of each of the design principles. The concentration of white space is itself "heavy," and tends to counterbalance the dark elements on the other side of the page. Square-shaped photographs appear on a rectangular page. Scrambled pictures precede a column of type that moves in the conventional way from top to bottom. Visual confusion is confined only to the display types. One cluttered article fits into an issue filled otherwise with pages stark and clean. Even-size pictures, no one of them standing out from the others, form one large mass that overpowers a smaller copy block, providing contrast to the page after all.

It would be more accurate to say that the designer using the diversified approach does not so much ignore design principles as emphasize one over the others.

The diversified approach is the experimental approach. And experiment is best conducted by those who are grounded in the fundamentals.

Two of the most honored practitioners of the diversified

approach were Allen Hurlburt of *Look* and Otto Storch of *McCall's*. *Look*'s imaginative handling of photographs in sequence caused *Life* to revitalize its appearance. *McCall's* brought new life to the women's magazines.

"It is more interesting for the reader if the visual pace of the magazine varies," Storch said. "Some pages can be quiet and others bold, some restful and others exciting, some with pictures dominating the layout and others with no pictures at all."

The diversified approach works best for large-format publications. The *Digest* size of some magazines tends to cramp the style of the freewheeling designer. But *Westward*, a publication of Kaiser Steel, Oakland, manages the diversified look despite its miniature pages.

Visualization

The designer, as he takes on a magazine assignment, first makes a decision on format (chapter 3). Then he decides which of the two basic approaches to design he will take: the ordered or diversified.

Already, he has placed some limitations on himself. Additional limitations may come from the editor. The designer gets a manuscript of, say, 2,500 words, a title, and four photographs, and five pages in the magazine where he can put them. He makes of this what he can, deciding which photograph to play up, how far down on the page to start the article, where subheads will go, how much white space to allow. Other articles will follow. And similar restrictions will accompany them.

The designer in this case is not much more than a layout artist. He gets some satisfaction out of fitting these things together, but clearly, he is not fully engaged in graphic design. He is not exercising his creative talent.

Far better is the arrangement whereby the designer plans the issue with the editor, helping decide subject areas for articles and stories. Occasionally he may plan the art and lay out the pages before the article is written; the article is tailored to fit.

Most important in the visualization process is the setting of the mood. The designer decides: photographs or drawings or no art at all? color? sans serif or roman type for the title? two-column or three-column pages? initial letters or subheads?

Realism might be better served through photography. Clarity might be better served through drawings. Color has psychological effects. Sans serifs may say "now"; romans may say "yesterday." Wide columns may suggest urgency, but narrow columns may be more immediate. Initial letters can be decorated to suggest the period of the piece.

He considers all of this, keeping in mind, always, production problems likely to result. Color adds to costs. Wide columns take more space because type has to be set larger.

Designers faced a difficult assignment in the mid-1960s with the "Death of God" debate. Nearly every magazine dealt with the matter; the question was, how to illustrate it. Designers could run mug shots of the theologians quoted, but these would not make very good opening spreads. And photographs of God Himself were hard to come by. Most designers took this way out: beautiful display of the article titles in old roman type. This seemed appropriate to the mood. *Time* (April 8, 1966), doing a major story on the debate, settled, for the first time in its history, on an all-type cover.

Whether art follows copy or copy follows art, the two must work in harmony. An article on the hippies features psychedelic lettering and art. An article about the computer age appears under a title in a typeface we associate with punch cards. One on the navy appears under a title done in stencil letters. An article on the population explosion swells out to the edge of a crowded page.

The art accompanying the article should say the same thing the title says. For an article on "The Hectic Life of the College President," for instance, the designer would not select a routine shot of a well-dressed executive, hands folded, behind a cleared-off desk. For fiction, the designer usually uses a drawing or painting for the opening spread; for nonfiction, photography. For fiction, the designer can reach deep into the story for a scene to illustrate. The scene need not be thematic. For nonfiction, the main piece of art should *typify* what's in type.

The designer usually reads the manuscript before it is set in type to decide what kind of typographic and illustrative treatment it should have. He may have a copy made for the illustrator and entrust the decision on illustration technique to him.

With some idea of what the picture or pictures will be, and how much space the manuscript will take, the designer begins with a series of thumbnail sketches of his pages, toying with space divisions. When he has thumbnails that show promise, he redraws them actual size so that he can begin figuring exact dimensions.

Mike Salisbury, art director of *West*, tells how he does it:

I don't rework any layouts. The first ideas I sketch out are usually the ones produced.

I work very loose and spontaneously, trying to keep a good pacing of layout styles throughout the book.

The less attention I give a layout's styling the better it will look.

I spend more time getting the proper photos, illustrations, and research material organized. The layout is usually secondary in importance to the material used in the layout.[1]

In some cases, especially for letterpress books, the designer does his designing with galley proofs and photostats of the art, cutting and pasting and moving items around until they give him the fit and the look he desires. He may ask the editor to cut down or increase wordage as an aid to fitting the manuscript to the page. This is one area where the editor who serves as his own designer has an advantage; he can do the cutting and the padding exactly where he needs it, when he needs it.

The ups and downs of camera movements

… ON SEESAWS, SWINGS, AND SLIDES

BY BOB DUNCAN

PHOTOGRAPHS BY HARVEY V. FONDILLER

The swipe file

A cartoonist copies the strong outlines and the lithographic grays of Herblock, and his colleagues, if not his readers, will spot the plagiarism. An illustrator copies the delicate line, the flat colors, and the decorative look of Milton Glaser or the virile, freshly painted look of Al Parker, and his fellow painters will see at once the influence of the master. And the appropriation of another man's style or technique seldom results in work that is the equal of the original.

In the area of graphic design, lifting ideas comes easier and

1. Letter to the author from Mike Salisbury, Nov. 27, 1970.

Popular Photography combines three same-size pictures and one big one, all in square format, with some column rules for an opening spread in the back of the book. The main picture is cropped to lead the reader down the teeter-totter to the beginning of the article's title. Note that art director George N. Soppelsa was able to retain formally balanced sections (the title and the right-hand page) in an informally balanced context.

with less stigma attached. Nobody can successfully trace design to its source. It is the rare designer who is not influenced—and not just subconsciously—by the work of other designers. Nor is this bad. The innovators—Herb Lubalin, Henry Wolf, Peter Palazzo, Paul Rand, and the others—have doubtless had great influence on the look of magazines other than those they've designed, and they must be pleased to have played a role in upgrading the general level of graphic design; they do not have exclusive interest in any one solution, anyway. Their great satisfaction lies in moving on to unexplored design plateaus.

Even these men maintain swipe files—printed portfolios of prize-winning work, if not the more obvious folders of clippings. Every designer and editor should build up his own collection of designs that please, inspire, and, most important, communicate clearly.

For scholastic editors who stand in awe of the job of graphic design one publisher brought out a book frankly devoted to the techniques of applying the page designs of the slick magazines to the pages of high school yearbooks.[2]

There is such a thing as creative copying. No beginning designer can get much satisfaction out of lifting a spread, whole, out of one publication and putting it down in his own magazine with a mere substitution of pictures and wording. He will try to change facings and picture sizes, adjust title length and placement, and so on; not solely to disguise the fact that he lifted the design, but to try to improve on it. He should use another design primarily as a starting point. And he should remember that good design is tailored to the needs of a specific article or story.

A designer will draw inspiration not only from other graphic designs but from architectural structures, oil paintings (they are designed, too), and, of course, Nature's landscapes.

He may find some stimulus from that classic set of ready-made designs: the alphabet. An *L* or a *U* or an *A* or an *R* , or a number, or one of the letters turned sideways or upside-down might suggest a pattern for a page or spread. Of course the reader will not see the letter or figure. The designer will not be bound by it. He will merely use it as a beginning.

Obviously, much of magazine design springs from advertising design. Advertising designers, probably more than magazine designers, take chances with graphics. The magazine designer who borrows from advertisers will at least keep abreast of graphic design trends. He should remember, though, that many of these "trends" turn out to be short-lived fads.

2. James Magmer and Franklin Ronan, *Look and Life as Guides for the Successful Yearbook Editor*, Midwest Publications Company, Inc., Birmingham, Mich., 1964.

Suggested further reading

ADAMS, ROBERT, *Creativity in Communications*, New York Graphic Society Ltd., Greenwich, Conn., 1971.

ARNHEIM, RUDOLPH, *Visual Thinking*, University of California Press, Berkeley, 1969.

BALLINGER, RAYMOND A., *Layout and Graphic Design*, Van Nostrand Reinhold Company, New York, 1970. (Revised Edition)

CATALDO, JOHN W., *Graphic Design & Visual Communication*, International Textbook Company, Scranton, Penna., 1966.

DE SAUSMAREZ, MAURICE, *Basic Design: The Dynamics of Visual Form*, Reinhold Publishing Corporation, New York, 1964.

GARRETT, LILLIAN, *Visual Design: A Problem Solving Approach*, Reinhold Publishing Corporation, New York, 1966.

HAMILTON, EDWARD A., *Graphic Design for the Computer Age: Visual Communication for All Media*, Van Nostrand Reinhold Company, New York, 1970.

HOFMANN, ARMIN, *Graphic Design Manual: Principles and Practice*, Reinhold Publishing Corporation, New York, 1965.

MCLEAN, RAURI, *Magazine Design*, Oxford University Press, New York, 1969.

MOUSTAKAS, CLARK E., *Creativity and Conformity*, D. Van Nostrand Company, Inc., Princeton, N.J., 1967.

MULVEY, FRANK, *Graphic Perception of Space*, Van Nostrand Reinhold Company, New York, 1969.

MURGATROYD, KEITH, *Modern Graphics*, E. P. Dutton & Co., New York, 1969.

NELSON, GEORGE, *Problems of Design*, Whitney Publications, New York, 1965. (Second Edition)

NIECE, ROBERT C., *Art: An Approach*, Wm. C. Brown Company Publishers, Dubuque, Iowa, 1963.

WEYL, NATHANIEL, *The Creative Elite in America*, Public Affairs Press, Washington, D.C., 1966.

WILSON, ROBERT CURTIS, *An Alphabet of Visual Experience: An Examination of the Basic Principles of Design*, International Textbook Company, Scranton, Penna., 1966.

Chapter 6
Typography

"Too much is said about good typography and not enough set," Herb Lubalin has observed. Still, for readers of this book, some additional advice on the use of types may be in order.

Readability

The point cannot be made too often: the one overriding consideration in typography is readability. If it's not readable, it's not good typography.

Type arranged in tricky formation may work for an occasional heading, but for most headings and for long columns of text matter, the traditional types, traditionally spaced, work best. The reader's reaction should be "What an interesting article!" not "What interesting typography!"

Some typographers make a point of distinguishing between readability and legibility. Legibility has to do with the ease with which the reader distinguishes one letter from another. Readability, a broader term, has to do with the ease with which the reader takes in a column or page of type. Readability also has to do with the way the story or article is written.

Readability, from a typographic standpoint, is affected by these factors:

1. *The style of the typeface.* Familiar styles are usually the most readable.

2. *The size of the typeface.* Within reason, the larger the face, the better.

3. *The length of the line.* Comfortably narrow columns are better than wide columns.

4. *The amount of leading (pronounced "ledding") between lines.* Most body sizes can use at least two points.

5. *The pattern of the column of type.* It should be even-toned.

6. *The contrast between the darkness of the type and the lightness of the paper.* The more contrast the better.

7. *The texture of the paper.* It shouldn't be intrusive.

8. *The relationship of the type to other elements on the page.* The relationship should be obvious.

9. *The suitability of type to content.* The art director should exploit the "personality" of types.

Of course, it isn't all that simple. More on readability later.

Type development

The early types were designed to approximate the handwriting —the calligraphy—of the countries in which they developed. The first German types of Gutenberg and his followers in the fifteenth century were harsh, black, and close-fitting—the German blackletter we today mistakenly refer to as "Old English." (A more accurate term for these types is "text," taken from the "texture" of the page, with its heavy, woven look.)

In Italy the faces were lighter, more delicate, after the Humanistic hand of Plutarch. These types were the forerunners of what we today call roman (small "r") types.

The first two centuries of printing in Europe (1450–1650) saw these two faces—blackletter and roman—used extensively. One other took its place beside them. It was italic, introduced by Aldus Manutius in 1501.

The advantage of italic, as Manutius designed it, was that it was close-fitting. That meant you could get more type per page. That was important because paper was scarce. And italic looked more like handwriting, which added to its desirability. Italic became an auxiliary face to roman, borrowing its caps from roman fonts. The two together became the most popular face everywhere in Europe except for Germany.

Typesetting

The types of Gutenberg and Manutius were set by hand. Today we still set some types this way. But, thanks to Ottmar Mergenthaler's invention (1884) and some follow-up inventions in both America and Great Britain, most types are set now by machine.

Hand-set types (foundry type and Ludlow) and machine-set types (Linotype, Intertype, and Monotype) were all developed for letterpress printing. The later printing process, offset lithography, brought about new methods of typesetting. Type produced by these new methods is called "cold type."

Cold type systems, which have cut typesetting costs in some cases to one-fourth of what they would be by "hot type" systems, have broadened considerably the art director's choice of faces, and given him great flexibility in designing his pages. Of the cold type systems, the chief is photocomposition.

Photocomposition has these advantages over hot type:

1. The type can be blown up to several times the original size without losing its sharpness. Repros of hot type, when blown up, would show irregularities. Furthermore, the type can be expanded in width, condensed, slanted, or otherwise distorted to make it fit a given space.

2. Characters can be closely fitted. In fact, they can even be made to overlap. If the art director wants close fitting in his hot type composition, he has to ask for repro proofs, then cut and paste them together.

3. The type can be set in wider measure. Most Linotype machines go out to only 30 picas.

4. The type is cheaper.

5. A photocomposition house is likely to offer a wider selection of types than a hot type house.

As early as 1950 type houses were bringing out new faces on a trial basis on film for photocomposition before putting them on metal. The Dom Casual face was introduced in this way. Today most of the familiar types are available on photocomposition machines. In addition, photocomposition houses have brought out hundreds of faces of their own. That's why type recognition these days is so difficult.

While phototypesetting has made great gains over hot type methods of composition, it has not eliminated them. In America and Europe there is still room for both systems. But in undeveloped countries, where type composing systems start from scratch, the old, conventional systems do not have a chance. It costs a lot less money to set up photocomposition houses. And the presses are almost always likely to be offset.

Unfortunately, much of the cold type composition is, from an aesthetic standpoint, less than satisfactory. The villain has not been photocomposition. The various phototypesetters produce type every bit as good as that produced by Linotype, Intertype, and Monotype machines. The villain has been certain typewriter-like machines with their unsuitable types and their awkward spacing.

Many of the typewriter-composers produce letters designed to fit a single width or, at best, three or four widths. Letters in their ideal state occupy a great variety of widths. A typewriter composition system clearly superior to most others is IBM's Selectric Composer. Its Press Roman face is especially useful.

If the art director has been using one of the inferior typewriter systems, he should consider carefully the money he has been saving and ask himself if the saving is worth the loss of quality he has to put up with. Sometimes, on close analysis, with the inconvenience of making corrections and cutting and pasting them into place, it turns out that "economical" typesetting systems are not so economical after all.

Computer typesetting

When type was set only by hand, a speed of one character per second was possible. Mechanical typesetters increased the speed to five characters per second. Photographic typesetters since World War II brought it up to 500 characters per second. Now electronic-computer typesetting can reach a speed of 10,000 characters per second.[1]

With computer composition, McGraw-Hill in its book-publishing operation has found it can cut production time for a book (after the manuscript has been copyedited) from a normal seven months to a spectacular seven weeks. The savings in time come not so much from the faster typesetting as from the doing away with all the steps that follow it—especially the back and forth movement of proofs of all kinds.[2]

Computers have changed—and will change—typesetting procedures for magazines, but they won't change the basic role of the art director, which is to pick the right types and the right art and put them together to give the best possible display to editorial matter. "Computers have been called 'very fast idiots'," says Paul J. Sampson, associate editor of *Inland Printer/American Lithographer.* "They can make it easier for the careless editor to rush into print with a poor product. They are completely neutral. It's still up to the editor to use his tools, new or old, to serve his field."

What to tell the typesetter

When the art director sends copy to the typesetter or printer, he must specify the following:

1. Point size.[3]
2. Name of the typeface.
3. Weight of the typeface, if other than regular (light, book, medium, bold, demibold, ultrabold, black).
4. Style, if other than upright (italic, condensed, expanded; it could be both italic *and* condensed or expanded).
5. Amount of leading between lines (the art director should specify "set solid" if no leading is desired).
6. Amount of letterspacing, if any.

1. Gerald O. Walter, "Typesetting," *Scientific American,* May 1969, p. 61.
2. Leonard Shatzkin, "The Secrets of Computer Printing," *Editor's Notebook,* May–June 1970, p. 8.
3. The typesetter or printer uses *points* to measure type sizes, *picas* to measure column widths. There are 72 points to one inch. There are 12 points to a pica, hence 6 picas to an inch.

7. Any special instructions on paragraph indentions and margins (flush left? flush right?)

8. Width of column (in picas).

Copyediting marks will take care of such matters as occasional use of italics, small caps, etc.

To save space the author of this book will not reproduce the various copyreading and proofreading marks used to communicate with the typesetter and printer. These marks, basically standardized, are shown in most good dictionaries, style books, editing books, and type specimen books.

Copyediting marks are made right on the original copy, which has been double spaced—triple spaced if for a newspaper—to provide the necessary write-in area. Proofreading marks are made in the margins of galley or page proofs.

One piece of advice is in order here: both copyreading and proofreading marks should be made with a soft pencil to facilitate erasures. The copyreader or proofreader sometimes has second thoughts about his changes.

Categories of type

There are many ways to classify type. If one were to do it from an historical standpoint he would classify them one way. Were he to do it from a utilitarian standpoint, he would do it another.

This book will classify types according to *use*.

We start by dividing types into two broad categories:

1. Body types (up to 14 points).

2. Display types (14 points and larger).

While many faces come in both body and display sizes, some come only as body types and some come only as display types. In a face designed for both categories one often detects subtle changes as it moves from the large to the small. For instance, the interior area of the loop of the "e" has to be proportionately larger in the smaller sizes of a face. Otherwise it would fill in with ink.

The body faces are divided into *book* faces (the most common faces and the faces used for texts of magazines) and *news* faces. News faces have been especially designed for letterpress printing in small sizes on newsprint. They are bold faces, essentially, with large x-heights.[4] They do not come in display sizes.

We can break down typefaces, body and display, into several broad categories called "races." The "races" include:

1. *Roman.* These faces have two distinguishing characteristics: (a) thick and thin strokes and (b) serifs at the stroke terminals. Where the differences in the strokes are minimal and

---

4. The x-height is the height of the lowercase "x."

where serifs blend into the letters, the romans are "old style"; where the differences are pronounced and where the serifs appear almost tacked on as an afterthought, the romans are "modern." In-between styles are "transitional" or "traditional."[5]

2. *Sans serif.* Sans serif types came along first in the early 1800s and were revived by the Bauhaus in the 1920s. Their strokes are essentially of the same thickness. There are no serifs at the terminals. More recent sans serifs, with slight differences in stroke thickness and with a slightly squared look, are called "gothics" or "grotesques."[6]

3. *Slab serif.* Slab or square serif types have even-thickness strokes as do the sans serif types, and serifs as on the roman types. The most beautiful of the slab serifs, because they lean toward the romans, are the Clarendons. Slab serifs were developed in England at a time when the country was taken by Egyptian culture, and the term "Egyptian," for no particular reason, was applied to them. Many of the slab serif faces are named after Egyptian cities. These faces have also been referred to as "antiques." Slab serif faces enjoyed popularity in the 1930s, but their use now is limited.

4. *Ornamental.* To keep the list workable, the author lumps a number of faces under this one category. There are the text or black letters (Old English), the scripts (which are intended to look like handwriting), and the gimmick letters (made to look like logs, pieces of furniture, etc.).

In each of these "races" are hundreds of "families"—adding up to several thousand types. For instance, in the sans serif race are such families as Franklin Gothic, Futura, Helvetica, News Gothic, Record Gothic, Spartan, Tempo, Trade Gothic, Standard, and Univers.

One of the interesting features of Univers is that the designer of the face, instead of giving the various versions descriptive names like "light" and "heavy" and "expanded," gave them numbers. He reserved odd numbers in Univers for upright letters, even numbers for italics. One of the newest families among the sans serifs is Avant Garde Gothic, designed by Herb Lubalin and Tom Carnase for International Typeface Corporation. The face is named after *Avant Garde*, drawing its character from the logo for that magazine. The face, available in several weights, is noteworthy for its close-fitting characters, its large x-height, and the unusual number of ligatures and alternate characters.[7]

---

5. The term "roman" is used by some printers to designate all upright types (as opposed to italic—or slanted—types).
6. The word "gothic" has been applied to many new—and hence controversial—types, including the type we know as Old English.
7. A ligature is a combination of two or more characters designed in a way to make them one unit.

Avant Garde Gothic, designed by Herb Lubalin and Tom Carnase, offers a great variety of ligatures and alternate characters. It comes in five weights. Shown here is medium. (Reprinted with permission of International Typeface Corporation. Copyright 1970 by International Typeface Corporation.)

Not only does the art director find it difficult to distinguish among the various families (exactly how does Granjon differ from Janson?), he also has difficulty distinguishing among variations in the same family of type. Linotype's Garamond differs from Ludlow's Garamond which differs from the Garamond issued by a foundry type manufacturer.

The Mergenthaler Linotype Corporation currently has two kinds of Garamond: regular and Garamond #3. Garamond #3 is very similar to a version of Garamond offered by Intertype, but Linotype's regular Garamond is quite different from the other two.

Some more recent faces have been designed exclusively for one company or the other. Caledonia is exclusively Linotype. Century Schoolbook is an Intertype exclusive.

Most families of type come in more than one weight (light, regular, bold, ultrabold) and more than one width (regular, expanded, condensed).

The italics

Although from an historical standpoint italics deserve their own category, typographers do not consider them as a "race." The reason: italics have become more a style variation than a type in their own right. Almost every face has its italic version.

For some types the italics are exactly like the uprights, but slanted. For other types, the italics are quite different—so different, in fact, that they appear to be of a different design. Many art directors prefer italics different in design from their uprights because then they are more useful as contrast types.

Italics, as conceived by Manutius, were narrower than the uprights, but in some faces today they are actually wider. In Linotype and Intertype faces they are equal in width to their uprights. That's because both the upright and the italic version of each letter are on the same mat, one underneath the other.

Because they are designed on a diagonal, italics tend to project a mood of restlessness or haste. Italics are not quite as easy to read as uprights. Art directors find italics useful for captions, for emphasis in body copy, for foreign phraseology, and for names of publications, plays, ships, and works of art. Used column after column, solid italics can be fatiguing. Nor does the reader appreciate them as occasional paragraphs in body copy; when readers move back into the uprights they get the optical illusion of reading type that bends over to the left.

When the editor or art director underlines a word in a manuscript, he is telling the typesetter to set the word in italics. He should make sure italics are *available* in that face; if not, the printer may set the word in boldface. It is a mistake to set names of publications in boldface. It makes them stand out unnecessarily from other words. If no italics are available, names of publications should be set in ordinary uprights.

Some magazines run the names of publications in italics but they run their own names, when they're mentioned in the copy, in caps and small caps. Like this: PUBLICATION DESIGN.

Small caps, only as tall as the x-height of the letters, are also useful for jobs ordinarily assigned to full-size caps: for instance, headlines quoted from newspapers and telegrams from letters-to-the-editor writers.

The character of types

Some types are versatile enough to be appropriate for almost any job. Others are more limited in what they can do. But all types have some special qualities that set them apart. Art directors are not in agreement about these qualities, but here are a few familiar faces, along with descriptions of the moods they seem to convey:

Baskerville
Bodoni
Caslon
Century
Cheltenham
Franklin Gothic
Futura
Garamond
Standard
Stymie
Times Roman

1. *Baskerville*—beauty, quality, urbanity.
2. *Bodoni*—formality, aristocracy, modernity.
3. *Caslon*—dignity, character, maturity.
4. *Century*—elegance, clarity.
5. *Cheltenham*—honesty, reliability, awkwardness.
6. *Franklin Gothic*—urgency, bluntness.
7. *Futura*—severity, utility.
8. *Garamond*—grace, worth, fragility.
9. *Standard*—order, newness.
10. *Stymie*—precision, construction.
11. *Times Roman*—tradition, efficiency.

These qualities, if indeed they come across at all to readers, come across only vaguely. Furthermore, a single face can have qualities that tend to cancel out each other. (Can a type be both tradition-oriented and efficient?) While the art director should be conscious of these qualities and make whatever use he can of them, he should not feel bound to any one type because of a mood he wants to convey.

Assume he is designing a radical, militant magazine like *Ramparts*. Baskerville seems an unlikely choice for such a magazine, and yet it has been used effectively by *Ramparts*. As it has been used by *Reader's Digest*!

Sometimes the best answer to the question "What type to use in title display?" is to go with a stately, readable type—like Baskerville—and rely upon the *words* in the title to express the mood of the piece.

Type Revivals

What may be good for one period of time in typography may

not be good in another. Type preferences change. Types come and go—and come back again.

A case in point is Bookman, rediscovered in the mid-1960s as a display face. Bookman is a face adapted from an oldstyle antique face of the 1860s. It is like Clarendon, but it has more roundness.

At the turn of the century it had become so popular that a reaction set in against it. Designers began to consider it monotonous. It was kept alive by offset and gravure, because its strong lines and serifs stood up well in that kind of printing. (The old *Collier's* magazine used it.) As these processes became more sophisticated and better able to handle more fragile types, Bookman died out.

In revival, it gives display matter a solid, strong look. In its italic version, with swash caps, it has a charm that has captivated some of our leading designers. (See the *New York* logo in chapter 8.)

Other types that have made a comeback in magazine design include Cooper Black, Cheltenham, and Futura.

The variety of typefaces

In all, the art director faces a choice of several thousand typefaces. The beginning art director has a tendency to want to use them all; they all look so good! Eventually he will develop strong prejudices against many of them. He will conclude that only a few fit his magazine. And he will change his mind from time to time as to which ones those are.

Because he works for a magazine that runs articles on subject matter that "ranges literally from pickles to politics," Herb Bleiweiss, art director of *Ladies' Home Journal*, uses a great variety of typefaces, as many as thirty in a single issue. ". . . An art director must let a natural variety develop without preconceptions which might limit effectiveness," he says.

He has even tried running headlines or titles that were smaller than the body type. Once he had a heading set on a piece of acetate and frozen into a cake of ice. That was for a feature with the title: "Work Wonders with Canned and Frozen Poultry Products." Resting on top of the ice were assorted products.

An art director like Herb Bleiweiss can get away with such innovation, but the beginning art director is wise to stick with only a few faces in traditional arrangements. A magazine's pages can easily turn into what Will Burton has described as "visual riddles." The reader will not have the patience for them.

"If . . . [editors] have a good art director who can handle the new tricks [made possible with phototypesetting] with taste and punch, editors can benefit from the new freedom. If not,

GREECE
JAMAICA
Ceylon
China
MEXICO
France
Tahiti
Canada
Hong Kong
Ireland
Scotland
𝔇enmark
Japan
PORTUGAL
BRITAIN

Some attempts by art directors to find typefaces or letterforms appropriate to specific countries or places.

An illustration from a whimsical ad sponsored by Quad Typographers, New York. The company has matched typefaces with illustration styles. These characters supposedly attended the typesetting company's "posh Fifth Anniversary Party." From left: European industrialist Claude Graphique, society columnist Lightline Gothic, impresario Futura Black, Baroness Excelsior Script, health faddist 20th Century Ultrabold, unidentified maid (her face is the company insignia), Texas tycoon Windsor Elongated, underground film star Prisma, Italian futurist designer Sig. Modern Roman No. 20, former channel swimmer Samantha Smoke, and her escort, Seventh Ave. mogul Max Balloon. Concept and design by Peter Rauch and Herb Levitt; illustration by Tim Lewis.

they may have only new ropes with which to hang themselves," says Paul J. Sampson, associate editor of *Inland Printer/American Lithographer.*

What type to use

The art director selects his types largely on the basis of personal preference. Still he has some rules to guide him.

"Objective research has produced few dramatic results," says Herbert Spencer, "but it has provided a wealth of information about factors of typography which contribute to greater reader efficiency, and it has confirmed the validity of many established typographic conventions, but not of all."[8]

Among findings verified by research are these:

1. All caps slow reading speed. They also occupy 40–50 percent more space.

2. Italics are harder to read than uprights.

3. Very short lines—and very long lines—are hard to read.

8. Herbert Spencer, *The Visible Word*, Hastings House, Publishers, New York, 1969, p. 6.

4. Unjustified lines do *not* hurt readability, especially now that we are getting used to them.

Most art directors decide on a body type and stick with it issue after issue. Occasionally an art director runs a special article in a different face. Or he uses one face for articles and another for standing features like columns and departments.

In making his original choice for body type or types, the art director takes paper stock into consideration. For instance, old style romans work better on rough paper stock; modern romans reproduce best on smooth or coated stocks.

The choice of typeface should also be influenced by the printing process to be used. Some of the Bodoni faces, because of their hairline serifs, do not show up well in offset.[9] Typefaces in gravure tend to darken; hence for a text face the art director might not want to start out with a type already boldface. That everything in gravure is screened, including the type, suggests he would want to use a face without frills.

Once the art director makes his choice of type or types for

9. See the typography in the first edition of Theodore Peterson's *Magazines in the Twentieth Century*, University of Illinois Press, Urbana, 1956. The editors changed the face in the second edition, 1964.

ABCDEFGHIJKL
MNOPQRSTUV
WXYZ
abcdefghijklmnopq
rstuvwxyz
1234567890

ABCDEFGHIJ
KLMNOPQRS
TUVWXYZ
abcdefghijklmno
pqrstuvwxyz
1234567890

ABCDEFGHIJ
KLMNOPQR
STUVWXYZ
abcdefghijklmn
opqrstuvwxyz
1234567890

body copy, he lives with it for a period of several years, perhaps even for the duration of the magazine. Choosing type for titles, on the other hand, represents a continuing problem. Often he chooses the type to match the mood of the article.

That the display type does not match the body type shouldn't bother him. But he should see to it that the various display types for a spread come from the same family. The display types should be obviously related and perfectly matched. If that's not possible, then they should be clearly *unrelated*. The art director should not put display types together that are *almost* related. *Almost* related types create the illusion that a mistake was made in setting.

An art director could combine an old style roman with a sans serif very nicely, but he would almost never combine an old style roman with a modern roman.

The you-can't-go-wrong types

Every art director has his favorite typeface, and one favorite may differ radically from another. Most art directors, however, could agree on a half dozen or so faces that form the standards against which other types are measured. A Basic Seven, so far as this author is concerned, would include these:

1. *Baskerville.* This face has to rank as one of the most beautiful ever designed. It comes now in many versions, but it was originally designed by John Baskerville, a British calligrapher, around 1760. Considered a threat to Caslon when it was introduced, Baskerville represented a break with the past, a move to a more modern look. It is a transitional face, more precise than the old style romans but not so precise as Bodoni.

A "wide set" type, it needs some leading. It looks best on smooth paper.

A quirk in the design results in a lowercase *g* with an incomplete bottom loop.

2. *Bodoni.* Italian designer Giambattista Bodoni drew some inspiration from Baskerville as he created Bodoni, a beautifully balanced if severe face, with marked differences in the thicks and thins of the strokes and with clean, harsh serifs.

The face looks best on slick paper and must be properly inked and printed. It is a little difficult to read in large doses. Like most faces, its beauty is lost in its bold and ultrabold versions.

3. *Caslon.* To most printers over the years, Caslon, designed in the eighteenth century by the Englishman, William Caslon, served as the No. 1 typeface. The rule was: "When in doubt, use Caslon."

The most familiar example of old style roman, this face still enjoys wide use. It has been described variously as "honest," "unobtrusive," and "classical."

Its caps, when you study them, are surprisingly wide, and its cap *A* seems to have a chip cut out of its top. The bottom loop on the lowercase *g* seems small. Otherwise, the face has no eccentricities.

4. *Clarendon.* The Clarendon faces are a cross between slab serifs and old style romans. The serifs, heavy as in slab serif letters, are bracketed, as in roman. They merge into the main strokes.

The first Clarendons appeared in England in the middle of the nineteenth century. Two recent versions are Hermann Eidenbenz's (1952) and Freeman Craw's (1954).

5. *Garamond.* This face was named after a sixteenth-century French typefounder, Claude Garamond, but it was probably designed by Jean Jannon. Equipped with unpredictable serifs, it is, nonetheless, beautiful and readable. It is a rather narrow face with a small x-height. It can be set solid.

6. *Helvetica.* Three great gothic faces came out of Europe in 1957: Univers, from France, designed by Adrian Frutiger; Folio, from Germany, designed by Konrad Bauer and Walter Baum; and Helvetica, from Switzerland, designed by Mas Miedinger. Clean and crisp, they look very much alike.

Helvetica, introduced in America in 1963 in body and display sizes, is perhaps the most available of the three. Unlike Univers, it is a close-fitting type, even on the Linotype. Like all the newer gothics, its rounds are slightly squared, and its strokes vary just a bit in thickness. The terminals on letters such as *e* and *s* are cut on the horizontal, aiding in readability. In all a handsome, modern face.

It comes in light, regular, regular italic, medium, bold, bold compact italic, regular extended, bold extended, extra bold extended, regular condensed, bold condensed, and extra bold condensed. The example shown here is Helvetica Regular.

7. *Times Roman.* Sometimes called *New Times Roman* or *Times New Roman*, this is the face designed by Stanley Morison for *The Times* of London in 1931. It is very much a twentieth-century type, not a revival, good for all kinds of jobs, although it is more of a body than a display face. Essentially an old style roman, it could, with its sharp-cut serifs, be classified as a transitional face. A peculiarity is the rounded bottom of the *b*.

Its large x-height makes some leading necessary. With its bold look, it was first a newspaper face, becoming popular later as a magazine and book face, particularly in America.

Allen Hutt reported in 1970 that after 1975 *The Times* will no longer use Times Roman as a text face. A new face will be

ABCDEFGH IJKLMNOP QRSTUVW XYZ abcdefghijkl mnopqrstuv wxyz 1234567890

ABCDEFGHIJKL MNOPQRSTUV WXYZ abcdefghijklmnop qrstuvwxyz 1234567890

ABCDEFGHIJK LMNOPQRSTU VWXYZ abcdefghijklmno pqrstuvwxyz 1234567890

ABCDEFGHIJ KLMNOPQRS TUVWXYZ abcdefghijklmno pqrstuvwxyz 1234567890

In an era of diminishing ranges, Western reserves are the best places to find our wildest animals—moose, bear or bison

by Joe Van Wormer

One sunny afternoon last September, five moose, three bulls and two cows, walked out of the timber to feed in willow-covered Pelican Creek marsh in Yellowstone National Park. In a matter of minutes excited visitors blocked a nearby road to take advantage of this rare opportunity to see and photograph specimens of our largest deer. Because big game species are generally both shy and scarce, there aren't many places where they can readily be seen at close range. However, in a few areas they have lost most of their fear of man. Yellowstone National Park is one such place. I have never failed to see moose there.

Chevron USA's *art director, Roger Waterman, for this right-hand page opener, was able to come up with a typeface that perfectly matched his drawing of a moose. Or maybe it was the other way around: he drew his moose to take on the look of the type.*

designed. Hutt says the trouble with Times Roman as a body face is that it requires good presswork and paper.[10]

Title display

Titles for magazine articles differ from newspaper headlines in that their shape and placement are not dictated by a *headline schedule.* Only the designer's lack of imagination limits what may be done.

Many art directors fail to take advantage of the greater flexibility magazines have over newspapers. The trade magazines, especially, seem wedded to old newspaper ideas about titles or headlines. They use the same old flush left, multi-line settings. Even the jargon of the headlines is the same. On the

10. Allen Hutt, "Times Roman: A Re-assessment," *The Journal of Typographic Research*, Summer 1970, pp. 259–70.

other hand, some magazines resort to so much typographic and design trickery that their readers become bewildered. And that isn't good either.

A good rule to start off with: *Magazine titles should occupy a single line of type in a size only slightly larger than the body copy.* Ideally, they should be set in the same face as the body copy. They should never be tipped, curved, or made to run sideways or up-and-down on the page. They should remain on the horizontal.

With that in mind, the art director can occasionally introduce a variation. When the mood of the article seems to call for a particular typeface or when the impact of the title can be improved with a bit of typographic emphasis, the art director can innovate.

Let's say one word in the title is more important than the others. The art director can bring out its importance in many ways: by setting it in a different face, a different size, a different weight; by printing it in color; by putting a box around it or underlining it; by reversing it in a black box or a color block; by separating it from the other words with a small piece of art; by showing it in perspective; by running it out of alignment. The important thing to remember is: only that one word should get the treatment. When two different words are made to stand out they cancel each other out. Carl Webb of the University of Oregon used to tell his students: "All display is no display." A worthy observation.

Should the art director want to innovate with the entire title, he can try setting it in giant letters; building it with letters cut from a photographic background; surprinting or reversing it in a photograph or tint block; wrapping it around a photograph; arranging the lines in a piggyback fashion; nesting the lines partially inside other lines; fitting them inside the text;

One case where Old English, in a simplified form, is appropriate as trade magazine typography. An opening spread from Fleet Owner. *Note the pleasing proportion of white space to title-and-text on the left-hand page. Art editor Bud Clarke ties the pages together with a large photo running across the gutter and with a two-page box. (With permission from* Fleet Owner. *Copyright 1970 by McGraw-Hill, Inc. All rights reserved.)*

Publishers' Weekly *for an article on university presses uses hand lettering rather than type in order to give the title a chalk-on-blackboard look.*

alternating the letters in black and color; superimposing them —the list is endless.

When *Sunset* sets a title in giant letters, it screens the letters to gray to keep them from looking cheap or loud. Another idea is to set giant-size titles in lowercase. Lowercase letters are more complicated in design and more interesting to view in large sizes.

Titles should ordinarily be set in lowercase anyway, with only the first word and all proper nouns capitalized. Lowercase is easier to read than all caps because lowercase letters are easier to distinguish from one another. Lowercase is easier to read than caps and lowercase because caps and lowercase cause the eye to move up and down, like the springs on a car moving along a bumpy road. Besides, writing caps-and-lowercase titles takes longer than writing all-lowercase titles: the title writer faces a complicated set of rules on which words to capitalize, which ones to leave lowercase.

When the art director has a multi-line title to deal with, he can show it flush left, flush right, or centered. It is not a good idea to run it flush left-flush right. To make it come out even on both sides usually takes some fancy and unnatural spacing. The most intriguing multi-line titles are those set in a staggered pattern to form an irregular silhouette. The lines should be kept close enough together so the title reads as a unit.

In multi-line titles it is almost never desirable to single out one word for emphasis. Asking the reader to jump from line to line is interruption enough. Asking him to accept a change in type style in the middle of it is asking too much.

If the art director *must* have one word in a multi-line title stand out, he can put it in a line by itself, and without changing the typeface. To make it stand out more, in a flush-left title, he can run it a little to the left of the axis.

In planning a multi-line title, the art director should pay more attention to the logic of the arrangement than its looks. It is desirable, of course, that lines be reasonably equal in length, but it is more important by far that they be easily read.

Most magazines run blurbs with their titles. Blurbs, which can go above or below the titles, are always longer than the titles and always in a smaller type. The designer should make certain the difference in size is great enough to assure the reader's seeing the title and blurb as two units.

When the title comes as two sentences, the designer cannot very well separate them with a period (unless the magazine's style is to end titles with periods), so he has to resort to some other device. He can use a semicolon, as a newspaper would do; he can use a typographic dingbat at the beginning of each sentence; he can use some extra white space; he can change to another typeface or size for the second sentence; he can change to color; he can change the position.

Punctuation up large

While the editor bears the primary responsibility for punctuation, the art director should be concerned about punctuation, too, especially as he letters in the titles and headlines, where errors are most glaring. Oddly, in his haste in checking proofs, the editor often misses punctuation errors that creep into display type.

The art director must be particularly careful to letter in apostrophes where they're called for. The word is *it's* when *it* and *is* are contracted. Only the possessive is *its*. The possessive for *men* is *men's*, never *mens*.

When the title carries a quote, the art director uses double quote marks, as in the body copy, unless he's working for a newspaper. Newspapers use single quote marks to save space. If the title consists of several flush-left lines, the art director may elect to put the quote marks outside the line of the axis.

If he uses an initial letter to begin an article, and the article begins with a quote, he'll probably want to leave the quote mark out. If he uses a quote mark, it should be in the same font as the initial letter.

The art director must not make the mistake of using a hyphen when he needs a dash (long or short—there are two sizes). And he should avoid the cliché of using a series of periods to end a line, like this . . .

The late Carl Dair made an interesting contribution to the typography of punctuation. He introduced an upright, straight line, the height of the x-height, set off with extra white space, to help readers make a distinction between a broken word (broken because it wouldn't fit at the end of the line) and a compound word (like world-wide). He used the ordinary hyphen for compound words only.[11]

Another punctuation contribution comes from American Type Founders Company, which recently introduced the interabang, special punctuation combining both the question mark and the exclamation mark (for use in such sentences as "Are you kidding?").

Body copy

In choosing a typeface for body copy, the art director is not quite so concerned with the beauty of the face as when he chooses display type. His primary concern should be: Is the type readable column after column? Further: What kind of pattern does the type make over a large area? The pattern should be even-textured, not spotty.

11. See how the system works in his book, *Design with Type*, University of Toronto Press, Toronto, Canada, 1967.

Most art directors prefer roman to sans serif faces for body copy simply because readers are used to them. Novelty hurts readability. But as sans serif finds increasing acceptance among readers of avant-garde magazines it will find increasing acceptance among readers of all magazines. Indeed, sans serif has in recent years become almost commonplace as body copy for some general circulation magazines.

One objection to sans serif used to be that it was too "vertical"; it did not have serifs to help move the reader horizontally across the line. But the newer sans serifs feature terminals that are sliced horizontally, and this tends to do the job serifs do.

A spread from United Church Herald *showing that interesting design is possible without artwork. Good display of type on the left-hand page and pleasant proportions and subtle use of ruled lines on the right-hand page give the spread plenty of impact. A second color helped, too.*

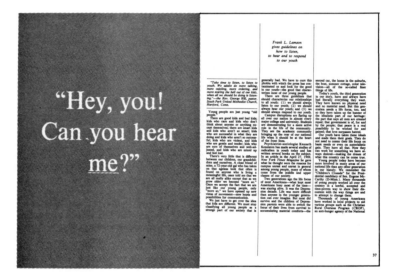

Also, the strokes of the newer sans serifs vary slightly in thickness, just as roman strokes do; sans serif type now is less monotonous in large doses.

Sans serifs, because of their solid character, are especially recommended where printing quality is inferior. Types with intricate serifs need superior printing in order to reproduce well.

Art directors have also changed their minds about unjustified lines. More and more magazines use them. Advertisers in their copy often get away with unjustified *left-hand* margins. Magazines avoid this. In magazine editorial matter, the lack of justification occurs on the *right*. In long blocks of copy, the reader needs a constant margin at the left to which he can return, line after line.

Some types need more space between words than others. Expanded types need more space between words than condensed types. Types with large x-heights need more space between words than those with small x-heights.

No need to line up the bottoms of the columns, as art director Raymond Waites, Jr., shows with this United Church Herald *spread. No need, either, to run the title at the top left of the spread.*

The spacing between words should never exceed the space between lines.

Copy needs extra spacing between lines when

1. the type has a large x-height;

2. the type has a pronounced vertical stress, as with Bodoni and with most of the sans serifs, and

3. the line length is longer than usual.

If copy is set in a single width, leading should be consistent throughout. It is best to specify the amount of leading before copy is set, as: "Set 10 on 12" (which means, "Set it in 10-point type on a 12-point slug."). Adding leading between lines afterwards costs more. Newspapers sometimes "lead out" the beginning or ending of a story to make it fit—a practice magazines should avoid. Leading part of a story tends to make the type in that part of the story look bigger than the remaining type.

Many art directors no longer consider a widow—a less than full-length line at the top of a column in a multicolumn spread —as the typographic monstrosity it was thought to be. But when a widow consists of a single word or syllable, the left-over space is great enough to spoil the horizontal axis at the top of the columns. The art director then should do some rearranging of his lines to get rid of the widow.

But readers appreciate an occasional oasis deep into long columns of copy. Art directors supply it with subheadings or— better still—just a little extra white space. Sometimes an initial letter helps.

Initial letters

An initial letter used at the beginning of an article or story

For a class in calligraphy, Jo-anne Hasegawa, student at the University of Oregon, creates an experimental design with old style roman letters in various sizes. A feel for letterform should be part of the training of every potential magazine art director.

or at each of its breaks beckons the reader, whose interest may have waned, and at the same time provides typographic relief.

An initial letter should match the face used for the title.

It is called a two-, three-, four-, or five-line initial, depending upon how deep in lines it is. It can be bigger than the title size and often is. The art director may find it necessary to help the reader make the step from the initial to the body copy by giving him a first word or two in all caps, or small caps. Body copy should fit snugly around initial letters. Sometimes this takes some fancy work by the composing room.

The art director may want to consider initial letters that project out or up from the body copy rather than fit down into it. *Mainliner,* the publication of United Air Lines, sometimes uses an initial *word* at the beginning of an article. It can be no more than a two- or three-letter word.

Captions

Picture captions are ordinarily set in type slightly smaller than body copy. Sometimes they are set in italics or in boldface.

Captions can be set in type larger than body copy if the pictures are not run in connection with articles and if they have no display type to set them off. The captions then serve also as titles.

Some editors seem to feel that caption writers should even out the last line so that it is fully filled and flush with the other lines. This is folly. The time spent counting characters and rewriting to make that last line fit can be spent better on other editorial matters.

By-lines

United Church Herald often combines by-lines with blurbs about the author. Example: "Mathew S. Ogawa shows how after-midnight broadcasts are reaching Japanese youth." The authors' names are underlined to make them stand out. Other magazines run blurbs about the authors in small type at the bottoms of article openings, sort of as footnotes. Still others, such as *Esquire*, run separate columns combining information about all the contributors.

The New Yorker places by-lines at the ends of articles or stories, apparently in the belief that readers should get into editorial material without regard to who wrote it. Most magazines, if they use by-lines, place them at the beginnings. *The New Republic*, for example, runs by-lines well removed from the titles of articles and right next to the articles' beginnings. Because both title and by-line are in boldface, the reader's eye moves from title across white space to by-line—and to the beginning of the article.

By-lines are set in type smaller than that used for article or story titles but larger, usually, than type used for body copy.

Credit lines

Some magazines run credit lines in a box on the table of contents page or somewhere else in the magazine. It is surprising that companies granting permission to reprint photographs or other illustrations would settle for that kind of credit. Few readers study such a box to find out who took what picture.

The more common practice is to run credit lines right next to the photographs, whether they be original or borrowed. Credit-line type is usually smaller than caption type, to keep the two entirely separate; often a sans serif type is used. Some magazines run credit lines up the sides of pictures to keep the lines from interfering with captions.

Credit lines can be reversed or surprinted inside the photographs at their bottom edges.

If a magazine does not want to be bothered with separate settings for credit lines, it can run them as last lines of captions, set off by parentheses.

When one photographer takes all the pictures for a feature, he gets a by-line rather than a credit line, just as illustrators get. The photographer's or illustrator's by-line may be slightly smaller than the author's and placed away from the story's opening.

Typographic endings

Like a good cup of coffee after a meal, some writer has said. That's what an article's ending should be. The reader should know when he's reached the end of the article or story; he should walk away inspired, shocked, amused, instructed, perhaps even moved to some course of action.

Many editors feel that the writing alone may not be enough to signal that the encounter between the writer and reader is over. Some typographic accessory should announce, in effect: this is The End. This is especially true now that so few magazines provide a cushion of fillers at the ends of articles. They end at the bottoms of pages.

The standard typographic device is the small, square box, available on any linecasting machine. Some magazines design their own end device and see that special matrices are available to the Linotype operator. *Playboy,* for instance, uses its rabbit symbol, reversed in a small black square with rounded corners. *Popular Photography* uses a stylized rendering of a lens opening. *Esquire* uses three vertical lines with a horizontal line running through them in the middle. *Sweden Now* uses a tiny, slightly altered version of its logo. *Scene,* published by Southwestern Bell Telephone Company, and *Sports Illustrated,* among other magazines, use the word "End" set in tiny letters.

Suggested further reading

BAIN, ERIC K., *Display Typography: Theory and Practice,* Hastings House, Publishers, New York, 1970.

BERRY, W. TURNER; JOHNSON, A. F.; AND JASPERT, W. P., *Encyclopedia of Typefaces,* Pitman Publishing Corporation, New York, 1962.

BIGGS, JOHN, *Basic Typography,* Watson-Guptill Publications, New York, 1969.

BIEGELEISEN, J. I., *Art Directors' Book of Type Faces,* Arco Publishing Co., Inc., New York, 1970.

DAIR, CARL, *Design with Type,* University of Toronto Press, Toronto, Canada, 1967. (Revised Edition)

DOWDING, GEOFFREY, *Finer Points in the Spacing and Arrangement of Type,* Wace and Company, Ltd., London, 1966. (Third Edition)

FYFFE, CHARLES, *Basic Copyfitting,* Watson-Guptill Publications, New York, 1969.

GATES, DAVID, *Lettering for Reproduction,* Watson-Guptill Publications, New York, 1969.

HAAB, ARMIN, AND HAETTENSCHWEILER, WALTER, *Lettera 3,* Hastings House, Publishers, New York, 1968.

HANSON, GLENN, *How to Take the Fits Out of Copyfitting,* Mul-T-Rul Co., Ft. Morgan, Colo., 1967.

HUTCHINGS, R. S., ed., *A Manual of Decorated Types,* Hastings House, Publishers, New York, 1965.

————, *A Manual of Script Typefaces: A Definitive Guide to Series in Current Use,* Hastings House, Publishers, New York, 1965.

————, *A Manual of Sans Serif Typefaces,* Hastings House, Publishers, New York, 1966.

LAMBERT, FREDERICK, *Letter Forms: Alphabets for Designers,* Hastings House, Publishers, New York, 1964.

LAWSON, ALEXANDER, *Printing Types,* Beacon Press, Boston, 1971.

LEWIS, JOHN, *Typography: Basic Principles, Influences and Trends,* Reinhold Publishing Corporation, New York, 1964.

LIEBERMAN, J. BEN, *Types of Typefaces and How to Recognize Them,* Sterling Publishing Company, Inc., New York, 1967.

LONGYEAR, WILLIAM LEVWYN, *Type & Lettering,* Watson-Guptill Publications, New York, 1966. (Fourth Edition)

OGG, OSCAR, *The 26 Letters,* Thomas Y. Crowell Company, New York, 1971. (Revised Edition)

ROBERTS, RAYMOND, *Typographic Design,* Ernest Benn Limited, London, 1966.

ROSEN, BEN, *Type and Typography: The Designer's Type Book,* Reinhold Publishing Corporation, New York, 1967.

RUDER, EMIL, *Typography: A Manual of Design,* Hastings House, Publishers, New York, 1967.

SPENCER, HERBERT, *The Visible Word: Problems of Legibility,* Hastings House, Publishers, Inc., New York, 1969. (Second Edition)

SUTTON, JAMES, AND BARTRAM, ALAN, *An Atlas of Typeforms,* Hastings House, Publishers, New York, 1968.

SWANN, CAL, *The Techniques of Typography,* Watson-Guptill Publications, New York, 1969.

TSCHICHOLD, JAN, *Treasury of Alphabets and Lettering,* Reinhold Publishing Corporation, New York, 1966.

ZACHRISSON, BROR, *Studies in the Legibility of Printed Text,* Almqvist and Wiksell, Stockholm, 1965.

ZAPF, HERMANN, *About Alphabets: Some Marginal Notes on Type Design,* M. I. T. Press, Cambridge, Mass., 1970.

Banta Book of Typographical Tips, George Banta Company, Inc., Menasha, Wis., 1969.

Graphic Arts Typebook, Reinhold Publishing Corporation, New York, 1965. (Several volumes)

Visible Language, Cleveland Museum of Art, Cleveland. (Quarterly)

Chapter 7
Art

One of the big advantages of offset is that almost anything from almost any source can be reproduced with little or no additional expense. In fact the flexibility and adaptability of offset has tempted editors of marginal publications to steal printed photographs and artwork from the more affluent publications. The only reason these editors are not prosecuted is that their publications attract virtually no attention outside their own exceedingly limited audiences. But clearly they are violating the law if the material they appropriate is copyrighted, and often it is.

There are enough low-cost art and photographic services around to make such illegal activity unnecessary, even for the most mendicant of editors.

Stock art

Art directors of company magazines can, for $15 a year, subscribe to *Service for Company Publications*, a monthly published by the National Association of Manufacturers, 277 Park Avenue, New York, N.Y. 10017. It is a clip sheet containing, among other features, cartoons, sketches, and short articles on slick paper, ready for pasteup.

Redi-Art, Inc., 30 E. 10th St., New York, N.Y. 10003, and Harry C. Volk Art Studio, Box 4098, Rockford, Ill. 61110, provide low-cost clip books of contemporary stock drawings classified by subject matter.

Of course any art that is in the public domain can be clipped or copied from books and magazines and used freely without fear of reprisal. Congress has for years been thinking about revising the copyright law, but as of this writing the law still provides protection for only twenty-eight years, plus an addi-

Two sample drawings from "Human Relations," one of scores of clip books available from Harry Volk Art Studio, Rockford, Ill. Editors can purchase clip books by subject area for a few dollars each, and each book contains about two dozen drawings from which to choose. There are no limitations on how they are used, or on frequency of use. Of course, no editor or advertiser who uses the Volk service, or some similar service, gets exclusive rights to the material.

tional twenty-eight years if the copyright owner applies for a renewal of protection. After fifty-six years any published material is up for grabs.

Dover Publications, New York, makes available a number of paperback collections of public-domain art. For a few dollars the magazine art director can build a library of old-time art.

Once he buys any of this stock art, the art director can use it however he wishes, and as often as he wishes. In the case of stock photographs, he is more restricted. He usually buys one-time use and is charged on the basis of his publication's circulation and the intended use.

Harold M. Lambert Studios, Philadelphia, offers him a choice of 500,000 black-and-white photographs and 50,000 color transparencies. H. Armstrong Roberts, New York, offers a similiar number.

For his photographs the art director can also turn to the picture libraries of other publications. Some publications lending pictures ask only for a credit line, some ask fees. *Life* charges $5 per print and a $45 one-time reproduction fee.

The art director can also deal with the wire services and with photo services like Black Star and Magnum. Fees here are likely to be steep, especially when photographs are made to order.

He can also turn to public and private libraries, museums, and historical societies.

For free photographs he can turn to various state and federal agencies, chambers of commerce, and public relations departments of companies, institutions, and trade organizations.

Literary Market Place, published annually by R. R. Bowker Co., New York, and found in most libraries, carries a list of more than fifty "Photo & Picture Sources"—places that sell stock photographs and drawings, contemporary and historical.

Writer's Market, published annually by *Writer's Digest*, Cincinnati, also contains a list of "Picture Sources."

Two books that are particularly helpful in this regard are *Picture Sources*, Special Libraries Assn., 31 East 10th Street, New York, N.Y. 10003, and *Pictures Unlimited*, Photographic Trade News Corp., 41 East 28th St., New York, N.Y. 10016. Price of each is nominal.

Stock art, then, is almost everywhere available, and at various prices. But stock art has two chief disadvantages: (1) it never fits the exact need of the art director, and (2) it is not available on an exclusive basis. Another publication—even a competing publication—could conceivably come out with the same art.

Art from within

On many small magazines and some big ones, the art director takes his own pictures or does his own illustrations.

If he takes his own pictures, he will want a good 35 mm camera with a fast lens, a telephoto lens, and a wide-angle lens. With today's fast film, he can usually get along without flash equipment.

The art director taking his own pictures has an advantage over a free-lancer in that he knows exactly what to watch for— what is needed—for an effective page layout.

It is necessary for the art director to line up a better-than-drug-store processor. The best procedure is to first order contact prints, then enlargements from those prints that seem most promising. Enlargements, even at $1 or $2 a print, are cheap enough; the art director must have more than he really needs so he can boil down his choices to the really outstanding photographs.

If the art director has a staff artist or photographer, he will work with him much as he would work with a free-lancer. The big advantage is that the staffer will be readily available and at a comparatively modest cost. But there has to be a continuous flow of work to make such an arrangement pay off.

Art from free-lancers

Many art directors feel that the ideal arrangement is to buy all art—photography and illustration—from free-lancers.

Free-lancers are everywhere. Once the word gets out that the magazine is in the market, the art director will face a steady stream of them—illustrators and photographers nervously clutching their portfolios of examples. "Sorry Mr.—what's the name again?—we really don't have many assignments that call for charcoal renderings of nudes." In case the art director

". . . Each story calls for its own individual technique," says Robert Quackenbush, who did the illustration for this right-hand opener for Clipper. "For this reason, I experiment with many mediums and tools to find the 'right' technique for a story. I have worked in nearly all mediums . . . from woodcuts, to etchings, to water colors . . . even to . . . a five-cent pencil." Note how well the art is integrated with the display type: each has a bold, hand-carved look. (Reproduced by permission from Clipper Magazine, published and copyrighted by Pan American World Airways.)

Walt Whirl, magazine and advertising illustrator, uses an ordinary pencil to make this sensitive line drawing. He combines a fine outline with areas of texture, letting the edges of the texture areas define some of the outline of the figure. He distorts the perspective in order to create tension in the drawing.

doesn't find the free-lancer he wants, he can turn to several directories.

Art Direction publishes a useful one: *Annual Buyers Guide*, listing 2,500 persons and organizations "classified by specialties, making it easy for the buyer to find just the talent or service he's seeking." *Literary Market Place* also runs names and addresses of free-lance artists.

It is one thing for the art director to pick out prints or drawings from among those submitted to him on speculation. It is another to pick out a photographer or illustrator from among those available and send him off on an assignment. A man's portfolio may not be representative of what he can do under adverse conditions.

Bob Pliskin, vice-president in charge of art for Benton & Bowles, the advertising agency, has a unique test for the photographer who sees him for an assignment. He has the man empty his pockets—the change, the handkerchief, and whatever else he may be carrying, and then asks him to arrange these things and take photos, up to fifty of them. The photographer then submits his half dozen best prints. If he can make such a collection of materials exciting and stimulating, he probably can handle any other assignment, Pliskin reasons.

Another problem has to do with deadlines. The art director can't be sure that a new man will deliver his work on time. So he tends to stick to a small stable of free-lancers whose work and working habits he is familiar with.

Younger artists, those who are not established, may feel there is a conspiracy against them.

Consider what the young cartoonist must feel as in issue after issue of the opinion magazines he sees only the work of Herblock or Bill Mauldin reprinted. Or if there are original drawings, they always seem to be done by Robert Osborn, he with the sparse brush style editors seem to like. Can no one else do as well?

In more recent years art directors have discovered David Levine, the fine-line caricaturist, and his biting portrayals have appeared regularly in *Esquire, The New York Review of Books,* and other publications. In one week, he did cover drawings for both *Time* and *Newsweek.*

Samuel Antupit, who was one of Levine's discoverers, says art directors have been negligent in developing new talent. They should be willing to try the work of the lesser-knowns. Only the small specialized magazines seem willing to heed his advice, if for no other reason than that they can't afford the big names.

The big magazines have lately shown interest in using name artists in unfamiliar roles. Herb Bleiweiss, art director for *Ladies' Home Journal,* likes to use photographers on assignments they've not tried before. "These people when working in a new area approach problems with a fresh eye," he says. When *LHJ* ran Truman Capote's "A Christmas Memory," Bleiweiss used a fine art painting by Andrew Wyeth to illustrate it. When *Ramparts* in May 1967 ran a cover on the controversial Bertrand Russell, the then art director, Dugald Stermer, commissioned an unlikely artist to do the portrait: the American-As-Apple-Pie illustrator Norman Rockwell.

Whether he works with a name artist or one just getting his start, the art director finds there is always some tension generated as the two try to reconcile their differences. And there are always differences.

The art director often sees the photographer, for instance, as temperamental, unwilling to follow instructions, and perennially late with his assignments. The photographer sees the art director as unreasonable in his demands and unconscionable in his readiness to discard and mutilate through cropping the photos he does accept. But final decision on photographs must rest with the art director. He is doing the buying.

This does not mean the two cannot work congenially together. The good art director has to be something of a public relations man and personnel director. He must put himself in the place of the photographer. He may find that the photographer has much more to offer than an ability to follow directions. A good photographer may have ideas for illustrating the story or article that the art director has not thought of. The art director should be willing to listen. And he should be willing to consider alternate shots submitted by the photographer when he submits the shots he went out of the studio to get. The photographer often finds new illustrative possibilities at the scene that neither he nor the art director envisioned when they worked out plans for photographic coverage.

The art director owes it to his photographer to explain the nature of the article or story being illustrated, the reasons for the pictures, their intended use and placement, and the nature of other art for that issue. Often the art director provides the photographer with a rough layout of the pages when the assignment is given.

Settling on rates

The staff artist or staff photographer works on a regular salary, so rates are not a problem. The free-lancer works differently. His rates are negotiable.

The free-lance illustrator may be attached to a studio or he may work independently. He is often willing to accept less for his work for a magazine than for an advertising agency simply because he finds magazine work more gratifying.

Sam Berman earned a national reputation for his World War II caricatures of Nazi leaders for Collier's. Later, as head of his own map-making firm, he created the largest global relief map ever made, copies of which sold to more than sixty-five museums and colleges. Now he combines his interest in three-dimensional art with his first love, caricature. The bust of Attorney General John Mitchell (with Martha) was one of a series done for Lithopinion, *the graphic arts and public affairs journal of Local One, Amalgamated Lithographers of America.*

The usual procedure is to give the illustrator a copy of the manuscript with the request that he submit a series of rough sketches.[1] From these the art director orders the finished drawings or paintings he wants, specifying any necessary changes. Often the magazine and the illustrator settle on a price in advance. A magazine, depending upon its size, can expect to pay anywhere from $10 or $20 to several hundred dollars per drawing or painting. Sometimes it's a matter of saying, "We have $150 to spend on a cover illustration. Interested?"

Photographers' rates are a little more standardized. Routine

---

1. Samuel Antupit suggests that the artist should have *more* than the manuscript to read; he should have the writer's research as well so that he will know more than the reader. Then the artist can really make a contribution.

Mario Micossi of Italy, whose works form part of the permanent collections of at least a dozen museums in Europe and in America, frequently does his scratchboard drawings for American magazines, especially The New Yorker. *This one is from* The Reporter, *a magazine that wasn't very well designed but which featured excellent artwork.*

photography costs very little, the art director finds, when he compares that cost to what he'd have to pay a good illustrator. But when he hires a professional magazine photographer, he should expect to pay some healthy fees. The American Society of Magazine Photographers, representing some 700 members, set new rates in 1966, their first change since 1952. For one day's work, a photographer should get between $100 and $150, plus expenses, the ASMP said. For stock pictures, he should get from $25 to $35 for a black-and-white print, $125 for color. The Society said the rates were justified because the typical free-lance magazine photographer did not work every day. Besides, he took extra time to organize and caption pictures. And camera equipment costs were rising. Some lenses cost $1500. A photographer needed $10,000 in equipment in order to function properly.[2]

It used to be that photographers sold all rights to their photographs for double the price of the one-time use. Now they are less willing to do that. Many photographers feel that photographs should earn something for them each time they're used, and the price should fluctuate according to use.

Using art imaginatively

The usual procedure is to do the article or story first, then go out after the pictures to illustrate it. But sometimes it's better to do it the other way around: tell the story in pictures, using words only where facts or statistics are not clear without them.

What the art director tries to do is come up with the one visualization that will tell the story immediately and forcefully. A measure of Otto Storch's genius was the illustration he commissioned for a May 1966 *McCall's* article on infidelity: a big red apple with a couple of bites taken out of it. Nothing else.

When Herb Bleiweiss of *Ladies' Home Journal* had the job of

2. See Charles E. Rotkin, "A Photographer Pleads His Case," *Publishers' Weekly*, Feb. 6, 1967, pp. 90 ff.

illustrating a feature on women's nightgowns, he didn't show the girls in just typical poses; he caught them in action, including one girl being rescued from a burning building.

When *Life* for its May 8, 1970, issue ran a feature on the dress styles of Pat Nixon and daughters, it showed doll-like drawings of each, with drawings of dresses alongside. The dresses had little flaps on them, the kind you find in paper doll clothes. In keeping with the illustrations, the article started out with the line: "Once upon a time. . . ." One might read into the feature the condescending attitude of the major magazines (*Reader's Digest* excepted) toward Nixon.

For an article entitled "What To Do in Case of Armed Robbery," *Go*, Goodyear's dealer magazine, showed a frightening close-up of a gun pointing straight out at the reader. No question about it: it compelled attention.

For a feature on "9 Ways to Beat Winter," *Small World*, house organ for Volkswagen owners, showed a drawing of a

Marilyn McKenzie Chaffee, an art teacher, shows how to make a realistic portrait by pasting down pieces of black paper where she wants deep shadows and pieces of printed body copy where she wants lighter shadows. The technique is particularly appropriate for this portrait: it is of Graham Greene, the writer.

VW, head on, enclosed in giant earmuffs. What better way to set the mood?

Sometimes the art stands by itself. *Minutes*, the magazine once published by Nationwide Insurance, ran two pages of pictures of manhole covers. There was no copy, there were no captions. The variety of patterns stamped on the covers was story enough.

Another idea is to concentrate on texture rather than form. If the subject is "Forests," the art director can make a rubbing or painting from a piece of bark and use it as a piece of line art. If the subject is "Accidents," he can make a rubbing or printing from a piece of bandage cloth.

But the style or technique of illustration doesn't have to have an obvious connection with the subject matter. Art Young, the socialist cartoonist, used an outdated drawing style, not unlike that of a crude woodcut, to fight capitalism and social injustice. Young considered the matter later in one of his autobiographies. "Here I was, a man commonly thought to be 'ahead of the procession' in ideas, who was for progress and change, and with little reverence for tradition, and yet my style was 'archaic,' reminiscent of the ancient past."[3]

Nor does the artist have to use traditional media. Art directors recently have encouraged their illustrators to experiment. The collage has lately become popular: the pasting together of fragments of art, already printed art, or papers and textiles. These can be used to form an abstraction or something that, viewed from a distance, looks quite representational. Some art directors are even using photographs of pieces of sculpture done especially for their magazines. For its March 15, 1971, cover on "Suburbia: A Myth Challenged," *Time* used a color photo of a needlepoint picture.

What kind of art the art director settles for depends upon what he wants his art to do. Does he want it to be informative? Then he asks for realism, either in photographs or illustrations. Does he want it to supply mood for the article or story? Then he asks for abstraction, something as simple, say, as a black border to symbolize death. Does he want it simply to decorate his page? Then he asks for ornament.

Involving the reader

How often have we been disappointed when a radio announcer whose voice we've admired shows up on the TV screen! He doesn't look at all as we imagined! If it's possible to leave the "illustrating" to the reader, the art director should do it. Charles Schulz will never show us the little red-headed girl or the inside

3. Art Young, *On My Way*, Horace Liveright, New York, 1928, p. 193.

of Snoopy's doghouse. We can be grateful. We already have our own ideas of what she—and what it—look like.

The art director can directly involve the reader in the use of illustrations. *Playboy* for February 1968 ran an article on possible winners of the 1968 presidential election. On a left-hand page was a painting of the president seated at his desk. A blank white box blocked out his head. At the right were portraits of the various candidates boxed in with dotted lines. It

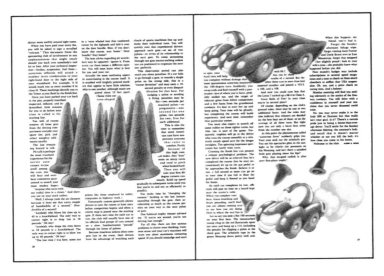

The last two pages of a four-page article on "Autocross: Amateur Indy," in the Second Quarter 1970 issue of **The Humble Way,** *a 9 x 12 external house organ published by Humble Oil & Refining Company, Houston. The opening spread features an illustration similar to those on this spread. The artwork appears in color, with a sort of 1930s-crayon-look. The copy is set to fit around the illustrations. Note the by-line—at the end of the article. Design by Baxter + Korge, Inc.*

was a sort of do-it-yourself spread; the reader presumably was tempted to cut out one of the faces and paste it in place.

The cartoon

The cartoon continues to play an important role—sometimes diversionary, sometimes propagandistic—for many publications. Newspapers run editorial cartoons on their editorial pages to bring current events into sharp, if distorted, focus. And they give over most of a page daily to a selection of comic strips purchased from feature syndicates.

Gag cartoons are largely the province of magazines. Where editorial cartoons and comic strips are done on a salary or contract basis, gag cartoons are done on speculation by freelancers. The cartoon editors on magazines buy them occasionally and keep them ready to drop into holes in the back of the book. These cartoons are used primarily as fillers. But *The New Yorker*, the magazine that really developed this art form in America, continues to use gag cartoons as a principal element of editorial display.

The magazines published in New York have designated Wednesday as market day for cartoonists in the area. On that day, dozens of cartoonists carry their "roughs" from magazine office to magazine office hoping to sell a few of them or at least to get some "O.K."'s from editors. But cartoonists sell their work through the mails, too, especially to the smaller, specialized magazines. An editor can pick out what he wants from a batch (a batch consists of about a dozen cartoons) and send the rest back. If he wants them done in a more finished form, he can mark "O.K."'s on those he likes and give the cartoonist instructions on what medium to use (ink or ink-and-wash) and indicate whether he wants verticals or horizontals. If nothing in the batch looks promising, the editor simply puts the roughs and a rejection slip into the self-addressed, stamped envelope provided by the cartoonist.

Once the editor uses gag cartoons he may find himself swamped with submissions. Cartoonists can smell a market from clear across the country. To get submissions started, the editor can have his magazine listed at no charge at the end of Jack Markow's regular column on cartooning in *Writer's Digest*.

Editors pay anywhere from $5 to $200 or more per cartoon. A common rate is $20. The top gag cartoonists have organized a Magazine Cartoonists Guild, with offices at 202 W. 78th Street, New York 10024.

Charts, graphs, tables, and maps

When the text matter deals with statistics, the art director can amplify, clarify, or summarize them with charts, graphs, or tables. Purely abstract thoughts and information already simple enough to understand do not lend themselves to charts, graphs, or tables, but almost everything else does. What the art director needs to look for is what Matthew P. Murgio in *Communications Graphics* has described as a "visual handle."

The art director can use a *flow chart* to show how machinery works, an *organization chart* to show how a company functions, a *line graph* or *bar chart* to show growth in numbers over a given period of time, or a *pie chart* to show percentages of a whole.

Ordinary charts and graphs are clear enough, but an artist can heighten their impact by changing them to *pictographs:* drawings in which lines, bars, or circles have been converted to representational art shown in perspective. For instance, he can draw people in place of bars or a silver dollar in place of a pie chart. But when using pictographs the art director must make certain the scale is not distorted.[4]

John Simon in his theater column in the Aug. 3, 1970, issue of New York, *makes the point that critics should not feel obligated to report on the length or loudness of the laughter of the audience for any given play. "For that you could install laugh-and-applause meters in the theatres and publish graphs instead of reviews." To illustrate the column, Beth Charney lettered a laugh complete with some imaginary measurements. Milton Glaser is design director of* New York; *Walter Bernard is art director.*

4. See Darrell Huff's *How to Lie with Statistics*, W. W. Norton & Company, Inc., New York, 1954.

The art director can make a *table* more useful by careful organization of material and skillful use of color, tint blocks, and rules. (See the tables carried in *U.S. News & World Report*.)

He can add drama to a *map* by showing it in perspective, by showing its topography as well as its outline, or by simplifying and stylizing its outline. It may even be desirable to distort a map to make a point (provided the reader understands), as one of the airlines did in its advertising in the late 1960s to dramatize the fact that its fast planes had brought Europe and America closer together.

Hendrik Hertzberg built an entire book around a single graph—page after page of dots, one million of them. "This book is a yardstick, a ruler divided into a million parts instead of a dozen," he said in his introduction. "The chief value of the book is as an aid to comprehension, and to contemplation. By riffling slowly through its pages, the reader may discover precisely what is meant by one million." At various intervals the reader finds a blank spot where a dot is supposed to be; a line runs from that blank spot out into the margin, and there the dot is reproduced with a caption. Dot No. 2, for instance, represents the "Population of the Garden of Eden," Dot No. 46,399 the "Number of times the word 'and' appears in the King James Bible," Dot No. 407,316 the number of "U.S. soldiers killed in World War II."[5]

To illustrate "What a Way to Make a Living," an article about the injuries suffered by the running backs in professional football, *Sports Illustrated* for Nov. 16, 1970, ran a drawing of a player, standing, facing to the front. The various injuries to the players were listed at the side. Ruled lines connected the various listings to various parts of the body, allowing readers to see at a glance where the concentration of injuries was. The diagram in a minimum amount of space summarized information that, in ordinary prose, would have taken a lot more space and told the story a lot less vividly.

Photographs or illustrations?

Illustrators enjoyed a "golden age" in the 1930s, 1940s, and early 1950s. But in the mid-1950s, their magazine market shriveled. Magazines were hard-hit by that new medium, television, and in their search for a new identity they turned to the camera. Fiction was no longer a major part of magazines; nonfiction seemed better served by photographs. The illustrator, if he got a magazine assignment at all, had to offer some-

5. See Hendrik Hertzberg, *One Million*, Simon & Schuster, Inc., New York, 1970.

thing the camera could not. One illustrator, Mark English, remarked in an interview in *The National Observer* (Aug. 21, 1967): "The camera has helped the artist see the direction he shouldn't be going in."

No doubt about it: the camera put many illustrators out of work. Art directors preferred photographs because they were more realistic, when realism was important; and they were more readily available and at less cost. Furthermore, the photographer gave the art director a choice of many poses and scenes.

But there is some evidence that the illustration has made a comeback. In 1957 Samuel Antupit said, "Illustration is far more interesting today than photography; the exciting, experimental things are being done in drawings, not photographs." Donald Holden, art book editor for Watson-Guptill Publications, said that photography "is becoming a very fatiguing medium." Art directors, he observed, were constantly looking for new ways to use the camera; using it in focus, using it out of focus, changing the angle. "I sense a certain desperateness in their efforts," he said. ". . . The fatigue factor may force the art director to rediscover illustration."

Allen Hurlburt, as art director of *Look*, preferred photographs to illustrations, but *Look*, like *Life*, was essentially a

Art director Dan Marr of San Francisco uses some closeup photography (by Lloyd Johnson) for this article on drug rehabilitation. The blurb in reverse letters is carefully placed inside the photo. A tint of yellow spreads over the photo except where the type is and gives the photo an eerie quality.

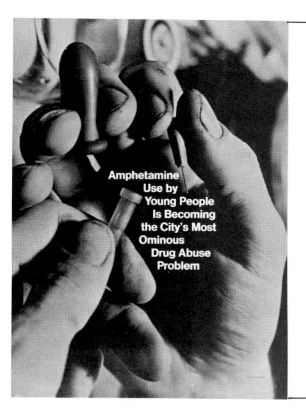

Amphetamine
Use by
Young People
Is Becoming
the City's Most
Ominous
Drug Abuse
Problem

THE FAMILY
at Mendocino State Hospital
Helps 'Speed Freaks'
Slow Down and Learn
to Live Without Drugs.

by Bernice Scharlach

"I MET MY HUSBAND three years ago. He turned me on to grass." Terri is 15, speaks hardly above a whisper. She has the eyes of a woman twice her age. "Then I dropped acid and ended up shooting speed. We considered ourselves part of the hippie scene, not the dope scene." Things have changed in the City since she left a year ago. "When I went to San Francisco on my last pass, I thought three-fourths of the people belonged up here."

At Mendocino State Hospital, where she is part of The Family—an innovative approach to treatment of young drug addicts—Terri has stayed clean, earned her high school diploma and is in the process of getting a divorce. She refers to the fact that use of speed—methamphetamine—is growing explosively here.

According to a report by the Central City Office of Economic Opportunity, $100,000 worth of speed was purchased in the Tenderloin alone in 1967. That year, nearly 3000 acute meth cases were handled at San Francisco General Hospital's Alcohol and Drug Abuse Center. There are thousands more users in the City, and the situation has worsened.

Dave is 20, a Vietnam veteran who tried marijuana and opium overseas and when he returned started shooting speed. Dave, like Terri, came to Ward 15 voluntarily—the only way a person can enter the program—to "clean up and get off the streets." In becoming a part of The Family, he had to do more than that—he had to change his life.

So did Brigette, another Family mem-

ber. "Most of us are used to living such rotten lives," she says, "to learn about trust and love and people caring about you is really beautiful. I want to take that out in the street and teach other people." She's 22, pretty enough to be a *Seventeen* model; she emphasizes her remarks with a toss of her long, brown hair. Her "rotten life" began when she dropped out of college, got strung out on benzedrine and began using cocaine and methedrine. As a "senior" she's on the panel of Family members who speak at schools all over Northern California and she hopes to join the 12 Family graduates now working as salaried counsellors in Bay Area clinics and hospitals, including San Francisco General Hospital.

Recently, two busloads of San Francisco teachers gave up a Saturday to go to Ukiah to learn about the program. Among the teachers was Mrs. Helen Youngclaus, counsellor at James Lick Junior High and teacher of the school's health and family life classes. Drug abuse has filtered down to her sixth grade classes and she wanted to observe The Family and find out about the program.

"I'm not sure about what good they (the panel of Family members) can do," said Mrs. Youngclaus. "I didn't have to be at the Constitutional Convention to teach history, or with Benjamin Franklin when he flew his kite to learn about electricity."

But Dr. Frances Todd, director of Family Life Education for the San Francisco Unified School District, and her as-

sistant, Eugene Huber, were more hopeful.

"We realized," said Huber, "that we are giving the students the same old information—hogwash, one teacher called it—about the physiological and psychological effects of drugs, but not offering the type of preventive education that would really deter them. With the number of juvenile narcotics arrests rising sharply each year since 1963, we obviously haven't been getting through. What we are looking for is a program of prevention that the kids can identify with. Perhaps Mendocino has the answer."

The Mendocino Drug Abuse Program was started two and a half years ago as an adjunct to a successful, if unorthodox, alcoholic program directed by Wayne Wilson. Wilson stressed voluntary admissions and maximum participation by patients. Dr. Joel Fort, then head of the City's Center for Special Problems, and Dr. J. J. Stubblebine, chief of the community mental health services, wanted a place for young addicts away from the drug scene in a neutral setting and hoped Wilson could apply his approach to the growing drug abuse problem.

Beginning with a small group of heroin addicts, Wilson went on to tackle the speed freaks, or meth heads—patients suffering from methamphetamine-induced psychosis.

Speed freaks use a prescription compound called methedrine, or any black market variation of the drug known generically as methamphetamine. The prescrip-

39

Art director Raymond Waites, Jr., for United Church Herald *uses a stark illustration to emphasize the aloneness of a man of principle. The horizon line carries the reader across the page and unifies the illustration with the copy. The illustration uses a second color, olive green, for the sky. There are no initial letters, no subheads to interrupt the mood.*

photographic magazine. Even on *Look*, Hurlburt saw situations where illustrations were called for. For instance: carrying a camera sometimes can be dangerous or even illegal, or sometimes it is difficult or impossible to gain model releases. An example of Hurlburt's imaginative approach to illustration was his commissioning of Norman Rockwell to do a series of paintings on integration. Hurlburt reasoned that because Rockwell had so long been trusted and admired by the middle class as an upholder of traditional American values, his work in this area would be all the more effective.

Now that we have some photographers who have abandoned realism for abstraction and we have some painters who have come back to realism—in some cases to hyperrealism—the line between photography and illustration is blurred. It's still the policy of most art directors to order photography for non-fiction and illustrations for fiction, but that is no hard-and-fast rule. An obvious exception is the use of cartoons to illustrate a piece of nonfiction on, say, human foibles.

So the only answer the art director can give to the question, Should we use photographs or illustrations? has to be: It depends.

Realism or abstraction?

The penchant for realism in art goes back a long way. The closer a piece of art was to real life, the better. *Time* (Jan. 27, 1967) tells the story of Zeuxis, fifth century, B.C., Greek artist, competing with another artist to see who could paint the most realistic picture. When his painting of grapes was unveiled, birds flew down and pecked at them. Surely he had won. But when the judges started to unveil the other painting, they were stunned. *The veil was the painting.* Zeuxis had fooled the birds, but his opponent had fooled the judges.

The coming of photography in the 1800s brought into question the idea that art was imitation. The camera was an instrument that could do the job better. So, many artists assumed a new role. Art became more than imitation; it became something with a value of its own.

Abstraction followed. Not that artists had not worked in abstractions before. But now abstraction became a dominant movement in art. Eventually, almost anything could pass for art: pieces of junk, objects that moved, combinations of common artifacts.

Not everyone was impressed. A writer in *True* tells the story of a man who told Pablo Picasso that he didn't like modern paintings because they weren't realistic. When the man later showed Picasso a snapshot of his girl friend, Picasso asked: "My word, is she really as small as all that?"

With the Armory Show in 1913, when modern art made its debut in America, artists favoring realism as an art form went into a decline, as far as the critics were concerned. But the average person continued to admire the Norman Rockwell kind of artist. Late in his career, perhaps because Americans then enjoyed a "vogue for the old,"[6] partly because Andrew Wyeth had made realism respectable again, Rockwell staged a comeback in the magazines. And at least two major books came out offering his collected works—at premium prices. Even the critics reassessed the man.

"It is difficult for the art world to take the people's choice very seriously, almost impossible if that choice has ignored all approved innovations," wrote Thomas Buechner, director of the Brooklyn Museum. "But Rockwell is the choice. He's the best of his kind and to some of us that's what art is all about."

He added: "If the democratization of the arts is to avoid the ultimate absurdity of accepting everything and therefore nothing, it must take Rockwell into account. He has the artist's capacity to communicate with people—lots of them—rather than simply to innovate for a historically oriented elite."[7]

Art as it has appeared in magazines has been slow to give up realism. Only in recent years have magazines made the move toward abstraction. But now the leaders among them and the smaller, specialized magazines, too, seem willing to experiment with any art form that can stand up to the printing process.

It would be difficult—certainly this book will not attempt it—to make a case for one kind of art as preferable to another.

6. See the Dec. 28, 1970, issue of *Newsweek*.
7. Thomas Buechner, "If We All Like It, Is It Art?" *Life*, Nov. 3, 1970, p. 16.

There is a place for all kinds of art in American magazines. For some magazines, for some articles, for some audiences—realism would be the ideal choice. In other circumstances, abstract art would be preferable. For some magazines the art might best follow current trends. For others, the art director might encourage among his contributors a highly original approach.

All these approaches in art are defensible. What the art director must guard against is making decisions based entirely on his own taste or preference without regard for the needs of the article or story and the preferences of his readers.

The purpose of art

Art can be used merely to set a mood. It can be used merely to decorate. It can also have a more specific purpose. It can (1) restate or amplify the text or (2) "make a separate statement," to use Dugald Stermer's phrasing. He likes the "separate statement" idea. So does William Hamilton Jones, editor of the *Yale Alumni News*.

"I really think photography should give an article an additional dimension," he says. "You can follow one line of thought in your text and you can deal with another in your visual material, and they'll reinforce each other and each will add to the dimensions of the other."

Final two pages of a six-page article in San Francisco *on busing of school children. Art director Dan Marr uses Earl Thollander's line sketches—ten of them—throughout to tie the pages together and, of course, to make them visually alive. Drawings can be a refreshing change in a magazine, even for articles that seem to call for photographs. It is not a good idea to use both drawings and photographs in a single* article, *but there is no reason why an art director can't use both in a single* issue.

But there is a question in this approach. An illustration *illustrates*; it does not exist of itself. If it does, it is something else. Perhaps it is all a matter of placement on the page. If the illustration or photograph makes "a separate statement," the reader can, one supposes, consider it a separate feature. What we have then in the original feature is one that is not illustrated.

And that isn't necessarily bad.

Style

Art style preferences change—for magazine art as well as gallery art. At the turn of the century the look was Art Nouveau:

West's art director, Mike Salisbury, flew from Los Angeles to Atlanta to dig up the art for this article on Coca-Cola and its advertising gimmicks. "The signs, bottles, matchbooks and trays—some of which are now collectors items—are as American as . . . well . . . Coke itself," says the blurb. "Soda-Pop Art" was laid out to be "as documentary as possible," Salisbury reports, "—very straight." (The article is copyrighted by Lawrence Dietz. Used by permission.)

sinuous, decorative, curvy. In the 1920s the Bauhaus made its influence felt; the look was orderly, geometric, functional. The Bauhaus look never did die out. It took a slightly more elegant turn in the 1950s with the introduction of Swiss design: the magazine page was still tightly organized, but some of the stiffness was gone.

Art Nouveau made a comeback in the 1960s, as did almost every art style. The 1960s were a decade of revival and experimentation. Among the new styles: Op Art, with its illusions in color and shape; Pop Art, with its attachment to the comic strip and high-Camp packaging; and the psychedelic look, with its sliding blobs of color in weird combinations, its illegible typefaces expanded, condensed, and contorted to fit curved spaces. Fortunately for readers, many of these styles died young.

For their art and their design—when it comes to style it's hard to separate the two—magazine art directors in the late 1960s turned increasingly to the 1920s and 1930s for inspiration. They simplified line and form, chose pastel rather than bold colors, arranged type and art symmetrically rather than bisymmetrically. Much of the art took on a rainbow motif. Futura type faces were back. Bevis Hillier in a book in 1968 called the look "Art Deco." (The *Deco* was short for *decoration*.)

If one had to use a single term to describe the art that came out of Push Pin Studios, the term might well be "Art Deco." Magazines that at the beginning of the 1970s had an Art Deco look included *Evergreen Review, Rags, Gentlemen's Quarterly,* and, to a lesser extent, *Avant Garde.*[8]

Technique

Preferences in techniques change, too. Brush painting, pallet knife painting, wash drawing, line drawing, scratchboard drawing, pencil drawing, felt- and nylon-tip drawing: they all have a place. Some techniques require tight handling, some a loose flair. Every imaginable tool is used on every kind of surface. In the 1960s, for instance, many illustrators were working in washes on glossy paper not meant to take washes. This resulted in tones that seemed to shrivel, like water on an oily surface.

Print in its July/August 1967 issue thought illustrators were preoccupied with techniques—at the expense of content. Maybe so. But illustrators need to constantly experiment with their styles and techniques, and art directors should encourage them to do so.

One way an artist can get tone into a line drawing is by doing the art in ink on textured paper and then using a grease crayon for shading. This is Horace Greeley, drawn by the author on Glarco No. 12 paper.

8. Jean W. Progner, "Art Deco: Anatomy of a Revival," *Print,* January/February, 1971, pp. 27–36.

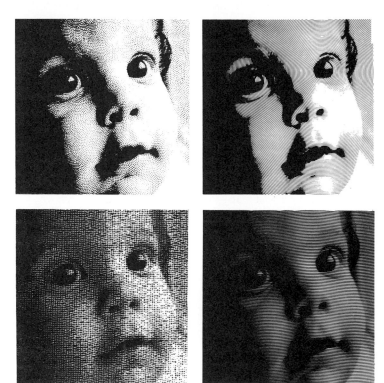

The original photograph and four line art conversions made by Line Art Unlimited (1101 State Road, Princeton, N.J.). The firm offers conversions in eleven other screens, including herringbone and denim.

Design of the art

Art directors cannot agree what style is best for magazines or what techniques best do the job. They cannot agree on whether art should be realistic or abstract. But they can agree on this: *The illustration should be well designed.* The principles of design that govern the arrangement of type and illustration on a page or spread also govern the placement of figures, props, and background within an illustration. Every illustration, from the crudest cartoon to the finest painting, should be well designed.

To most art directors, design in illustration is more important than draftsmanship.

Reproducing the art

In working with line art, the art director should see to it that it all takes the same reduction. This is desirable not only to save costs but also to keep consistent the strength of the artist's line. It is not a good idea to use both fine-line art and thick-line art in the same feature. This means that the art director must decide where he wants big art and where he wants small art before giving out his assignments.

Line art—and halftone art, too—generally turns out best when reduced to about two-thirds of original size. The slight imperfections or irregularities are thus minimized. For a change of pace, though, the art director ought to try *blowing up* in size his line artwork. This adds greatly to its strength and sometimes gives the art a refreshingly crude, bold look it doesn't have in its original state.

One of the advantages of line art over halftone art is that line art, at least when it is run actual size, always comes out as the art director expects. With a halftone, the art director can never be quite sure.

Art directors soon learn that a photograph that has the necessary qualities to hang in an art gallery is not always the photograph that reproduces well. Some art directors feel that a photograph a little on the gray side reproduces better than one a little on the black side. Sometimes the photoengraver or offset cameraman can bring out a gray photograph by overexposing it; there is not much they can do with an already overexposed print.

The art director must choose his photographs not so much on the basis of how well they look in hand as on the basis of how well they will reproduce. Only long experience with photographs can really teach him this.

Art directors used to salvage unsatisfactory photographs by retouching them, but this is not done as much as formerly. Thanks to the 35 mm camera, the art director has many prints to choose from.

Photographs do not reproduce well in letterpress unless a fine screen is used in making the halftone and a smooth paper is used in the printing. Newspaper halftones are often inferior to magazine halftones because newspapers, at least the big ones, are printed letterpress on cheap, rough-textured newsprint. The screen used to make each plate has to be coarse; otherwise the paper stock would not be able to receive it. As a consequence, much of the detail is lost.

The ordinary newspaper halftone takes a 65-line screen, the magazine halftone a 133-line screen. Offset lithography makes possible the use of finer screens—for both newspapers and magazines.

For four-color process work, offset printers often use a 150-line screen, better than a 133-line screen but still not as fine as they can go. The new offset process can handle a 200-line screen, and art directors should ask that such a screen be used, especially if they are using coated stock.

Polaroid has made it possible for photographers working for offset publications to produce their own prescreened halftones, ready for pasteup as line art. It makes available a camera that houses its own screen in any coarseness, from 45 to 133 lines. The Polaroid camera is not an ideal camera for newspaper or magazine work—it is bulkier than a 35 mm, does not have the accessories, and the pictures it produces are sometimes flatter than those made with other cameras—but for small weekly newspapers, especially, the prescreen feature may more than compensate for these disadvantages.

While the usual halftone for both letterpress and offset appears in a dot pattern, newer developments in both photo preparation and photo reproduction make possible halftones in various line patterns and textures. *Newsweek,* when it did a cover story Nov. 24, 1969, "Does TV Tell It Straight?" ran photographs of four TV newsmen—all in ruled-line halftones. Because the photos were cut to a shape resembling a TV screen, the pattern related the halftones even more meaningfully to the subject.

Sometimes the art director must use—may prefer to use—an already-screened halftone. If his publication is offset, he can paste the halftone repro proof in place along with the type repros, and the printer will treat it as line art.

If the screened halftone is from a newspaper, he may find the screening too coarse for his needs. He should then have the halftone reduced. This will bring the dots closer together, making the picture clearer.

If the halftone is not clear or the screening is too fine, it may be necessary to rescreen it. In rescreening, the platemaker must make sure he avoids a moire pattern—a sort of swirl—in the final print. Sometimes you get a moire pattern even when working with an original photograph, as when a figure in that

The first four pages of a major feature in Fleet Owner. *Art editor Bud Clarke uses large, closely-cropped photographs to hold pages together. Note his adaptation of the peace symbol to form the first letter of his title. The use of sans serif helps say "youth" in this article. The opening might have started more easily for the reader if a little white space had been used to separate the blurb from the lead. (With permission from* Fleet Owner. *Copyright 1970 by McGraw-Hill, Inc. All rights reserved.)*

photograph wears a suit or dress with a pronounced pattern. The platemaker may be able to eliminate the moire in a second shooting by adjusting the angle of the screen.

Art directors have a number of ways to turn an ordinary photograph into something that looks like the work of an illustrator or painter. The most common practice—it has almost become a cliché—is to make a line reproduction from the photograph rather than a halftone reproduction. The platemaker simply handles the photograph as if it were a line drawing. He doesn't use a screen. What happens is: all the middle tones of gray drop out. You get a high-contrast print—stark, dramatic, bold. And sections of it, if desired, can easily be painted out or retouched. A variation is to take the bold line art and screen it to, say, 60 percent of black or combine it with a block of solid second color.

The art director can get an unusual effect, too, by ordering his halftone in a jumbo size screen, so that the dots are much larger than normal. From a distance, the art looks like a photograph. Up close, it looks like a piece of Pop Art.

Or he can send the photograph to one of the studios that specialize in making exotic prints from photographs through use of screens with pronounced textures: crosshatches, irregular dots, wavy lines, etc. The prints are turned over to the platemaker who handles them as he would any piece of line art. The photographs are, in effect, prescreened.

Photography in magazines

The halftone was developed in the 1880s. One of the first magazines to use halftones regularly was the *National Geographic*, beginning in 1903. The photographs in this magazine even today are technically superior to those in other magazines; but none of the *National Geographic* photographs has been memorable. Interestingly enough, *National Geographic*, for all its stodginess, is remembered by some for its photographs of female breasts in an age when other magazines recoiled at such photographs. The girls of course were always dark-skinned natives of foreign countries. One writer observes,

> . . . During the grim nineteen-thirties and forties, curious youth turned to *The Geographic*. Certain pictures are burned deep into the brain of countless thousands of men who were adolescents in those years. . . . [Some of the photographs were] the stuff of multidimensional sexual fantasy beside whom the girls in *Playboy* are poor plastic things indeed.[9]

Life's contribution to the development of photography in magazines is undoubtedly greater than *National Geographic's*. Started in 1936 as a sort of illustrated *Time, Life* gradually changed from a news magazine to a magazine of special features. More than any other publication it developed the idea of photojournalism: great photographs taken on the spot, where and when important things were happening. Sometimes the photographs merely reported, sometimes they expressed a form of opinion. Often their greatness was accidental.

Acting as moderator of a seminar sponsored by the American Society of Magazine Editors in 1969, Harold Hayes, editor of *Esquire*, noted the demise of photojournalism. TV has killed photojournalism, he said.

What's important for magazines these days, he said, is photographic *art*. Photos are no longer just shot; they are *arranged*—by art directors and photographers working together.

9. Tom Buckley, "With the National Geographic On Its Endless, Cloudless Voyage," *The New York Times Magazine*, Sept. 6, 1970, p. 20.

There are those who **would argue with this. They point out** that photographs are nothing more, nothing less, than a journalistic tool. Like written journalism, the photograph informs, expresses opinion, entertains. Let those photographers who would do their own thing or make their "statements" do it—but not for publication.

A lot of readers and some editors and art directors disapprove of some of the recent trends in photography.

The magazines' infatuation with blurred photographs in the early 1970s became the subject of some satire in *Saturday Review*. "What has happened," wrote Dereck Williamson,

. . . is that the improperly exposed and badly focused photograph has become Art. The bad picture is now good, and the good picture is bad. For amateur 35-millimeter photographers like myself, this is distressing news. For years I've been culling my slides and throwing away Art.

Many of my mistakes would now be worth big money in the modern magazine market place.

He cites a number of his culls, including "One Tennis Shoe, with Kneecap," "Child Unrolling Agfachrome at High Noon," and "Daughter's Birthday Party with Failing Flashcube." His "Giant Redwoods and Finger," had it been sent to a magazine, would have been accepted and probably captioned: "A personal statement of the photographer concerning man's ruthless attitude toward his environment."[10]

But there is still plenty of room in magazines for sharply focused, well-lighted photographs. Editors and art directors like them because they say things that need to be said. And they are readily available. While only a few persons can turn out usable drawings or paintings, almost anyone can turn out publishable photographs, not the kind that would delight the heart of a W. Eugene Smith, perhaps, but publishable nevertheless. To many, photography represents "instant art"; and everyone can participate. Out of thousands upon thousands of routine photographs, there just have to be some that, if they don't qualify as works of art, at least have enough clarity or meaning to justify reproduction in some publication.

Among the most popular courses offered on college campuses these days—and in the high schools, too—are the courses in photography. Moholy-Nagy once said, prophetically: "The illiterate of the future will be the man who does not know how to take a photograph."

The photo essay

For many years the photograph, like the painting or drawing,

10. Dereck Williamson, "Shutter Shudders," Phoenix Nest column of *Saturday Review*, Dec. 5, 1970, p. 4.

was used merely to *illustrate* an article or story. It still is used that way. But in the 1930s some editors, especially those at *Life*, worked out an additional use for photographs, putting them into a spread or a series of spreads and letting them tell their own story, sometimes without captions. The photo essay was born.

Like a piece of prose, a photo essay has a story to tell or a point to make. The pictures all revolve around a central theme. They may be uniform in size, or they may vary greatly in both size and shape. There is always a key photograph for the series, but there may be a sub-key photograph for each spread, too. It is up to the art director to unify the photographs.

Any combination of pictures is likely to say something different from what each picture by itself says. The sum is different from its parts. So the art director must share with the photographer the responsibility for developing the theme of the essay. The order of presentation and the juxtaposition of one picture with another greatly affect what the essay says.

Deciding on photographs

The art director should make sure the photographer fully understands any assignment and knows how the pictures will be used, whether for illustration or essay purposes.

If he wants to emphasize height, the art director should direct the photographer to take his picture from a worm's-eye angle. If he wants to show an item in context with its surrounding, he may ask for a bird's-eye view.

Often a photograph does not tell the complete story unless scale is included. A photograph of a tree seedling may not mean much unless a knife or shovel or some other item whose size is understood is included in the picture. When *Posh*, the quarterly published by P & O Lines, Inc., ran an article on sculptures in miniature, the art director saw to it that photographs showed the various pieces held in hands. Closeup shots were made from different angles to heighten interest.

The art director should insist on a wide selection of prints. Contact sheets are good enough. The art director can study the prints with an 8-power magnifier. He should ask for more blow-ups than he can use—three or four times as many—because no matter how well he reads the prints, he'll see new things when they're bigger. He should have some choices at that level, too.

When *Time* decided to devote a cover story to air pollution for its Jan. 27, 1967, issue, 23 photographers were sent out and kept shooting for three days. In all, the team shot 160 rolls of black-and-white and color film. When it was all over, when all the selections had been made, the magazine used only 13 shots, including the shot for the cover.

Other magazines can't afford such luxury of choice. Small magazines often settle for the single picture or two that are available. Often the art director uses a picture he knows is inferior; but it is the only one that is offered him.

Sometimes he has two or three excellent shots, but there is not much difference among them in camera angle, camera distance, or subject matter. He should resist the impulse to use them all. Redundancy spoils good photography.

There is some merit, however, in using a series of similar shots of an individual who is the subject of an interview. A series of photographs tells the reader more about the interviewee than a single photograph can. Besides, the several similar pictures give the reader a nice feel of visual continuity.

When he needs a mug shot to go with an article or story and he has several to choose from, the art director should choose the one which has an expression appropriate to the mood of the article. The reader can't help being puzzled when, while reading about someone involved in a tragedy, he sees the person with a silly grin on his face. At the least the reader should be made to realize, perhaps in the caption, that the picture was taken on some earlier occasion.

Photographing money

It used to be illegal to show U.S. folding money in a photograph. When a bill could be seen, a retouch artist had to obliterate it before the plate was made. If a closeup was desired, the photographer made sure his subjects used play money rather than real money.

The government has relaxed its rules. Within reason, it is now possible to show money. The money should be shown only in black and white, reproduced in a size either larger or smaller than actual size; and the editor should be prepared to justify the use of the photo on educational or news grounds. To be on the safe side, the art director should check with the Treasury Department.

Reproducing photographs of coins and stamps entails some risk, too, but restrictions here are more relaxed.

Color photography

For certain kinds of magazines—those dealing with exquisite scenery and luxurious travel, for instance—full-color photography is a must. But, as chapter 4 points out, it is expensive.

Another problem with full-color photography is that it makes *everything* look beautiful. By focusing close, the photographer makes the pattern and the splash of color more important than the content of his picture. Ugly things, like filth washing up on a river bank, become works of art to be admired. For this reason, the art director, even when he can afford color, chooses to stay with black and white for some of his features.

Photographic clichés

While any pose, from any angle, with any focus, can find a place in today's magazines, certain pictures, at least in ordinary usage, should be avoided by the art director if for no other reason than that they have been used too often. These pictures include the following poses:

1. people shaking hands during award ceremonies.
2. public officials signing proclamations and other papers.
3. people studying documents.
4. people pointing to maps, to trees, to anything.
5. committees at work.
6. public speakers at the rostrum.

Whoever arranged for this picture got a professional model to show pages of a newspaper while the managing editor of that newspaper (center), looking a little foolish, accepted an award from an association executive. While it may appear that this picture was staged to show how not to do it, it was for real. It ran on the pages of a trade magazine. The accepting-the-award picture will, unfortunately, always be with us, and in many cases it will be in a form no less awkward than this.

But even the photographic cliché has its place in well-designed magazines. The fact that a picture may be "Camp" might be reason enough to run it. Or maybe the nature of the article calls for a photograph that, under other circumstances, would be considered as too stilted to use. Magazine art directors of the early 1970s seemed more willing than in the past to run group shots, with subjects looking straight ahead into the lens of the camera. An example of this was the family picture—a father with his wife and nine children—on pages 30 and 31 of the Oct. 2, 1970, issue of *Life*.

The Western Art Directors Club in a publicity stunt in 1970 got away with a photographic cliché when it sent out a formal group shot of newly-elected officers. All persons but one were looking straight ahead into the camera, painfully serious. One, in the middle of the front row, had his back facing the camera. He was the outgoing president.

Handling photographs

When finally laying out his pages, the art director works with 8 x 10 glossies. Using a grease crayon, he makes his crop marks in the margin. He does not write on the backs of photos for fear of denting the front surfaces. Dents, bends, and folds show up in the final printing.

The art director is particularly careful in his handling of transparencies. When a black-and-white print is lost, a new one can be made easily. But when a transparency is lost, all is lost.

In indicating sizes to the photographer or printer, the art director always gives width first, then depth. (The British do it just the opposite.) The art director can make sure there is no misunderstanding when he writes down a size by marking a short horizontal line above the width and a short vertical line above the depth.

Cropping photographs

Most art directors feel they can improve on the original composition of photographs, dramatize them, make them more "readable," change the emphasis, by cropping—cutting away unnecessary detail and background. This is the age of the closeup. It is also the age of the strongly vertical or the strongly horizontal shape—anything to get away from the rectangle of average proportions.

Much of this cropping is good. But some of it is unnecessary and, worse, destructive of good photography. What appears to be monotonous background or foreground may be vital to a photograph's proportion.

When an art director is convinced that cropping is desirable, he should make his crop marks in the margins, not on the photograph itself. He may want to use the photograph again with some new cropping.

The art director must never crop a photograph of a painting. The reader assumes that when he sees one in a magazine he is seeing it in its entirety. But it is acceptable to run only a section of a painting and label it as a detail from the original.

Doctoring photographs

Inexperienced art directors often cut photographs into odd shapes because squares and rectangles are "monotonous." These art directors make the mistake of thinking that readers are more interested in shape than in content.

Nothing—nothing—beats the rectangle or square as a shape for a photograph. A circle, a triangle, a star, a free form—these may have occasional impact; but as a general rule, they should be avoided. If the art director wants some added impact he can crop his photographs into extremely wide or tall rectangles.

Some art directors like to outline their photographs with thin black lines, but the edge formed by the photograph itself is usually best.

A silhouette halftone—the reproduction of a photograph in which a figure is outlined against a pure white background—provides an effective change of pace for the art director. The silhouette is much preferred to the photograph with doctored edges because it does not represent shape for the sake of shape; it emphasizes content. A single silhouette can be used for contrast on a spread of photographs in the usual rectangular and square shapes.

If the art director feels that one element in a picture should "walk out" from the rest of the picture, he can put that element—or part of it—into a silhouette and square off the rest of the picture.

When silhouetting (also referred to as outlining) a photograph, the art director may find it necessary to do his own cutting or opaquing. He should be sure the figure or object in the photograph is large enough to take the silhouetting. He should avoid intricate silhouettes, such as a girl with wind-blown hair.

For the infrequent occasion when he finds it necessary to cut a photograph into an odd shape, the art director can best do it by drawing the shape first on a sheet of tissue paper, which he then rubber cements over the photo. He then follows the outline with his knife or scissors, and concludes by peeling off the sheet and rubbing away any dried rubber cement that remains.

Bleeding photographs

Bleeding photographs—running them off the edge of the page—tends to dramatize them and make them appear larger than they really are. Not only does a bleed picture occupy extra white space that would be used as margins; it also seems to stretch beyond the page. There is no optical fence to contain it.

Generally speaking, only large photographs should be bled. It is never advisable to bleed small mug shots. Nor is it necessary, when he uses bleeds, for the art director to bleed consistently throughout the magazine. Sometimes a combination of bleed and nonbleed pictures is best.

The art director must order his halftones with an extra one-eighth to one-quarter inch strip (final halftone size) for each edge that bleeds. Because extra trimming may be involved and an oversize sheet must be used, the printer may charge more for bleed pages.

An art director seldom bleeds a painted illustration, and he never bleeds a photograph of a painting.

Art directors favor bleeding for a while, then abandon the

Because this nearly full-page photograph appeared on a left-hand page of a college magazine, the editor flopped it to make it face the gutter. But in the process he made a left-hander out of singer-guitarist Ric Masten, changed the arrangement of strings on his guitar, buttoned the man's shirt the wrong way, and moved the pocket over to the other side. It would have been much better to let the picture face off the page. The flopping was made all the more ludicrous by a picture elsewhere on the spread that showed Masten playing the guitar in his normal way—from his right side.

practice, then pick it up again. As the 1970s began, the trend seemed to be away from bleeding.

The practice of running boxes around photographs flourished for a while, then died out; and now it's back again. In some cases, the lines are more than lines; they are bold bars, butted up against the photograph's edges. A variation is the boxing of silhouetted photographs, as practiced especially by the Sunday New York *Times* in its "Week in Review" section.

Sometimes the silhouette does not touch the box; sometimes it is cropped so that at least one flat edge butts against the box. (See *Newsweek's* Oct. 5, 1970, treatment of a series of football pictures, beginning on p. 58.)

Flopping photographs

The art director may be tempted to flop a photograph—change its facing—if it seems to point off a page. But this is tricky business.

Flop a portrait, and the part in the hair is on the wrong side. The suit is buttoned on the wrong side. If a sign is included in the picture, it will read from right to left.

Scholastic Magazine for March 1970 ran a photograph of the cover of *Onondagan*, the yearbook of Syracuse University. On the yearbook's cover was a picture of a light switch turned on. The "ON" in caps showed plainly (*On* is a shortened version of the yearbook's name). But for the sake of a facing, the editor of *Scholastic Editor* flopped his photograph. And the "ON" came out reading "NO."

Arranging photos on the page

It might be useful here to consider chapter 5's design principles as they apply to the use of photographs.

To bring order to his pages, the art director should use fewer pictures—perhaps fewer than he would consider desirable—and he should use them in large sizes. A large photograph is many times more effective than a smaller one. The impact does not increase arithmetically; it increases by geometric progression.

Big photographs also save money. It costs as much to take a small picture as it does to take a big one. As much thinking and effort go into a small picture.

For the sake of unity, the art director should bring related photographs together in his layout. Organization for content is more important than organization based on the way photographs happen to face.

When he uses several photographs per page or spread, the art director places the closeups at the bottom because this conforms more naturally to the way we see things in perspective. He keeps his photographs all the same size—or he makes them obviously different in size. He avoids making them almost —but not quite—equal. In most cases he has some large, some middle size, some small photographs; and he combines squares with rectangles, and among his rectangles he has some horizontals and some verticals.

It is not a good idea to run full-page pictures on both left- and right-hand pages, especially if they bleed on three sides and run into the gutter. The two then appear to be a single, massive, photograph. A small band of white should separate them at the gutter.

Here is a summary of techniques for combining several photographs on a page, unifying them and yet allowing them to stand separately:

1. *Run a small band of white between them.* The band may vary in width, or it can stay the same throughout the spread. Art directors used to prefer separations of no more than an eighth of an inch, but now they seem to prefer a wider band: a quarter of an inch or more.

2. *Butt the photos up against each other.* This works well if the photos are of different sizes; some of the photo edges will be printed against a field of white. Some art directors like to run a thin black line where the photographs join.

3. *Overlap the photos.* This means cutting mortises into photos and slipping portions of other photos into the holes. The overlap can fit snugly. Or it can have a small white line around it to help separate one photo from the other.

Overlapping is not always desirable because it calls attention to shape rather than content. When you overlap, you get photos that are L- or U-shaped. This spoils the composition of the photos, even when what is mortised out appears to be unimportant foreground or sky.

The usual overlap allows only one of the photographs to print in the shared area. For an unusual effect the art director can print one photograph in black, one in color, without bothering to mortise; he can let them both show. Or he can print one photograph in one color, one in another, and where they overlap he will get a third color.

4. *Fit one photo inside the other.* The art director can do this when the center of interest of the base photograph is concentrated in one area. His base photograph would be one he would otherwise crop. The smaller photo would fit into an internal mortise. Again it could fit snugly, or it could carry a thin white outline.

Are captions necessary?

The art director should use as much care in the placement of captions as in the placement of the photographs themselves.

He can line his captions up against an edge—or both edges—of the photograph, or he can line them up against an edge inside the photograph. Captions should fit up close to the photographs they describe so that the reader will have no trouble correctly associating them.

Some photographers are beginning to question the need for captions. "If the pictures aren't good enough to stand by themselves, why run them?" a photographer might ask his art director. If all the editor wants to do is to convey a mood or provide a visual oasis, perhaps captions are not necessary. And certainly many of the captions that editors write these days—captions seem to get only last-minute attention in busy editorial offices—are innocuous or insulting to the reader's intelligence.

Still most photographs need captions to bring out what the camera cannot, to identify persons shown, to tie the photo-

When a magazine reproduces paintings, especially fine arts paintings, it should not change their basic proportions. Nelson Gruppo, art director for Famous Artists Magazine, *faced this problem when he designed this four-page feature. He devotes one page to each of four artists, and on the first page he is able to add two paragraphs of general introduction without disturbing the organizational pattern. He is also able to combine different kinds of mug shots. Note that the second two pages repeat the title, not in the display face but in the body face, and in a size slightly smaller than body type size. Columns are unjustified.*

Christmas 1969 Sketchbook by J. Sentell   An angel was sent to a virgin, betrothed to a man whose name was Joseph; and the virgin's name was Mary.

A spread for a Christmas issue of United Church Herald. *J. Sentell's powerful dry-brush illustration is followed by others on subsequent pages. No color for this spread, just black on newsprint-like stock. Offset lithography makes possible the large areas of solid black.*

graphs to the text of the article or story. The photographer should not look upon captions as demeaning of his ability to communicate. Well-written captions give photographs an additional dimension.

The caption can tell what happened before the picture was taken. Or what happened afterwards.

In most cases mug shots need captions. When a magazine runs a mug shot with a standing column, the reader can't tell whether the picture is of the columnist or the man being written about unless the shot carries a caption.

Is art necessary?

Not every article and story needs art in the traditional sense. Carefully selected display typography, tastefully arranged with generous amounts of white space, can be art enough.

Some subjects simply do not lend themselves to art. A subject can be too momentous, too tragic, too lofty. Art would be at best redundant, at worse anticlimactic.

And when an art director can't afford art or finds he has on hand for a particular feature only mediocre-quality photography, he should be willing to design his pages without art. A quiet, even stilted page is preferable to an amateurish one.

Nation's Cities *uses a piece of line art to supply visual interest to a right-hand opener,* **and** *then, where the article continues, reuses part of the art* **to** *help the reader adjust to the new page. Actually, the magazine reuses* two *parts of the art—the bottom five figures and* two *more figures ahead of them* in *the line. Art directors are Louise Levine and Evelyn Sanford.*

Suggested further reading

BERGIN, DAVID P., *Photo Journalism Manual*, Morgan & Morgan, Inc., Publishers, Hastings-on-Hudson, N.Y., 1967.

BOAS, GEORGE, AND WRENN, HAROLD HOLMES, *What Is a Picture?* Schocken Books, Inc., New York, 1966.

BOWMAN, WILLIAM J., *Graphic Communication*, John Wiley & Sons, Inc., New York, 1968. (How to translate ideas into "visual statements.")

BUSH, CHILTON R., *Writing Captions for Newspictures*, American Newspaper Publishers Association, New York, 1966. (Booklet)

CARRAHER, RONALD G., AND THURSTON, JACQUELINE B., *Optical Illusions and the Visual Arts*, Reinhold Publishing Corporation, New York, 1966.

CHERNOFF, GEORGE, AND SARBIN, HERSHEL, *Photography and the Law*, Chilton Book Company, Philadelphia, 1971. (Fourth Edition)

CROY, PETER, *The Layout of Illustrative Materials*, Hastings House, Publishers, New York, 1965.

FEININGER, ANDREAS, *The Color Photo Book*, Prentice-Hall, Inc., Englewood Cliffs, N.J., 1970.

FOX, RODNEY, AND KERNS, ROBERT, *Creative News Photography*, Iowa State University Press, Ames, Iowa, 1961.

GILL, BOB, *Illustration: Aspects and Directions*, Reinhold Publishing Corporation, New York, 1964.

GLYCK, ZVONKO, *Photographic Vision*, Chilton Book Company, Philadelphia, 1966.

GRAHAM, DONALD W., *Composing Pictures*, Van Nostrand Reinhold Company, New York, 1970.

GUITAR, MARY ANNE, *22 Famous Painters and Illustrators Tell How They Work*, David McKay Company, Inc., New York, 1964.

HESS, STEPHEN, AND KAPLAN, MILTON, *The Ungentlemanly Art*, The Macmillan Company, New York, 1968.

HILLIER, BEVIS, *Art Deco*, E. P. Dutton, New York, 1968.

HOGARTH, PAUL, *The Artist as Reporter: A Survey of Art in Journalism*, Reinhold Publishing Corporation, New York, 1967.

JACOBS, LOU, JR., *Free Lance Magazine Photography*, Hastings House, Publishers, New York, 1970. (Revised Edition)

LINDERMAN, E. W., *Invitation to Vision: Ideas and Imaginations for Art*, Wm. C. Brown Company Publishers, Dubuque, Iowa, 1967.

LUCKIESH, M., *Visual Illusions: Their Causes, Characteristics and Applications*, Dover Publications, Inc., New York, 1965.

LYONS, NATHAN, ed., *Photographers on Photography*, Prentice-Hall, Inc., Englewood Cliffs, N.J., 1966.

LYONS, NATHAN, ed., *Seeing Photographically*, Prentice-Hall, Inc., Englewood Cliffs, N.J., 1966.

MARKOW, JACK, *Cartoonist's and Gag Writer's Handbook*, Writer's Digest, Cincinnati, 1967.

MEYER, HANS, *150 Techniques in Art*, Reinhold Publishing Corporation, New York, 1963.

MILLS, JOHN FITZ-MAURICE, *Studio and Art-Room Techniques*, Pitman Publishing Corp., New York, 1965.

MURGIO, MATTHEW P., *Communications Graphics*, Van Nostrand Reinhold Company, New York, 1969. (Charts and graphs and other visual presentations.)

NELSON, ROY PAUL, *Fell's Guide to the Art of Cartooning*, Frederick Fell, Inc., New York, 1962.

———, and FERRIS, BYRON, *Fell's Guide to Commercial Art*, Frederick Fell, Inc., New York, 1966.

NIECE, ROBERT C., *Photo-imagination*, Chilton Book Company, Philadelphia, 1966. (Use of photography in commercial art.)

PAPP, CHARLES S., *Scientific Illustration: Theory and Practice*, Wm. C. Brown Company Publishers, Dubuque, Iowa, 1968.

POLLACK, PETER, *The Picture History of Photography*, Harry N. Abrams, Inc., New York, 1970. (Revised Edition)

QUICK, JOHN, *Artists' and Illustrators' Encyclopedia*, McGraw-Hill Book Company, New York, 1969.

RHODE, ROBERT B., AND McCALL, FLOYD H., *Introduction to Photography*, Macmillan Company, New York, 1971. (Second Edition)

ROTHSTEIN, ARTHUR, *Photojournalism: Pictures for Magazines and Newspapers*, Chilton Book Company, Philadelphia, 1965. (New Edition)

RUBIN, LEN S., *Editor with a Camera*, A. S. Barnes & Company, Inc., Cranbury, N.J., 1968.

RODEWALD, FRED C., AND GOTTSCHALL, EDWARD, *Commercial Art as a Business*, Viking Press, Inc., New York, 1970. (Second Revised Edition)

SHEPPARD, JULIAN, *Photo Design Methods*, Hastings House, Publishers, New York, 1970.

SPENCER, OTHA C., *The Art and Techniques of Journalistic Photography*, Henington Publishing Company, Wolfe City, Texas, 1966.

STANKOWSKI, ANTON, *Visual Presentation of Invisible Processes*, Hastings House, Publishers, New York, 1966.

WEST, KITTY, *Modern Retouching Manual*, Chilton Book Company, Philadelphia, 1967.

Infinity, American Society of Magazine Photographers, New York. (Monthly)

National Press Photographer, National Press Photographers Association, Fargo, N.D. (Monthly)

Chapter 8
The magazine cover

You can't judge a book by its cover, they say. And you probably can't judge a magazine by its cover, either. But a lot of readers think they can, especially if they buy the magazine on the newsstand.

No feature is so important to a magazine as its cover, no matter how the magazine is circulated.

"Every business publication has a substantial body of what might best be termed uncommitted readership—denizens of the circulation who, depending on the level of their distraction, might or might not read a given issue of the magazine," says G. Barry Kay, editor of *Canadian Paint and Finishing*.

". . . The difficulty in overcoming this preoccupation [with things other than the magazine] is compounded for you by the fact that you must wage your entire battle on the strength and appeal of one page—your cover."[1]

What the cover does

A magazine cover does these things:

1. *It identifies the magazine.* The art director tries to come up with something in the cover design to set the magazine apart from all others.

2. *It attracts attention.* The art director must stop the reader somehow—and then get him inside.

3. *It creates a suitable mood for the reader.*

And if the magazine is displayed on newsstands, the cover has one more function:

---

1. G. Barry Kay, "Your Covers," *Better Editing*, Fall 1970, p. 5.

4. *It sells the magazine.* No wonder the circulation department takes more than a casual interest in the choice of art and the wording of titles and blurbs on the cover.

What goes on the cover

The typical magazine cover carries a logo (the name set or drawn in appropriate or memorable type); date of the issue and price per copy; art; and titles of major features, with names of authors.

Sometimes the art director has additional elements to contend with. *Freedom & Union* used to run the name of the editor on the cover.

Major display on covers takes any of these forms:

1. *A photograph or illustration tied to a feature inside.*

2. *Abstract art or a photograph or illustration that stands by itself.* The art director may want to keep such art free of all type, including the logo, so it will be suitable for framing. An explanation of the art can be carried in a blurb on the title page.

The cover of the *Bulletin of the Atomic Scientists* permanently accommodates a "doomsday" clock. The hands occasionally move back and forth as world conditions change. The hands, of course, are always close to midnight.

3. *Type only.* The type can be in the form of a title or two from articles inside, as in the case of opinion magazines like *The Nation;* or as a table of contents, a form *Reader's Digest* was instrumental in popularizing.

4. *The beginning of an article or editorial that continues inside.* *The New Republic* has used an occasional cover for this purpose. Some magazines—*Advertising Age,* for example—run several articles or stories on the cover, newspaper-style.

5. *An advertisement. Editor & Publisher* uses its cover for this purpose. A cover ad brings premium rates.

Making decisions about the cover

Covers require both a permanent decision on basic format and an issue-by-issue decision on art and typography.

For his basic format the art director must answer the following questions:

1. Should the cover be of the same stock as the remainder of the magazine? Or should it be of a heavier stock?

2. What process should be used to print the cover? The same as for the remainder of the magazine? Or some other?

3. What kind of a logo does the magazine need? Where should it go on the cover? Need it stay in the same place issue after issue?

united church herald

October '68   Candidates in November's race for the
White House are assessed by two prominent partymen in a HERALD interview.

united church herald

united church herald

Nov.'68

Ohio Edition

the groovy, lonely, way-out, up-tight, mini-skirted, maxi-active, turned-on world of the young

Three United Church Herald covers for late 1968 showing how the art director uses the same logo but gets variety through use of paintings, color photography, and dropout halftones. Sometimes the art bleeds, sometimes it doesn't. The magazine usually uses full color on the cover. The line running between the two women on the November cover reads: "the groovy, lonely, way-out, uptight, mini-skirted, maxi-active, turned-on world of the young."

4. Does the cover need art? Photograph or illustration? Must the art have a tie with an inside feature? Or can it stand on its own, like the old Norman Rockwell covers for *The Saturday Evening Post?*

5. Does the cover need color? Spot color or process color?

6. Are titles or blurbs necessary? Where should they go on the cover?

7. Will a regular cover do? Or is a gatefold called for? Or maybe an oversize cover, like those on the pulp magazines of the 1930s?

A major decision for each issue will be the selection of the art. "Perhaps the most frequently encountered error in cover design today, according to top editors and publishers, is committed by those who go all out to get attention with abstract or other unusual art but fail to direct the attention they have captured to anything that will entice the reader inside the magazine," observes *Better Editing.* "A magnificent window display may stop the shopper but it won't get him into the store unless it offers merchandise he wants."[2]

Newsstand considerations

A magazine sold on the newsstands, in contrast to one delivered only by mail, needs to (1) sell itself to the impulse buyer and (2) identify itself for the regular buyer. Where a through-the-mail magazine can run its logo anywhere on the cover and in different typefaces from issue to issue, the newsstand magazine needs a standard logo and in a standard position.

Most newsstand magazines are displayed in an upright position, often with only the left side showing. This is why many newsstand magazines have their logos crowded in the upper left. If the magazine is *Life*-size, it lies on its back, in stacks, often low in the stands.

What art and blurbs the art director puts on the cover seriously affect sales. "Trends in cover art change rapidly," said Norman P. Schoenfeld, when he was art director at *True.* "We have to keep close tabs on how a given cover sells on the newsstand. . . . Naturally, our circulation department takes a keen interest in our cover selection."

Timing

A magazine that features people in the news on its covers may be deeply embarrassed as news changes while the magazine is being printed and delivered.

The surprise victory of President Harry S Truman over

2. "The Most Important Page," *Better Editing,* Fall 1965, p. 5.

Thomas E. Dewey in 1948 caught a number of editors out on a limb. *Mad*, for an issue planned before the 1960 election but placed on newsstands right afterwards, appeared to have been prophetic by featuring John F. Kennedy on the cover with this line: "*Mad* congratulates John Kennedy upon his election as

A logo designed by Herb Lubalin for Family Circle. *This was one of the first of the "nestled" logos, with letters from one line fitting snugly against letters from another. The C actually overlaps the m. "Circle" is so placed that a couple of vertical axes are formed, one with the two i's, the other with the l and r. The tail of the y is clipped to fit the tail of the r. And of course the letters are unusually close-fitting horizontally. All of which makes for a tightly knit* Family Circle.

President. We were with you all the way, Jack!" But then you turned the magazine around and found another cover that said the same thing—for Richard Nixon!

The logo

A logo is much like a company trademark. Its adoption is a serious matter. Once adopted, it settles in for many years of service. Its value increases to the point where its owner feels reluctant to abandon it even when its design becomes outmoded.

In designing a logo, then, the art director avoids types or letterforms that soon will be out of date. Yet he picks type that is distinctive. More important, he picks type that is appropriate.

The Sporting News is an example of a magazine with an inappropriate logo face: Old English. The editors would argue that their weekly publication is newspaperlike in its approach, and Old English has been used, historically, for newspaper logos. But Old English has an ecclesiastical feel; it is far removed from the roughness and vitality of the sports world.

Whatever face the art director decides on, he roughs the idea for his logo on tissue, but because of a logo's specialized nature, its importance, and its permanence, he calls in a professional calligrapher or letterform artist to do the finish. He should not allow his logo to be hand-lettered by just anyone who knows how to draw. Illustrators as a rule are unfamiliar with type and letterform, and many of them do a poor job of lettering. *Nieman Reports*, at least at the time this was written, was an example of a magazine with a logo of poorly drawn roman letters that could just as easily have been set in type.

Settling for a regularly set typeface instead of hand lettering is always the best solution when professional lettering help is not available or affordable. The art director himself, without much ability as a lettering artist, can do some innovating with type. He can order reproduction proofs of the type and then cut the letters apart and respace them to bring to his logo a flair ordinary typography can't supply. Because logos involve only one or two words and because readers have a chance to study them issue after issue, the art director can do things with spacing that he wouldn't do when working on article and story titles. For instance, he can move two capitalized words together, with no space between.

LikeThis

He can doctor some of the letters, too, so that they would be unrecognizable were they not seen in context. Herb Lubalin, who designed *Sport*'s new tight-fitting all-cap logo, chopped off the bottom half of the main downstroke of the *R* and propped the letter up against the *O*.

Dare, a magazine once published for barbershops, ran its logo in mirror reverse, so that it read from right to left. It was in keeping with the nature of the magazine; it "dared" to be different.

Popular Photography for its logo found it necessary to separate the word "Photography." (The "Popular" in the title is run small and up the side, an inconspicuous part of the logo.) The dictionary separates "photography" between the *g* and the *r*. But that doesn't read right. The magazine wanted "Photo" to stand out. So it went ahead and separated the word like this: "Photo-graphy," even though the separation technically is wrong.

The logo can run in a different color each issue. It can even be embossed, as for *Venture* and occasional issues of *Playboy*. But most art directors feel it should appear in the same place on the cover, issue after issue, especially if the magazine sells on the newsstand. Of course, the logo could be so unique it could be spotted by potential buyers no matter where it's placed. *Family Circle*, wholly a newsstand magazine, has that kind of a logo. (Again, designed by Herb Lubalin.) *Woman's Day* moves its logo around from issue to issue, sometimes keeping it in a single line, sometimes in two lines.

Changing the logo

There comes a time in a magazine's growth when it must—it just must—change its logo.

Some magazines change suddenly, some gradually. *Newsweek* has made its changes gradually. Entering the 1960s

New York's *logo is adopted from an earlier one used by* New York *when it was part of the* Herald Tribune. *The original was in Caslon swash. Now, in a bolder version, it combines elements of both Caslon and Bookman. Designer: Tom Carnese. Art director: Walter Bernard.*

Close-fitting sans serif letters make up the logo for Print. *It is always run small and to the side at the top of the cover. Note that the* r *and* t *are designed to pick up the shape of the* n. *And note that the crossbar on the* t *is elongated to give the letter better balance in context with the other letters.*

the
Humble
Way

A close-fitting logo for Humble Oil & Refining Company's quarterly magazine. Note how one word fits inside another. Note too that the ay lines up with the top of the W rather than with the bottom. This helps unify the spacing. The face is a closed-up variation of Ultra Bodoni. Shown here in about its actual size, it floats anywhere on the 9 x 12 page to best complement the cover photo.

Blue Flame

For its house organ, Northwest Natural Gas Company uses a hand-drawn logo made of letters that look like flame. And of course the logo is printed in blue.

Change
IN HIGHER EDUCATION

Change is made from a set of ligatures. This handsome type is based on a photolettering face which the magazine uses for titles inside.

Newsweek had a slab serif logo that stretched most of the way —but not all the way—across the top, with a heavy underline that continued down the left side and across the bottom. The line formed sort of a flattened-out C. Then in the mid-1960s *Newsweek* dropped the left and bottom line and retained only the underline. Later the magazine dropped the underline. In 1970 only the word *Newsweek* was left (with the art and cover blurb). And the slab serif letters were modernized, made more expanded than before. The logo stretched all the way across the top.

Family Circle, on the other hand, when it changed its logo, changed it suddenly and dramatically.

Perhaps the rule should be: if the logo is salvageable, change it gradually, in order to retain what recognition value the logo holds for the reader. If the resistance to change has gone on too long and the logo is hopelessly outdated, go ahead and make a clean break.

Art in the cover

The late Joe Ratner, after considering the various claims for one kind of cover over another, concluded that as far as the art was concerned, the ideal cover would show a nude woman sitting on a braided rug, with a dog at her elbow, a rose in her teeth, holding a baby, and eating apple pie.

But cover art today tends to be less predictable than in the past. It is more direct and less cluttered. Art directors of newsstand magazines think of their covers as posters to be seen from 30 feet away. They look for closeup art with a strong silhouette —art not dissimilar from the art on billboards.

Whether the art director uses photographs or illustrations depends again on the nature of the magazine and its audience. A journalistic magazine would normally use photographs, a literary magazine illustrations. It is probably not a good idea to switch back and forth.

Photographs have virtually replaced illustrations as cover art on magazines because photographs are more readily available on short notice and, in most cases, cheaper.

When working out his cover format the art director is wise to pick a square rather than a rectangular hole for the photograph. Picking a rectangle, he has to commit himself to all horizontal or all vertical shots for his cover. Picking a square, he can, with judicious cropping, accommodate both horizontals and verticals, and of course he can run Rollei shots without any cropping. Whatever shape he chooses, the photograph should dominate the page, perhaps even bleeding all around.

If the art director uses art that ties in with something inside, he'll want to run a blurb on the cover pointing to that tie. If the art is independent, he'll somehow have to separate the cover blurbs, if any, from the art to prevent the reader from making a wrong—and sometimes incongruous—connection.

While abstraction in cover art—both in photography and illustration—is making gains, realism still works best for certain magazines. Petersen Publications, publishers of magazines for car buffs, gun lovers, and hot rodders, have experimented with arty covers but have found they do not sell as well as covers crowded with type and illustrated with no-nonsense, sleeves-rolled-up paintings. Albert H. Isaacs, art director, would probably rather commission the arty covers, but he tries to keep his audiences in mind. Good design for such audiences is not necessarily what good design would be for other audiences.

The use of offbeat art can unsettle the reader not used to it. When *Time* for its Feb. 16, 1968, cover ran a photograph of a papier-mâché bust of Kenneth Galbraith by Gerald Scarfe, one reader wrote in: "My five-year-old son looked at the cover picture and said: 'Well, I guess they did the best they could.'"

Even realism can be overdone. The July 10, 1967, issue of *Newsweek* carried a cover showing a map of Vietnam burning on an American flag background. This angered a reader. "Did you actually burn our flag? If so, I am now making a citizen's arrest." *Newsweek* placated the letter writer by pointing out that the stars and stripes were painted on cardboard; a paper cutout of Vietnam was set afire and dropped on the cardboard and a photographer took the picture.

For its logo, Alma Mater, *publication for alumni directors, overlaps the two words of its name. The overlapping "ma" takes on characters of letters both at the left and at the right. The result is a logo made up of three kinds of letters. Yet the designer succeeds in making it all look like one tightly ordered unit.*

Titles on the cover

Titles—or blurbs—on the cover are meant to lure the reader inside. Some magazines devote their entire cover to them. Others combine them with art. Obviously, the simpler the cover, the better. If titles and blurbs must be included, they should be held down to just a few words in two or three lines at the most.

Most annoying, from the reader's standpoint, is the practice of running a title on the cover and changing it when it appears over the article inside. Why do editors persist in doing it?

"The Magazine of Winter" almost buries its logo in snow. But enough of the type shows so that the name stands out adequately on the newsstands.

Color on the cover

If he doesn't use color anywhere else, an editor seems to feel he must use it at least on the cover. The possibilities include 3-D full color, ordinary process color, spot color, and one-color printing.

Time has developed a special red as a cover border to help readers instantly identify the magazine. *National Geographic* similarly has used a bright yellow.

If the cover is printed separately from the magazine itself,

Reach, *published by the Church of God, Anderson, Ind., for its logo, uses some trick typography to capture the spirit of the magazine.*

color on the cover is within the budget of most magazines even when they can't afford color throughout.

Small magazines usually go the second-color route, using a bright color that will contrast with the black-and-white photography. Often the second color consists of a band or block into which the logo or blurbs have been surprinted or reversed.

The art director who desperately wants a full-color cover but can't pay for the original art, color separations, and printing might want to consider the preprinted covers available, at least for some special issue. These are stock covers, with the art printed only on the front cover; the inside front and inside back covers and the outside back cover are blank. Sheets are shipped flat, ready for imprinting. The magazine runs its logo somewhere over the art, where it doesn't interfere. And it runs editorial matter or company ads on the blank pages. The cover is then bound in with the rest of the magazine.

Buildings, the construction and building management journal, moves its logo around each issue and completely changes its cover art. For this cover, art director John E. Sirotiak uses a montage of newspaper clippings behind two figures in full color. The logo and the blurb at the bottom are in bronze. Note that the figures are arranged to match the logo in width.

Covers to remember

The gatefold cover continues to intrigue art directors. The folded extra sheet not only makes possible a cover with a one-two punch but also an inside cover ad that stretches over three facing pages. A classic gatefold was *The Saturday Evening Post*'s for April 28, 1962. It showed first a lineup of ball players looking pious while the "Star Spangled Banner" was being played, then a wild fight involving the players and umpires.

Another classic was *Esquire*'s cover for November 1966. Hubert Humphrey, then Vice-President, was shown saying, "I have known for 16 years his courage, his wisdom, his tact, his persuasion, his judgment, and his leadership." When you turned the page you found Humphrey was really sitting on President Johnson's lap. He was a ventriloquist's puppet! Johnson is shown saying, "You tell 'em, Hubert."

It is easy to see the influence of *Esquire* on the covers of other magazines. One that was affected was *Seattle,* a courageous and controversial magazine that, unfortunately, died in 1970, when the whole economy of the city suffered with the cutbacks at Boeing. For a 1967 cover, *Seattle* showed a well-dressed businessman, seated, silhouetted against a white background. The cover blurb named him and added: "He is a local businessman. He is a homosexual." In an article inside, the businessman explains and defends his homosexuality.

Rivaling *Esquire* with the uniqueness of its covers is a younger magazine, *New York,* like *Esquire* an exponent of the "new journalism." For a cover promoting an article on ice cream, *New York* for Aug. 3, 1970, showed a nude girl holding out two ice cream cones, placed to look at first like a bra. The title, parodying a best-selling book at the time, went: "Every-

FLEET OWNER

7 70

A McGraW-HILL PUBLICATION

Special Issue:
Trucking in America

With its July 1970 issue, Fleet Owner *introduced a new logo designed by Appelbaum & Curtis, New York. The logo "reflects today's fleet operation: strong, bold, modern, progressive." Note that the cover identifies the month by number rather than by name. Colors for this issue were black, blue, and red. (With permission from* Fleet Owner. *Copyright 1970 by McGraw-Hill, Inc. All rights reserved.)*

thing You Always Wanted to Know About Ice Cream But Were Too Fat to Ask."

In its 1970 year-end issue, *New York* gave readers a 12-page handbook for consumers, telling them, among other things, "How to Break the Supermarket Code and Guarantee Your Food Is Fresh." The cover consisted of a drawing of a box one might find in his grocery store, gaudy in color, with a sunburst saying "Special" and a band with type running diagonally across the face. The designer even uglified the logo to make it appear as though it belonged on the package. The 40¢ price for this issue was stamped on the top of the box in the familiar purple indelible ink under the printed words, "You pay only." The box carried the line, "Net weight 6 oz.," which was about what that issue weighed.

West *is not afraid to change the size of the logo from issue to issue or to move it around on the cover. For this cover promoting an article on photography as "everyman's art form," art director Mike Salisbury puts his logo into a setting that approximates the Kodak logo. Photographer Ron Mesaros uses a Polaroid camera to take this picture of someone taking a picture.*

Even *The Atlantic* has become more innovative in its covers. For its October 1970 issue it ran a gatefold for the first time. It provided plenty of room to display a collage by Larry Rivers for a "Soldiers" feature. A title running across the bottom read: "The Army is the only damn thing [and then you had to turn the flap] holding this country together."

But it takes a magazine like *Psychology Today* to give something like a gatefold its ultimate impact. For July 1971 the magazine ran a *six*-page gatefold cover, which featured a game readers could play and also made possible an ad that spread over four open pages inside.

Cover traditions

The New Yorker once each February reruns its first cover designed in the early 1920s by the cartoonist Rea Irwin. It shows a foppish gentleman studying a butterfly. *The Saturday Evening Post* used to devote one cover each year to Benjamin

Franklin, even after historian Frank Luther Mott exposed the magazine's tie to Franklin as highly imaginary.

Many magazines like to tie their covers to the seasons of the year. *McCall's* has used the *M* and *C* of its name to spell out "Merry Christmas." The cover tradition that gets more attention than any other, perhaps, is *Time's* first cover of each year, which features its "Man of the Year" selection. During the last weeks before the selection, *Time's* letters column is filled with suggestions from readers.

Promotional considerations

The cover is important to both the circulation and advertising departments of a magazine.

The art and the blurbs on the cover strongly affect the number of copies sold on the newsstands. Sometimes the circulation department is not content with the cover as printed; it adds some promotional literature of its own.

As his model for this cover painting, Charles E. White III used an old Life cover photograph of a Los Angeles car hop, substituting one platter for another—a record for a tray—and adding the palm trees. Art director Mike Salisbury completed the illusion by putting the illustration in an old Life cover setting. Salisbury's idea here was to provide "a nice surrealistic image for Sunday readers . . . and something a bit different from the very abstract album cover type of art."

Art director Mike Salisbury took his own photograph for this West cover, but not on location. He took it in front of his house. He was careful to choose a pair of glasses, with blue lenses, that symbolized rebellious youth; that the glasses were broken symbolized retaliation by the Establishment. The original cover was in full color.

To sell copies or subscriptions or to urge renewals, a magazine attaches slips of paper to the cover and sews or staples notices into the binding. This practice got out of hand in the 1950s and 1960s as readers angrily ripped their magazines apart trying to dispose of all the come-ons. Now magazines show more consideration for their readers. They add stick-ons and stick-ins that, when removed, do not damage the magazine. An *Esquire* notice stuck on the cover, reminding a subscriber his subscription is about to expire, carries the note: "Pull card gently and cover will not be damaged." *Time* includes a reorder card not bound into—simply slipped into—the magazine, so that it falls out when the magazine is opened.

The stick-ons are often localized for newsstand display. They call attention to articles high in local interest. Even though the magazine puts out several regional editions, covers themselves stay the same.

But for one issue (June 1968) a new editor at *Esquire*, Harold Hayes, decided he needed seven different covers, one for most of the country, six others for selected large cities featured in an article. It was an experiment not often to be duplicated.[3]

When a magazine offers reprints of an article, it wraps the reprint with the cover for that issue. When an advertiser requests reprints of his ad for direct mail use, he expects the cover to accompany the reprint.

A picture of the cover may also be included in advertising directed to media buyers in advertising agencies. For that reason, the cover should be reproducible in a reduced size.

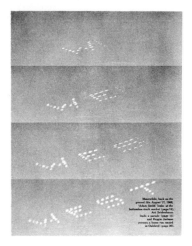

Marshall Lumsden, editor of West, dreamed up this cover, a series of photographs from the air showing lights spelling out the name of the magazine. The blurb at bottom right reads: "Meanwhile, back on the ground this August 17, 1969, 'Adam Smith' looks at the bottomless stock market (page 16), Art Seidenbaum leads a parade (page 11) and Reggie Jackson pursues a home run record in Oakland (page 36)." "One of our best remembered covers but a miss with the promotion department," reports art director Mike Salisbury, "[because it had] no logo." (Photos by Bill Bridges.)

The back cover

The back cover is an ideal place for advertising. For a magazine without advertising, it can present a problem: What to put there?

A house ad is often the answer—or possibly an ad for a public agency.

Or if he has no other use for the space, the art director can choose a strongly horizontal photograph for the front cover and wrap it around the back. Another possibility is to use the same art as on the front cover and flop it for the back.

The final touch

The art director puts a disproportionate amount of his time on the cover. He agonizes over the art. He worries about the

---

3. It must have been a production and distribution nightmare. It was tried because the new editor didn't know any better. Reported the magazine: ". . . so in the end it turned out to be easier to do than to make him understand why it couldn't be done."

placement of the type. He checks the color proofs—and checks them again. Finally, it all fits. Everything is perfect. The magazine is printed. The circulation department takes over.

And what happens? The subscriber gets his magazine, and plunked down right over the type and art is a mailing sticker.

A unique case involved an early November 1969 issue of *Time*, which featured a cover portrait of Vice-President Spiro T. Agnew right after his first attack on the news media. About 320,000 copies of the magazine (only part of the press run) went out with the label pasted across Agnew's mouth. A spokesman for the magazine said it was "a production error."

Suggested further reading

BUECHNER, THOMAS, *Norman Rockwell: Artist and Illustrator,* Harry N. Abrams, Inc., New York, 1970. (All 317 *Saturday Evening Post* covers plus other illustrations are reproduced.)

Chapter 9
Inside pages

The reader opens up a magazine and sees a left- and right-hand page together. It is up to the art director to arrange these two pages to form a single unit. He must do this and at the same time make each page readable of itself. He must create design within design.

Crossing the gutter

The big problem is the gutter running between the pages of a spread, a psychological as well as a physical barrier. When left and right pages are complete in themselves, the gutter actually helps the art director by acting as a separator; but for most spreads, he must build some kind of a graphic bridge to get the reader across.

He can be obvious about it, positioning a piece of art or a heading so that part is on one side of the gutter, part on another. Or he can do it with more subtlety, repeating on the right-hand page a style of art, a pattern, or a color from the left-hand page to help the reader make a visual association.

If he chooses to run art across the gutter, he should do it at a natural break. If a face or figure is involved, he should not let the gutter split it in two. He should not split any art down the middle, unless he wants it to stretch all the way across the spread and bleed left and right. In most cases more of the art should be put on one side of the gutter than the other.

Using art in this way puts design considerations ahead of art appreciation. Readers really don't like their art to go across the gutter. The art, somehow, seems damaged to them, bent—as indeed it is.

If the art director is not aware of production limitations, he may make the mistake of running art across the gutter at a spot on the signature, or between signatures, where perfect alignment is impossible. It is a good idea to check with the printer to determine where across-the-gutter placement will permit the best production.

When the art director uses a line of display type to bridge the gutter, he should use it in a large size. He should not separate the line between letters; he should separate it between words. He should also leave a little extra space at the point of separation, especially if the magazine is side stitched.

The two-opening spread

Sometimes it is necessary to run two article openers on one spread. The article on the left page is a one-pager. A new article begins on the right-hand page. Both articles contain illustrations. How does the art director keep them separated visually?

Some possibilities:

1. He runs a wider-than-usual river of white between the two. He can, of course, separate them horizontally rather than vertically, running one across the top of the two pages, the other across the bottom.

2. If he separates the articles vertically, keeping one on the left-hand page and the other on the right-, he can hold the illustrations for the one on the right until later in the article.

3. He can make the heading of one article bigger than the other.

4. He can put one in a box or run a tint block over it.

5. He can set the articles in different types or set one in two-column format, the other in three-column format.

6. He can establish an optical gap by using and positioning artwork for both articles that pulls the reader to the outside edges.

When he has to display *more* than two illustrated articles or stories on a spread, the art director almost *has* to use boxes or ruled lines.

The unevenly divided spread

Sometimes it is necessary to run two or more different articles on a spread—articles that occupy different amounts of space. One may take up a little more than a page, the other a little less. How does the art director separate these?

1. He can separate them with an extra wide band of white. Sometimes it is best to separate them horizontally rather than vertically. Each article runs all the way across the spread, the larger one at the top.

2. He can run a line or bar between them, in black or in color. Or put one in a box.

3. He can run a tint block over one of them.

4. He can run one in a different size type or in a different column width.

In most cases, wise use of white space is the best answer.

The right-hand start

An art director gets his most dramatic display when he uses a spread—a left- and right-hand page facing one another—to open an article or story. Often he uses one piece of art so big it stretches across the gutter, uniting the two pages.

Sometimes it is necessary to start an article on a right-hand page. If the left-hand page is an ad, the art director will have an easy enough time of it making the opening look different from the advertisement so the two will not be read together. If the left-hand page is the ending of a previous article, the art director should keep art off that page so the page will not compete with his new opening page.

To get the reader to turn the page the art director should direct the thrust of the page to the right. He might want a slug saying "continued" at the bottom of the page. But, please: no arrows.

Continuity

Designing facing pages so they go together is part of the problem. The art director also has to arrange the spreads so *they* go together.

Some magazines like to have all pages related. Others are content to unify only those pages used for a specific article; the collection of article units making up a single issue can represent any number of design approaches.

As the art director unites his spreads, he may well think of himself as performing a function similar to that of the *motion picture art director*. In fact a background in motion picture work would not be a bad background for a magazine art director. Asger Jerrild got his experience at Warner Brothers before he took over as art director of *The Saturday Evening Post*.

The art director achieves a continuity for each spread by sticking with the same typefaces and the same kind of art and by positioning these consistently on the pages. He sets up some horizontal visual axes and relates each spread to them.

Separating editorial matter from ads

Because advertisers don't like isolation, because they like to be up there with articles, stories, and editorials, magazines will

New York Faces Future Shock
By Alvin Toffler

". . . Future shock may turn out to be the most devastating urban disease of tomorrow, and millions of New Yorkers are first in line, as usual. The challenge: how to control change . . ."

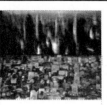

". . . It is impossible to understand what is happening to human relationships in America unless we examine their duration . . ."

". . . Instead of conversations, we send high-speed communiqués and search for all sorts of magic to accelerate friendship . . ."

The main illustration develops right before the reader's eyes as he moves through each spread of this 10-page New York *article. An accompanying boldface blurb changes position on each two pages as the illustration changes, adding to the feeling of movement. The original is in full color. Like many magazines,* New York *runs a small-size reproduction of its logo at the beginning of the main article in each issue. The reader has gone through a number of pages of distracting advertising and other front matter; the small logo refreshes his memory by reminding him what magazine he is reading. It also helps set aside editorial from advertising matter.*

continue their present practices of scattering advertisements throughout their pages.

Given the circumstances, Cortland Gray Smith, editor of *Better Editing,* has drawn up a list of rules for separating editorial matter from advertising.[1] Among them:

1. Make editorial matter look "as different as possible from the usual advertising pattern." Editorial usually has a quieter look.

The art director usually does not know what the advertising will look like until he sees the Vandyke or page proofs. Sometimes he must make adjustments at that point. He may even convince the business side to move an ad.

1. See Cortland Gray Smith, "Page Design for Flow-Through Makeup," *Better Editing,* Spring 1970, pp. 17–19.

A page of short items, united with strong ruled lines. The column heading art is appropriate to the mazazine: Fleet Owner. *Note that for headings within the column, the editor has simply put first words in boldface type. (With permission from* Fleet Owner. *Copyright 1970 by McGraw-Hill, Inc., All rights reserved.)*

If the advertiser has too successfully imitated editorial style, the magazine may run the line over the ad, "An Advertisement," to warn the reader.

2. Adopt an editorial look or pattern that is *consistent* in its use of type styles and spacing. What Smith is saying here, essentially, is that the formalized, highly ordered magazine has an easier time separating editorial from advertising than the more circuslike magazine.

3. Allow an extra measure of white space between editorial and advertising.

4. Concentrate ads *between* editorial features, not *within* them. He's asking here that the art director, representing the editorial department, work with the business and advertising department to establish a better lineup of page allocation.

Which brings us to one of the art director's most important jobs. Before each issue is put to bed, he should go over the Vandyke or page proofs as though he were one of the subscribers, this time not to check his design of editorial pages (he's already done this) but to see how the book looks as a unit—how the ads fit in with the articles and stories. Up until this point, he probably had no idea what each ad was to look like. Each was only a blank rectangle around which he had fit his own material. Advertising departments and editorial departments on magazines, for good reason, do not influence each other as an issue is put together.

This last-minute check can save much embarrassment. No tribute to a grand old lady will be juxtaposed with an ad for Playtex living bras. No article on the plight of the poor will start across the page from an ad for Cadillac. No antismoking article will be followed by an ad for Winston.

If you want a classic case, turn to pages 76 and 77 of the Jan. 24, 1967, issue of *Look*. The left-hand page, all copy, features the title: "Who Will Control the GOP in 1968?" The right-hand page has a full-color, three-quarter-page bleed closeup of a man yawning, presumably because he's comfortable on a United Air Lines flight, not because he's bored with the Republican Party.

Jerome Snyder, art director for *Scientific American*, says that when he skips this last check, sure enough, every time, an ad falls into place next to editorial matter wholly inappropriate to it. Not that the magazine should consciously work out relationships between ads and stories. But it should keep items separated that are obviously incompatible.

Much has been written about how placement of an ad affects readership, and some advertisers pay premium rates for op-ed placement, "Campbell Soup" position, up-front placement, and so on. Recent studies tend to show that placement has less effect than was originally supposed. Ads do not necessarily have to be next to "reading matter." Editors have been moving away from the practice of continuing articles and stories in the back of the book so they will trail through ads. Perhaps eventually they will bunch the ads completely in one section of the book so that art directors can arrange editorial material into a unified whole.

The case for departmentalizing

Routine stories—of deaths, job changes, etc.—should be gathered under collective headings. This makes the design job much easier. It also makes related items easy for the reader to identify.

An obit column with a single heading makes unnecessary an editor's hunt for synonyms for death. The subheadings over each item can simply name the person. Appropriate black borders may be included with the column.

The Delaware River Port Authority Log *uses strong art and overall tone to tie a spread together, then reuses part of the art for a carryover spread back in the book. Even with the art, the carryover spread stands out nicely from the advertising. Note that the blurb under the title is in the same type as the text; note also that the by-line and the "Continued" line are in a lighter face. (Design by Studio 3 of Philadelphia.)*

Carryover spread for a United Church Herald *article on the deserter. The article was printed on a gold-tinted textured stock in black and blue-gray inks. Note the use of an extra-coarse screen halftone. The inward-pointing arrows are a regular typographic device used to close articles in the magazine.*

On the letters-to-the-editor column it is not necessary to start each letter with "Dear Editor" or "To the Editor." The salutation is understood. Letters should be grouped by subject. Nor does each letter need a subheading. A new subheading is necessary only when the subject changes.

Look added art—and interest—to its letters column by taking sample quotes from letters and playing them up in display type—one for each page or column of letters. The type for this display was simulated typewriter type. The letters themselves were set in sans serif type.

Look also ran a box at the end of the column giving the magazine's address and explaining the policy on letters.

Column headings

The editor gives his imagination a brisk workout as he tries to come up with a name for a standing column. What he settles for is important when you consider that he will be using it for months, maybe years.

Some magazines use no-nonsense titles, like "Letters," on their letters-to-the-editor column. *Trans-action* shows a little more imagination with "Feedback from Our Readers," particularly appropriate in that "feedback" is an "in" word with social scientists, who read this magazine. (Several other magazines use "Feedback," too, for their letters columns.) *Trans-action's* version shows the title with two arrows, one pointing to the left, one to the right. *Essence,* the high-fashion magazine for black women, calls its letters column "Write On!"

The *Journal of the American Medical Association* uses "AMAgrams" for its column of short news items. "AMA" for the American Medical Association; "gram[s]" from a Greek word meaning "written." The art puts each letter in a block, and the blocks are slightly scattered to represent blocks used in the game of anagrams.

Live, a church-school publication of the Assembly of God, uses the heading "Assembly Lines" for a column of miscellanea. The art consists of the two words repeated several times in smaller type in a second color.

Fitness for Living heads its column of short news items on fitness with "All the News That's Fit," a takeoff on the slogan of the New York *Times*.

The title for a record column in *Senior Scholastic* is "DISCussions." The all-cap beginning is art enough for this one. The title for a record column in *Harper's* is "Music in the Round."

Oak Leaves, Oak Park, Ill., weekly, calls its birth announcement column "Hello World." (A good title, but it should have a comma after "Hello.")

Some magazines have even toyed with clever headings for obit columns. This seems a bit much. The author remembers seeing one once called "Pardon Our Dust." *National Review*'s "RIP" [Rest in Peace], perfectly proper, still is a little unsettling, especially with the new meaning "rip" has taken on.

The design of the column heading has to be as carefully considered as the naming of the column. Readers will see it many times. The art director should not hesitate to adjust the heading several times until he gets it right. He might well decide to leave off any art, to do the job with good typography only.

Whatever is decided, it is important that the style for all column and departmental headings be consistent.

News Meter, employee publication of the San Diego Gas & Electric Company, runs small pictures and narrow-measure captions for its personalities page, separating each item with column rules. The designer "hangs" two from the top and builds three of them up from the bottom. Sometimes the mug shot is over the caption, sometimes under. The result is a highly unified page. The original is in black and a second color (olive), but black alone would work as well.

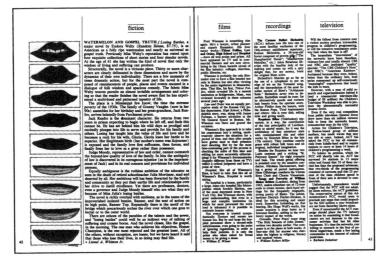

Several back-of-the-book departments are nicely combined in this one spread from United Church Herald.

The interior logo

A magazine should run its name in a small slug line on each spread if not on every page, along with the page number and date. Researchers, if not ordinary readers, appreciate this service.

At one or two spots early in the magazine the editor might also want to run the logo as it appears on the cover, but in a reduced size: on the table of contents or masthead page and, if the magazine has lots of advertising before the main features begin, on the opening page of the first article. *New York* magazine, for instance, gives the readers twenty-four or more pages of advertising, letters to the editor, movie schedules, etc., before it gets to its opening article. Perhaps to remind the reader that it is *New York* he's reading, the editors run a tiny version of the logo at the top of that opening article, complete with a section of the three-line rule the magazine runs above the logo on the cover. Actually, how well a logo will take reduction should be a consideration in its design.

United Church Herald devotes its inside front cover and page 3 to its masthead, an introduction to a major article, and the table of contents (illustrated). Note the unusual format for the table of contents.

The table-of-contents page

For many years the table of contents was a no-man's land in American magazines. No longer. Now the table of contents—and the entire table-of-contents page—is a magazine showpiece.

Saul Bass made a high art of motion picture titles and credits. Today many motion pictures run an additional credit line at the beginnings or ends: "Titles by _____." Magazines haven't gone that far, but their art directors have given more thought to the table-of-contents page than ever before.

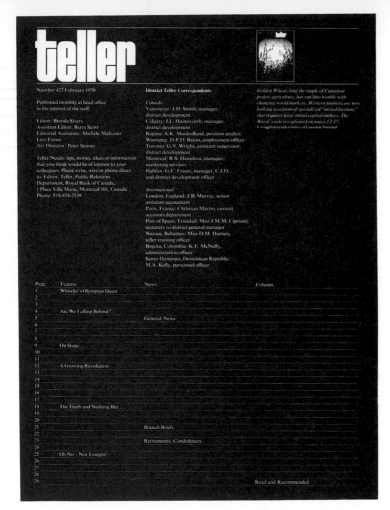

This is the inside front cover for Teller, *a 9 x 12 slick paper monthly published "in the interest of the staff" by the Royal Bank of Canada.* Teller *reproduces its logo and (in a small size) its cover and combines them with a masthead and a table of contents printed in reverse letters on a black background. Note that the editor has really made a* table *out of the table of contents. The blackness of the page complements a black border around art on the cover.*

What goes on that page varies from magazine to magazine, but on most magazines, the page includes (1) the table of contents, (2) the listing of staff members, (3) the masthead, and (4) a caption for the cover picture along with a miniature version of the cover. There may also be some copy on the page, as, for example, an editorial, a preface to the issue, statement from the publisher or editor, or an advertisement.

For some reason *The New Yorker*, alone among major magazines, did not for many years run a table of contents. For that matter it did not—nor does it yet—run by-lines, except at the ends of articles and stories. Nor do many of the opening spreads carry art. Perhaps the magazine expected readers to start at the beginning and read straight through. Perhaps it felt readers didn't have to be lured. Competition from *New York* and a general change in readers' attitudes changed *The New Yorker*, at least to the extent that in the late 1960s it began to carry a regular table of contents.

The table of contents for a magazine lists the titles of articles and stories, the names of the authors, and the page numbers where the articles and stories start. If the table is extensive, the editor divides it into sections, like "Articles," "Stories," and "Departments." *The New Yorker* and *Saturday Review* list the full names of cartoonists appearing in each issue—a worthwhile service when you consider the unreadability of most cartoonists' signatures.

For their tables of contents art directors increasingly are taking parts of illustrations inside the magazine and reproducing them with the table of contents. *New York* is a good example.

The listing of staff members should feature the main members in the order of their rank and in parallel terminology. It should not, for instance, use "editor" for one staff member and "production" for another. Many magazines find it desirable to list principal staff members in one size type, lesser staff members in another. Editorial staff members are usually run separately from business staff members. On many magazines, the three top editorial staffers are the editor, the managing editor, and the art director. The listing need not be in the form of a table; it can be "run in" to save space.

The masthead, usually in agate type, carries basic information about the magazine: date of issue, volume number, frequency of publication, name of publishing firm, editorial and business addresses, information on submitting manuscripts, information on circulation, price per copy, annual subscription rate, etc.

The masthead should make it easy for the contributor and subscriber to find the correct addresses (editorial offices often have addresses different from circulation offices). It might be a good idea to introduce each address with a boldface line: "If you want to submit a manuscript" for one and "If you want to subscribe to the magazine" for the other. Maybe a third will be needed: "If you want to place an advertisement." Every editor should take time once each year to rethink his masthead and work with his designer to better organize the material it contains.

Every magazine has to run at least an abbreviated version of a masthead, but if the magazine is thin enough, say with sixteen pages or fewer, it can probably skip the table of contents and the listing of staff members. Or it can compress the table of contents and masthead into a single column.

For big magazines, the table of contents can go on one page, the masthead on another, the listing of staff members on still another.

Teller combines colorful art and typography for lead articles with a more subdued look for standing features. This news section makes use of horizontal lines, sans serif headline faces, roman body copy, and numbered pictures. Part of the magazine is printed on glossy white paper; this section, and several other news-oriented sections, are printed on dull-finish, blue-tinted stock.

Chapter 10
Newspaper makeup

The typical daily or weekly newspaper is not designed, really; its parts are merely fitted together. They are fitted together customarily in such a way as to fill in all the available space— to the top, the sides, the bottom of the page.

Sort of like a jigsaw puzzle.

A little white space here and there relieves the congestion, but the white space is more accidental than planned.

The pity is that newspaper executives do not realize how lacking in design are the publications in their charge. These are word-oriented people, these executives—or business-oriented; and they take a hard-bitten attitude about newspaper format that, not seriously challenged in several centuries, will not quickly change now, even with mid-twentieth-century technological revolutions. Forget what's going on in magazines. On TV. The newspaper executive lives by the book.

And the book says:

1. The newspaper shall be broken up into narrow vertical columns, eight to the page.

2. The columns shall be separated by ruled lines.

3. Headlines shall be standardized.

4. At the top of the first page shall go the nameplate, in an Old English face, preferably in an inline or outline version.

5. Beginning on page 2, the ads; and they shall be arranged in half-pyramid form, with the greatest concentration on the right-hand side of the page.

6. With a border established uniformly for the pages, printed matter shall extend to all four sides and corners. No blank areas except in the ads, which the sponsors are free to do with as they wish.

Perhaps there is no better way to present the newspaper fare. So varied are the stories, and so numerous, they simply cannot be given the luxurious display treatment magazine features and stories get. And the demands of daily if not hourly deadlines discourage the kind of design experimentation one finds in the offices of more leisurely edited publications.

One man who has helped give newspapers a face-lifting is Edmund C. Arnold, head of the graphic arts department of Syracuse University's School of Journalism, newspaper publisher, and consultant to the Mergenthaler Linotype Corp. He has designed or redesigned the *National Observer, Christian Science Monitor*, Louisville *Courier-Journal*, St. Louis *Post-Dispatch, Today* (Cocoa, Fla.), and other papers. Carrying on the traditions established by John Allen and Albert Sutton in the 1930s and 1940s, Professor Arnold in his frequent lectures to conventions of newspapermen and in his numberless articles and books, first anesthetizes his audience with his wit, then pounds home his admirable dicta: wider columns, no column rules, more white space, all lowercase headlines.[1] But after several years he has succeeded only in substituting for some papers one set of rules, admittedly superior, for another. The newspaper look is still there.

Publisher Gardner Cowles put his finger on the problem at a meeting of the William Allen White Foundation at the University of Kansas. "A good newspaper needs a good art director. When I say this, most editors don't know what I am talking about."

He explained: Papers today are laid out or made up by editors or printers with no art background or training. Other media would not think of assigning so important a task to people not equipped for it.

On successful magazines, the art director ranks right below the top editor in importance and authority. He has a strong voice in helping decide how a story idea is to be developed. He suggests ways to give it maximum visual impact. He knows how to blend type and photographs so that each helps the other. His responsibility is to make each page come alive and intrigue the reader. Newspapers need this kind of talent. Too few have it.

Among newspapers that have art directors are the Chicago *Daily News*, Providence *Journal* and *Bulletin*, Miami *Herald*, *Newsday* (Long Island), and *Today* (Cocoa, Fla.). *The Bulletin* of the American Society of Newspaper Editors for January 1971 ran a report on the duties of these art directors and concluded that any newspaper with a circulation of more than 50,000 needs the services of an art director. *The Bulletin* predicted that the idea of art directors for newspapers would spread.

This 7-Up ad is one of the earliest of the FlexForm ads, run just before Christmas, 1968, in the Peoria, Ill., Journal Star, which originated FlexForm ads. When an advertiser buys a Flex-Form page, he can design his ad in any shape he chooses, zigzagging among the columns for up to 65 percent of the space, getting full-page dominance without full-page cost. His ad can appear in more than one piece, as in the ad above. When it first came out, FlexForm was hailed as "the first significant change in the use of regular newspaper pages in 50 years." More than 200 newspapers have experimented with FlexForm. The advertiser who uses it undoubtedly gets remarkable impact with the various shapes FlexForm allows, but because editorial matter has to be squeezed into the remaining holes, FlexForm makes even more difficult the display of editorial matter on the inside pages.

---

1. Another prodder is Howard B. Taylor, editorial consultant to the Copley International Corporation, and former writer of a weekly column on "Layout and Design" for *Editor & Publisher*.

When design help comes to newspapers it will come from outside the fraternity. It will come from graphic designers with magazine or advertising agency experience who are fast enough and flexible enough to deal with multiple daily deadlines and late-breaking news and, more important, who are capable of making editorial as well as art and design decisions. It will come from graphic designers who are verbally as well as visually literate.

Men with these traits are hard to find, because, as Clive Irving, the British designer, points out, "tradition has separated the two."

One paper found such a man. What happened on that paper, from a design standpoint, may have been a first step in revolutionizing the newspaper look.

The look of the late Herald Trib

It would be nice to report that because it tried harder the Avis of New York newspapers was able to catch up with the stodgy New York *Times*.[2] Unfortunately, the *Herald Tribune* not only failed to catch up; it failed to survive. And yet, in its last days, it was, by all odds, America's best-designed newspaper.

Once a near-equal to the *Times* in circulation in the New York morning field, the *Herald Tribune* by 1963 had fallen far behind. In desperation its management considered a number of editorial changes and—more important to the readers of this book—a number of design changes. Long a pacesetter in typographic excellence among newspapers, the *Herald Tribune* decided a *radical* change was in order.

The man management turned to was a stranger to newspapers: Peter Palazzo, an advertising and graphic designer. With no preconceived notions of what a newspaper should look like, Palazzo conducted a study and was surprised to find that newspapers—all newspapers—had scarcely changed at all in format over the years.

Convinced that in competition with magazines, newspapers, from the standpoint of quality, were running a poor second, Palazzo recommended changes for the *Herald Tribune* in both design and editorial content and treatment. To improve itself the paper would have to coordinate its editorial and design operations. And yet Palazzo asked for nothing revolutionary. He worried, rightly, about reader habit.

"One must be very careful about tampering with habits which have built up over a long period of time," he said. Perhaps he was thinking of the 1962 storm that followed the about-face made by *The Saturday Evening Post*.

---

2. The author omits from the discussion the *Daily News*, lively in spirit but deadly in design, America's No. 1 newspaper, but in circulation only.

OLD

NEW

To illustrate a speech he was to make to a group of newspaper executives, Dan Kelly, senior vice-president and creative director of the Chicago office of Foote, Cone & Belding, asked art directors at his agency to redesign some newspaper front pages, four of which are shown here. Original pages are shown at the left, redesigned pages at the right. Although the art directors admitted that their suggested formats might be impractical, they did feel that "newspapers can be more inviting, more interesting, and more relevant to their readers in the communications explosion of the '70's." The designers are Dave Hunter (Knoxville Journal), Pat Sindt (St. Louis Post-Dispatch), Jay Fisher (Tulsa Daily World), and Bert Hoddinott (Chicago Today). Chicago Today is a tabloid.

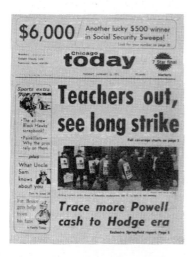

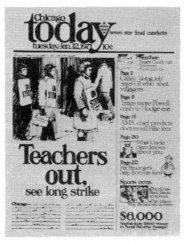

The Paper of Oshkosh, Wis., a short-lived small-circulation offset daily, was a pacesetter in newspaper design with its modular arrangement of its news stories and generous use of white space. Headlines were set in all-lowercase Bodoni Bold. Columns were set in a variety of widths. Captions were set narrow and placed to the right, leaving unusual amounts of white space at the left.

Page three of The Paper *was always a second "front" page, free of ads. Where page one devoted itself to national and international news, page three devoted itself to local news.*

What Palazzo asked for and got, essentially, was a magazine look for the paper. He concentrated on the Sunday issue, especially the Sunday magazine section and the front pages of the other sections.

He insisted that more thought be given to selection, editing, and placement of pictures. Cropping of pictures was often needed, he admitted, but he reminded his client that when you crop a picture you change what it says. Cropping does more than simply "move the reader in close."

For its headlines the *Herald Tribune* had been using Bodoni Bold, an "in" face among the better-designed newspapers in America. Palazzo requested Caslon, which, as far as management was concerned, was a face for advertising and book typography. Anyway, did it have the quality Palazzo ascribed to it? To convince the skeptics, Palazzo lettered a four-letter word, first in Bodoni, then in Caslon. And, by golly, in Caslon the word looked almost respectable!

Print, the prestigious magazine of graphic design, in its September/October 1964 issue, applauded the new *Trib* look, saying the change has been "widely hailed as a milestone in newspaper design." But other papers were not willing to emulate it because it was, essentially, a *magazine* look. Only in their locally produced magazine sections did the look take hold. Most editors of these sections recognized *New York*, the Sunday magazine of the *Herald Tribune*, as the most beautiful in the industry. Some of these editors, moved by what they saw, shortly after the appearance of the new *Trib*, began to make greater use of white space, heavy and light horizontal rules, old-style roman headline faces in lighter-than-usual weights, and even italic swash capitals where appropriate. *West*, the Sunday magazine of the Los Angeles *Times*, took on the look of the *Herald Trib*.

By the end of 1966 the New York *Herald Tribune*, its design already compromised through merger with other papers earlier in the year, gave up altogether. Good design—and some fine writing, especially in the magazine section—could not save the paper.

No one claims that design is the answer to "the disappearing daily." Design can only improve an already strong newspaper. Unfortunately, the strong papers, like the New York *Times*, do not feel compelled to give their readers the added dimension of good design. Innovation will continue to come from the runners up; when it finally takes hold, the leaders will have to follow.[3]

Design under existing conditions

To revolutionize the standard format for newspapers is too much of a job for a book dealing generally with all aspects of publication design. All this volume can do is point out that newspapers stand in *need* of change. That change will come eventually seems certain.

In the meantime, readers of this chapter will want to know how they can best operate under existing conditions. What follows is a discussion of the best current techniques for laying out the pages of a standard newspaper.

First, the editor—or makeup man— will have to understand newspaper production.

The printing of newspapers

The newspaper format lends itself to letterpress. Only since World War II has offset lithography posed any real threat to

3. Although the *Times* on a daily basis remains badly in need of a graphic overhaul, some of its Sunday sections now are elegant.

letterpress as the preferred method of printing. But in that short time it has replaced letterpress on most of the weeklies and about one-third of the dailies. Its advantages: better and cheaper picture reproduction on poor-quality paper, greater flexibility in design, less expensive typesetting, a more even laying on of solid color and black areas. Offset's advantages are particularly impressive on short press runs. They diminish as the runs get longer.

Letterpress in recent years has been able to adopt some of offset's advantages; and with the coming of computer typesetting, it may well regain some of its lost ground. At any rate, both processes seem firmly established in the industry.

Rotogravure, a third process, will continue to serve best the producers of syndicated Sunday magazine sections and Preprint and SpectaColor advertising inserts.

The dummy

In laying out the pages, some editors paste galley proofs onto full-size layout sheets. (The printer makes available simultaneously two sets of proofs: one to proofread, the other to clip and paste.) With a dark or bright-color pencil, the editor marks the number of the galley across the face of every story—perhaps every paragraph—then with scissors or razor blade cuts away excess paper, making a unit out of each story.

Other editors prefer to use half-size sheets, calibrated into inches and columns so that ½ inch on the sheet represents a full inch in the newspaper. To use such sheets, the editor takes measurements off the galleys and with boxes and lines marks story placement on his layout sheet. He can mark—rather than cut and paste—on full-size sheets, too, if he wishes.

The pasteups or drawn designs need not be 100 percent accurate. Lines need not be perfectly aligned. The dummy serves only as a *guide* to the printer; he squares things up and adjusts the fit as he handles the type and later pulls his page proofs.

The basic formats

During the lull just before Christmas, wire service operators fill the wires with art they compose at their keyboards. They use Xs for their basic designs, Ms and Ws for darker areas, periods and colons for lighter areas. The Library of Congress has recognized their efforts as an unusual art form and has accumulated a permanent file of designs. One of the most widely admired wire service artists is Charles Reeser of the Washington, D.C., Bureau of Associated Press. "Peace on Earth," at the right, was his contribution for 1970. Newspapers, which receive art like this with their regular wire service copy, sometimes reproduce it in their Christmas issues. Magazines can make use of this art form, too. An artist can produce such art using a typewriter.

The editor using a newspaper format has two basic choices: the full-size sheet, approximately 15 inches wide by 23 inches deep, usually with 8 columns to the page; and the tabloid sheet, approximately 11 inches by 15 inches, with 5 columns to the page. The tabloid, really a half-size paper, was developed to serve the strap-hangers on mass transit systems. It is less popular now, partly because of the demise of mass transit systems, partly because it was the format of the discredited sensational press. But it does have the advantages of giving better display to small ads and creating the impression of a "thick" paper. A number of newspapers publishing their own Sunday magazine sections choose the tabloid format because it provides greater layout flexibility.

Kinds of makeup

Authors dealing with newspaper makeup tend to categorize it under six headings:

1. *Symmetrical.* You'll be hard pressed to find examples of symmetrical newspaper pages today. Even the New York *Times* has pretty much abandoned them.

2. *Informal balance.* This is far more common and sensible; all the other kinds of makeup are really nothing but variations.

3. *Quadrant.* Informal balance is achieved on a page that is cut into imaginary quarters; each quarter has some art and some heavy typography.

4. *Brace.* Liberal use is made of stories that start out with multicolumn heds and leads, funneling down to single-column tails. One *L*-shaped story fits snugly into another; or a picture fits into the *L*. Stories look like braced wall shelves, hence the name.

5. *Circus.* Such makeup is loudly informal and gimmick-ridden. Otto Storch gave it magazine respectability on the pages of *McCall's* in the late 1950s.

6. *Horizontal.* This informal makeup has many multi-column heds and pictures, with stories blocked off into horizontal rectangles several columns wide. Horizontal, but not vertical, column rules are used.

To these Edmund Arnold has added:

7. *Functional.* There is increased emphasis on readability. Crowding is out; white space is in. Furthermore, the nature of the news determines the look of the page.

Which is as it should be.

"All bad newspaper layout is bad," says Clive Irving, "because the process is performed backwards; somebody dreams up some pretty shapes and then the poor material is massaged to fit."

Jumping the stories

The average 8-column paper runs about a dozen stories on its front page. The more stories, the more chance of providing something of interest to every reader; but the more need, then, of jumping stories to inside pages. The trend is toward fewer stories—and fewer jumps. An editor doesn't want a reader to leave the front page to follow a certain story—and not get back there again.

The editor can avoid jumps and still have plenty of front-page stories if he breaks long stories into two or several short

stories, putting the main one on page 1, putting others inside.

When stories must jump, they should jump, if possible, to the back page of the section they start in. The jump hed can either restate the original hed or take up the subject being dealt with at the jump. (The original hed usually deals with the lead paragraphs of the story.) Logic suggests the jump hed should be smaller or at least no bigger than the main hed.

You never run a "continued" slug when the story continues in the next column. The Chicago *Tribune* often continues a story from column 8 of page 1 to column 1 of page 2, and does it without a "continued" line.

A front page and an editorial page of the Minneapolis Tribune, redesigned in 1971 by British designer Frank Ariss. With its precise, clean, contemporary look, appropriate for computer-assisted production, the Tribune is one of the most attractive and readable newspapers in the United States. There are no column rules and no paragraph indentations. The most important front-page story appears at the top left rather than at the top right. The nameplate and headline face are in Helvetica. The symbol of the open newspaper (or of the sheet of paper on a web press; it depends upon how you look at it) appears on various pages.

No wonder some papers leave the design of inside pages to the printer. What can you do with a mere quarter-page news hole or less—the area left over after the ads are laid in place? You have little or no room for pictures or display heds. Worse, your small space is *L*- or *U*-shaped.

An answer—if the advertisers would sit still for it—lies in abandoning the every-ad-next-to-editorial-matter practice and adopting instead a pattern for ads that puts them all in a rectangle at the side or bottom of the page. Better still, keep all

ads on their own pages: a page or two of ads, a page then of news and editorial features, and so alternating through the paper. Readership studies of ad placement do not necessarily confirm the belief by advertisers that an ad gets poor readership when it is "buried."

Because advertisers, lacking confidence in their own works, insist that their ads appear next to editorial matter, newspapers arrange ads on inside pages in triangular patterns, leaving top-of-the-page triangles—"news holes"—for the newsman to fill. This makes real design of inside pages virtually impossible. Further complicating the problem of inside pages is the advertiser, still insistent that his advertising appear next to editorial matter, who buys not a *full* but a *near*-full page. What do you do with an *L*-shaped news hole 1-column deep and 8-columns x 1 inch across? To deal with this problem, some papers offer advertisers a "Scotch page"—a full page at the near-full-page rate.

Making it easy for the reader

Readers appreciate a news digest on the front page, boxed or otherwise set aside, perhaps over the nameplate, with single paragraphs devoted to each of the major stories. The wise editor is stingy with details here; he doesn't want to spoil his reader for the whole story. When page numbers follow each entry, the digest serves, too, as a special table of contents.

For large papers, there should be a general table of contents pointing the reader to regular features.

It is a good idea to establish regular placement for standing features and pages. Portland's *Oregonian* drives its readers mad by moving its editorial page around from issue to issue; but at least the paper always makes it a left-hand page. Because they take more time to read, editorial pages on most

Two versions of a heading for the letters column of the Minneapolis Tribune, *shown here actual size. When the column spreads over onto two pages, the paper runs one of these on the editorial page, the other on the op-ed page.*

Ellen Peck

Will Jones
after last night

Headings for regular columns in the Tribune *are look-alikes: each carries a line-conversion portrait, balanced at the right by a heavy bar that forms a near-box. Samples are shown here in actual size. Note that one heading only names the columnist; the other does that and carries a column title, too. Still, the headings clearly are related.*

papers (including the *Oregonian*) go toward the back; the skimmers can drop off then without missing the important stories—and the advertisements.

The thoughtful editor runs standing features and pages in the same position, issue after issue. And the reader thanks him for it. *Time* magazine proved that "departmentalizing" the news pays off after all.

Obits should be gathered in one section of the paper under a standing heading or between symbolic black bars. Obits need no individualized heds. How many ways can you say—would you want to say—that a person has died, anyway? The full name by itself is headline enough. Besides, you avoid awkward part-present tense, part-past tense heds like this: JOE SMITH DIES TUESDAY. (Sounds as if poor Joe is set to face a firing squad.)

So can engagements and weddings be gathered together under standing headings and run with label, name-only heds. And you can avoid hunting synonyms for "Wed."

Readers also appreciate an arrangement of material—possible only with large newspapers—that makes separate sections out of sports pages, financial pages, and other special pages. That way the whole family can enjoy the paper at the same time. Ideally, each section would be printed on its own tinted stock.

The question of emphasis

Makeup is largely a matter of assigning proper emphasis to stories. Usually, one story gets bigger emphasis than any other. On some days, however, the page may have two stories of equal significance. Maybe three.

It is a good idea to think of stories as falling into three general categories of importance—major stories, important stories, and fillers—and assign emphasis accordingly.

You can emphasize through placement. You can also emphasize through size, unusual handling, blackness, color.

Until recently, the No. 1 spot on the front page was always the top of the eighth column, because that was where the banner headline ended. With decreased emphasis on newsstand sales, the banner is less important and not often used; there is no reason, then, why the No. 1 story can't go at the top left of the page, where the eye normally first settles.

At one time, all the emphasis was confined to the top half of the page. Now the entire page is considered; editors take specific steps to get some typographic display "below the fold." Edmund Arnold talks about "anchoring" all four corners of a page with something heavy. Run dark headlines, boxes, pictures, or other typographic weights to "define" each corner, he advises. This seems a bit arbitrary. One wonders: What's so important or mysterious about corners that they need defining?

Newspaper typography

The character of the publication, the kind of paper it's printed on, the amount of space available—these considerations affect the designer's choice of typefaces. That the typical newspaper is published for persons of varying backgrounds and ages suggests types should be simple and familiar. That the paper stock used is cheap, absorbent newsprint suggests types should be open and somewhat heavy. That space is at a premium suggests types should be somewhat condensed.

Chapter 6 describes body faces available and tells how these types are set for both letterpress and offset newspapers.

Headlines

For headline type, newspapers—offset and letterpress—use sans serif, slab or square serif, or modern roman in display sizes. A few use old style or transitional romans, provided they are on the heavy side, like the Cheltenham used by the Milwaukee *Journal*. Most editors prefer a condensed face so that they can get a better "count" for their headlines. Among the sans serifs, Spartan is popular; among the slab serifs,

Stymie; among the moderns, Bodoni bold. For standing column heds, a paper is likely to turn to one of the decorative or miscellaneous (and, frankly, boorish) faces, like Kaufmann bold or Brush.

Letterpress papers rely on Ludlow for headline typography, offset papers on photographic headsetting machines.

All papers draw up a "hed chart" or "hed schedule," which reproduces sample heds in various sizes and arrangements, gives them numbers, and tells what the maximum count is per line. The count can only be approximate; it is based on a system which puts all letters, numbers and punctuation marks into four width categories: ½, 1, 1½, and 2. With some exceptions, punctuation marks are ½; lowercase letters, 1; numbers and capital letters, 1½; capitals M and W, 2. Depending on the typeface, lowercase letters f, i, j, t, and l usually count as ½, lowercase m and w as 1½; caps I and J as 1. The space between words can be ½ or 1 unit, but it should be consistently one or the other.

The advantage of a hed chart is this: Referring to it, the copyreader can pick quickly a "stock" style and size appropriate to the story, scribble the code number at the top of the sheet, shoot it over to the hed-writer. The code tells the hed-writer what style is wanted, how wide in columns the hed is to be, how many decks are wanted, how many lines are wanted in each deck—and what the maximum count is. He can't exceed the maximum count, but he can stay under it. Some newspapers insist that each line take up at least two-thirds of the maximum count and that in a multi-line hed the longest lines be kept at the top.

It could be worse.

The few newspapers who remain faithful to the geometric-shaped heds of an earlier era—flush-left-and-right, cross-line, step-line, hanging indention, inverted pyramid—require an *on-the-button* count. Fortunately, the flush-left heds now so universally used do not so seriously restrict the hed-writer. The heds are more readable. And they are better looking, too.

Edmund Arnold has recorded two important dates in newspaper design: Sept. 1, 1908, and Dec. 4, 1928. On the first date, the Minneapolis *Tribune* became what Arnold believes was the first newspaper to use caps-and-lowercase headlines. Until then, all newspaper headlines had been all-caps; and for years afterwards—on through most of the 1920s—most newspapers continued to use all-caps headlines. Unreadable though they are, they find favor on a few newspapers even today.

On that second date, the *Morning Telegraph*, a specialized newspaper in New York, became the first newspaper to use flush-left headlines. Until then, all newspaper headlines had been contorted into inverted pyramids, hanging indentions, and other stringent and crowded shapes. A few newspapers in the East today continue to use hard-to-read and hard-to-write heds. But only a few.

The argument now is over the adoption of all-lowercase heds. These are heds with only the first word and all proper nouns capitalized. Magazines have long since adopted such heds—or "titles," as they are called in that medium; newspapers gradually are coming around. A headline contains a subject and predicate. It is a sentence picked out from among the first few paragraphs and writ large. It follows, then, that it should *look* like a sentence. That each word should be capitalized does not help.

The modern newspaper has dropped the idea, too, of the multiple-deck headline. Today, on most papers, a headline consists of one or, at the most, two decks of two or three lines each. Headlines are not so deep as they were; but they are wider. They spread across several columns, adding to the horizontal look.

Subheds

Sub-headlines within the bodies of stories provide necessary typographic relief when stories are long. Four styles are common:

1. Flush left.
2. Centered.
3. Lined up with the paragraph indentions.
4. Run-in.

These are almost always in boldface type and often in capital letters. The first three must be displayed with sufficient white space above and below, preferably with more white space above than below.

The run-in subhed needs only a little white space above. Usually it begins at the regular paragraph indention. It can be a line complete in itself. Or it can be simply the first three words or so, set in boldface. An advantage of such a subhed is that it comes from the reporter already "written."

Some papers use, instead of or in addition to subheds, occasional complete paragraphs set in boldface type, often in a narrower measure than regular body type. Such paragraphs cheapen the look of the page and give arbitrary emphasis to parts of stories.

The nameplate

From journalism's beginnings, editors felt names of their newspapers should stand out as copies were peddled and hawked on city streets. About the only dark type known or available

was the blackletter, a face we know today as Old English. Even today, partly because of tradition, partly because of what editors consider the "dignity" of the face, many nameplates still appear in that same unlikely face.

It is time newspapers adopt a face for nameplates more in keeping with the times and with their headline and body types. Plenty of boldface types are available; and we know today that even small faces can stand out provided they are displayed with a generous amount of white space.

If a paper can't bring itself to give up Old English for its nameplate, it can at least simplify the type. The New York *Times* did this recently, greatly improving the looks of the nameplate. Compare it to that of the Washington *Post*, also Old English, but in an *outline* version.

The typeface in a nameplate can be in strong contrast to the headline face, or it can be in the same face, say in all caps where headlines are caps and lowercase.

Actually, a newspaper's nameplate is almost always drawn and photoengraved—that's why it's called a name*plate*. The

Bill Kuykendall for the Worthington, Minn., Daily Globe captures the mood of "the celebrated secular monk" Ralph Nader in this memorable photograph. The story accompanying the photo describes Nader on the platform: "As he speaks, his eyes lift up to meet the crowd, his back arches up, his voice gains in volume and authority. He does things with his hands. He folds them into prayer position. . . ."

drawing often incorporates a line sketch of an insignia or some local scene. An effective nameplate can be made of reproduction proofs of type cut and repasted and retouched by an artist familiar with letterform.

Many newspapers use a single design in more than one size. The nameplate may "float" to any location from issue to issue. Steve Sohmer, creative director of the Bureau of Advertising of the American Newspaper Publishers Association, suggests that newspapers incorporate the day of the week into the nameplate. Instead of the *Daily News*, you would have the *Monday News*, the *Tuesday News*, etc.

Pictures

Today's newspaper practice puts photographs in a secondary role. Editors use pictures to fill holes. The New York *Daily News*'s idea of great art, so Edwin Diamond reports in an article in *New York* (February 1971), is "a group color photo of the Mets."

Philip N. Douglis, photojournalism columnist for the now-defunct *ICE Reporting,* called the daily press "a photographic disaster area." What bothered Douglis and what bothers other critics is the preponderance of staged shots and meeting pictures that can interest only those who pose for them.

If art in newspapers is to improve, one place to start is with picture size.

If the case is strong for larger pictures in print media generally, the case is overwhelming for newspapers. The 65-line screen for reproducing photographs remains constant as the size increases. The larger the picture the finer, in proportion, will the dot pattern appear.

The photographer taking pictures for his paper now moves in close on his subject. If he doesn't, the picture editor crops the picture to emphasize what may be a small portion in the original. Even then, he runs the picture large. Most editors agree with their photographers that the paper is better off with fewer but larger pictures.

While in gallery photography the picture may speak for itself, in journalistic photography it must be explained in words. Under the halftone goes the caption (called by newspapermen "cutlines") in a width equal—or almost equal—to the picture width. Boldface or italic can be used, in a size that is a point or two smaller than body copy. For an unusually large picture, the caption may be set in two or more columns. Some newspapers use captions set considerably narrower than picture widths, with small multi-line headlines placed at the right side, flush left or flush right or centered. If a picture accompanies a story, it needs no headline; the story's headline is its umbrella.

Newspaper color

Despite valiant efforts by the newspaper industry to achieve magazine quality in color reproduction, newspapers remain hopelessly outclassed. No matter how much care is taken by the photographer and photoengraver in making separations for three-color process work, the inability to keep a fourth plate in register, the coarseness of the screens, and the inferiority of the paper stock make faithful reproduction of the original impossible. If the newspaper can't get its color through pre-printed rolls of rotogravure material, it might well consider confining its color to solid or even-screened areas—to flat color, in other words.

Indiscriminate use of process color does nothing to improve the communication. In fact, color can hurt rather than help. Why hold out for a washed-out, too-purple color halftone when a less-costly-to-produce black-and-white halftone shows up clearer?

The Worthington, Minn., Daily Globe regularly features some of the best photographs to be found in American newspapers. "We have sought to innovate and improve ways of displaying pictures and, very important, relate them to text," says Bill Kuykendall, photo editor. "We believe a gap has existed much too long among photo-people and word-people on newspapers. We seek to encourage by example the metamorphosis of photographers into photo-journalists and writers into visual-appreciationists. Anything less than a concerted effort to present clearly and concisely the visual and written components of story frustrates communication. Journalists have been treading water too long." In this picture by Kuykendall entitled "The Pigeon People," a group of boys, ages 9 through 13, show pigeons they captured to sell to citizens of Worthington at 25 cents each, "marked down from 35 cents." It was a late summer project for the youngsters.

ROY PAUL

A wash drawing is executed by the author in India ink. The ink was used in its original state for outlines and in a watered down state for tones. Such a drawing calls for highlight-halftone reproduction. The Eugene, Oreg., Register-Guard ran the drawing to illustrate a feature on a local crackdown on fathers who had deserted their families. It had to be a drawing; the story didn't lend itself to photographic coverage.

Nor does *flat* color necessarily improve the communication. Type in a too-light color becomes hard to read. Halftones in a too-light color lose their detail. Flat color is best when laid out in reasonably large areas in solid or screened tones to contrast with nearby type or art.

Newspapers printed by offset lithography get better results with color than newspapers printed by letterpress. Perhaps the best color to be found in any newspaper in America can be found in the Fairbanks, Alaska, *News-Miner*, a small offset daily.

The horizontal look

Until recent years the vertical look predominated among newspapers. Single-column, multiple-deck headlines plunged deep into each page, while unbroken black lines fenced off each column from its neighbor. Today on an increasing percentage of papers, the horizontal look prevails.

The first break with the past came with the extension of headlines across one column and into the next. Not only were multi-column heds better looking; they were also more readable. That the headline writer had more space to work with meant he could avoid some of the headline clichés—those miserable three-, four-, and five-letter words that only a deskman could love.

Another break came with the elimination of column rules. They had made pages monotonously vertical. But it was impossible to eliminate column rules without adding extra white space. Without rules, you needed as much as a full pica of space between columns. Otherwise, you sometimes had more space between words than you had between columns.

Where was the extra space to come from? Newspapers couldn't very well make their pages wider. Nor could they make their columns narrower. Columns were too narrow as it was. The standard column measured out at 11 or 12 picas, too narrow for good readability, even with copy set in small news type. Two Minnesota psychiatrists showed that columns set in 7- or 8-point types, common then, would be more readable if the columns were 15 or even 18 picas wide. Yet at the close of World War II, publishers, facing rising newsprint costs, trimmed another pica from their narrow columns. (It was a painless way to raise advertising rates; a column inch was still a column inch, even when it took up less space.) To compound the felony against readability, they increased body type size to 9 points.

The logical step was to cut down on the number of columns —from nine or eight columns to seven or six. Edmund Arnold saw value in the "7½" format, in which one column was slightly wider than the other six. The slightly wider column could be used for a feature column or a news roundup. Eventually publishers bought the idea of the wide column for newspapers. Today the six-column format is common.

The case for wider columns

It would be a mistake to write off the narrow column altogether. Under some circumstances, in limited doses, the narrow column serves the reader well, especially when it is set with an unjustified right edge.[4] But when columns stretch from top of page to bottom, row on row, page after page, narrow measure puts too much of a burden on the reader.

It holds him back.

A recent study conducted by Jack Nuchols, Jr., working under the direction of J. K. Hvistendahl, associate professor of journalism at South Dakota State University, showed that 9-point Imperial, a news face, could be read 4.1 percent faster in a 15-pica width than in an 11-pica width.

Moreover, narrow columns take longer to set. Albert Leicht, also working under the direction of Professor Hvistendahl, found that Linotype operators, using the same face, could set matter with 15-pica lines 35 percent faster than matter with 11-pica lines.

An editorial cartoon doesn't need labels and doesn't even need a caption to get its point across. This Eugene, Oreg., Register-Guard cartoon, drawn by the author, shows Richard Nixon's predicament with the peace movement at the beginning of the 1970s. A line drawing done for line reproduction. Zip-A-Tone was used for the pattern in Nixon's suit.

4. Cf. the 4-column-page design used in *Fell's Guide to Commercial Art* (Frederick Fell, Inc., New York, 1966), co-authored by this writer and Byron Ferris.

Wider columns mean fewer lines, less hyphenation at the ends of lines, and more consistent spacing between words.

Of all the suggestions for improvement of newspaper format made in recent years by Arnold, Hvistendahl, and others, the wide column stands the best chance for universal adoption. Despite what Arnold calls "the reluctance of the industry as a whole to break out of timeworn habit," newspapers one by one are adopting a six-column format for the regular eight-column-size sheet. The *Wall Street Journal* has long used the wide-column, six-column format. The *National Observer* chose the format when it started in 1961. The Louisville *Courier-Journal* and the Los Angeles *Times* have recently made the conversion.[5]

Two problems must be solved before the wide-column format really takes hold: The wire services will have to make available TTS tapes that will set 15-pica lines, and advertising agencies will have to adopt a new set of standard widths for advertisements.

The case for unjustified lines

In his first few years of teaching, this writer worked a great deal with high school journalists and teachers, many from small-town schools that could afford to produce only mimeographed newspapers. The young editors attached to these publications felt cheated, somehow; oh how they envied their peers at larger institutions who directed more glamorous offset or letterpress operations! Grimly they did what they could to make the mimeographed product look "printed." For one thing they insisted on justified body copy for all their stories.

This meant typing each column twice. On the first round, the typist carried each line as close to the maximum width as possible, filling in the end of the line with x's. She counted the number of x's for each line, then, on the second round, put the required number of extra spaces between words. The copy for these papers was typed in the same narrow measure newspapers used.

It was a senseless procedure, of course. It took far too much time. And the finished product was the worse for it.

The young editors could not accept the fact that ordinary typewriters are not flexible enough to produce natural-looking justified lines. Nor could they see that the 10- or 12-point typewriter typefaces (elite or pica) were too large for their narrow columns. They made a mistake all too common in the graphic

5. J. Clark Samuel, editor of the Foxboro, Mass., *Reporter*, a weekly, wrote to *The American Press*, January 1966 to point out that, so far as he knows, his paper has used the six-column format since its founding in 1884.

arts: they tried to make one medium fit the mold of another.[6]

Ironically, while the young editors were trying to emulate regular printed newspapers by justifying their columns, regular printed newspapers for their news columns were toying with the idea, already established in advertising, of ragged right edges.

The advantages of unjustified lines appear to be these: complete consistency of spacing between words, less need for hyphenation at ends of lines, less chance of the reader's "losing his place" as he moves from line to line, less expense in setting copy and making corrections. Research has not confirmed all these advantages, but Professor Hvistendahl, one of the few men to do any work in this area, suggests that you can read unjustified lines "a little faster" than you can read justified lines. But when you call the lack of justification to the attention of the reader, he is likely to say he prefers the lines justified.

The look of the future

Newspaper design will change as newspapering itself changes. TV will help. Most journalists admit now that the electronics media do a better job with spot news than the print media. The trend in newspapers will have to be away from the "what" to the "why." TV whets the appetite; newspapers deliver the details, the background. The interpretive newspaper will dispense with the hodgepodge and take on more and more the look of the magazine. Better design.

But change comes slowly.

Writes Clive Irving in the *Penrose Annual* 1967: ". . . Printing advances are being introduced whose potential is not even recognized [by newspapers] let alone exploited." Editors use offset and phototypesetting to produce papers that look just like the old standby letterpress papers. "Yet the mechanical restraints imposed by the use of hot metal and rotary presses are no longer there. The prison door has been opened but the prisoner refuses to leave the cell."

He adds: "Newspapers at the moment are a technically underdeveloped resource. Their place in life is so important that this neglect jeopardizes not only them, but the health of society."

It is easy to criticize the newspaper look of the 1970s. It is

---

6. The author is not above making the same mistake. As an artist for a high school newspaper in the days of linoleum block printing, he did everything he could—including the heating of the linoleum to make cutting easier—to make the block look like a regular line engraving. He failed to realize the inherent crude, strong, black look of a linoleum block could be the look of graphic art of a high order.

A swearing-in ceremony does not offer much chance for innovative photography. Nor would Eugene, Oreg., Register-Guard Photographer Paul Petersen place this shot among his best photographs. But compared to what an unimaginative photographer would do with an assignment like this, Petersen's photograph is a nicely designed piece of art.

not so easy to come up with anything more than superficial advice on how to change that look.

Perhaps the following three suggestions are not wholly practical, but it seems to this observer that if they were adopted newspapers would, in the phrasing of Clive Irving, "move from the Stone Age to the Space Age."

First, *the package itself—the size—must change.* The standard broadside newspaper (roughly 15" x 23") is too big for consecutive page design.[7] The tabloid size (half the regular size) provides a much more workable format. Unfortunately, we associate the tabloid with the cheap and sensational New York journalism of the 1920s: the *Graphic*, the *Mirror*, the *Daily News*. But you can't eschew a good thing just because someone in the past has misused it. It would be like abandoning the word "freedom" to the John Birch Society.

Among the more respected newspapers to use the tabloid format are the Chicago *Sun-Times* and Long Island's *Newsday*.

7. The oversize newspaper page was originally a tax dodge. Beginning in 1712 British papers were taxed by the page. Taxes eventually disappeared, but by then editors and readers had gotten used to the oversize page.

The latter, with a clean, crisp look and handsome typography (Century heds and Century Schoolbook body copy), is one of the nation's best-designed newspapers.

By 1970 fifty-five of the dailies and hundreds of the weeklies were tabloids. They enjoy an advantage over their full-size competitors in that they need to display fewer items on each page. Fewer items mean better organization.

Where a full-size newspaper has from six to eight columns per page, a tabloid has four or five.

A variation of the tabloid format is seen in *Rolling Stone*, which folds a second time—to a smaller size. This is to ensure itself a place on newsstands where space is at a premium. And it gives *Rolling Stone* a front page much like a magazine's.

Some advertisers who like full pages have raised objections to the tabloid format. You don't get the impact of a broadside, they say. But the *Reader's Digest* has shown repeatedly that in magazine formats full pages draw as well in pocket size as in *Life*-size. A full page is a full page is a full page.

Second, *ads must be arranged in solid blocks*. No more stacking them in half pyramids to put each "next to reading matter." News holes must be kept as horizontal or vertical rectangles, so that the designer will have a better field in which to arrange the elements. Another advantage of the tabloid is that it allows fewer ads per page: there is less need then for pyramiding them.

It should not be necessary to vary the weight of the headline according to the length of the story. A same-size headline face in several column widths is variety enough. Additional variety can be achieved through picture sizes and shapes, placement of white space, use of horizontal lines.

Nor should headlines be subject to arbitrary editorial rules that say they must always have a subject and a predicate, be written in present tense, be free of words like "and" or "the," and so on.

Finally, *hed schedules as drawn up by most newspapers must be abandoned*. Headlines should not be written to fit a space; they should be written to be appropriate to the stories. Lines should not be separated according to count; they should be separated according to sense. If that means a one- or two-word line followed by a six-word line, so be it. Better yet, put the whole headline into a single line.

Suggested further reading

ALLEN, JOHN E., *Newspaper Designing*, Harper & Brothers, Publishers, New York, 1947.

ARNOLD, EDMUND C., *Functional Newspaper Design*, Harper & Brothers, Publishers, New York, 1956.

————, *Modern Newspaper Design*, Harper & Row, Publishers, New York, 1969.

BASKETTE, FLOYD K., AND SISSORS, JACK Z., *The Art of Editing*, Macmillan Company, New York, 1971. (Some material on newspaper makeup)

BUSH, CHILTON R., ed., *News Research for Better Newspapers*, American Newspaper Publishers Association Foundation, New York. (Annual publication of research findings, some of which involve makeup and typography. Since 1966.)

CROWELL, ALFRED A., *Creative News Editing*, Wm. C. Brown Company Publishers, Dubuque, Iowa, 1969.

GILMORE, GENE, AND ROOT, ROBERT, *Modern Newspaper Editing*, Glendessary Press, Inc., Berkeley, Calif., 1971.

HULTENG, JOHN L., AND NELSON, ROY PAUL, *The Fourth Estate: An Informal Appraisal of the News and Opinion Media*, Harper & Row, Publishers, New York, 1971. (Chapters 2, 8, and 9)

HUTT, ALLEN, *Newspaper Design*, Oxford University Press, New York, 1967. (Second Edition)

HVISTENDAHL, J. K., ed., *Producing the Duplicated Newspaper*, Iowa State University Press, Ames, Iowa, 1966. (Second Edition)

MACDOUGALL, CURTIS D., *News Pictures Fit to Print—Or Are They?* Oklahoma State University Press, Stillwater, Okla., 1971.

SUTTON, ALBERT A., *Design and Makeup of the Newspaper*, Prentice-Hall, Inc., New York, 1948.

WOODS, ALLAN, *Modern Newspaper Production*, Harper & Row, Publishers, New York, 1963.

Chapter 11
Book design

This final chapter will attempt to cover some of the fundamentals of book design, production, and illustration. The reader who wants to get into this subject in depth will find an abundance of literature, more by far than for magazine and newspaper design, for the bibliophile has perhaps commanded more attention than he deserves from the book publishing industry. A once-a-month column on "Bookmaking" in *Publishers' Weekly* is especially instructive.

Understanding book publishing

To be effective the book designer should have some understanding of the book publishing industry and how it operates.

Think of a book publisher as essentially a middleman between the writer and his audience. It is the book publisher who arranges the details of publication and distribution of the manuscript and who finances the project. His job is to make money for both himself and the writer.

Under the standard contract between writer and publisher, the writer gets 10 percent of the retail price of every book sold, a little more if the book goes into high sales figures. The other 90 percent is used to pay for the editing, design, production, printing, promotion, and distribution of the book, and other business expenses, and to provide some profit to the publisher.

More disorganized, more hazardous than most businesses, book publishing is unique in that its product constantly changes. Each book published—some houses publish 600 or 700 titles a year—must be separately designed, produced, and promoted.

The book publishing industry tends to divide most of its output into two broad categories: tradebooks and textbooks.

Textbooks are those volumes, mostly nonfiction, published to meet the specific needs of students at all levels. Sales depend upon adoptions by teachers, departments, and boards of education. Tradebooks include most other books, fiction as well as nonfiction. They do not serve a captive audience; sales must be made on an individual basis, and they often depend upon impulse buying. For this reason, tradebooks, unlike textbooks, require jackets as an aid in selling. Sales are made through retail stores, through mail order, through book clubs. The markup on tradebooks is usually 40 percent, twice the markup on textbooks.

Reference books (dictionaries and encyclopedias) and children's books ("juveniles," as the trade calls them) are in categories of their own. They require different kinds of selling methods and different design and production approaches, too.

Some publishers specialize in one kind of book, some in another; and some publishers produce books in all categories. Several hundred book publishers in the United States produce between them more than 30,000 different titles each year.

In the early years of book publishing, the publisher, printer, and seller were one and the same. As the industry grew, each became a business by itself. Today few publishers do their own printing; and, except for mail order sales, the retailing of books is also a separate business.

The reappearance of design

Although good design was very much a part of early books, it was forgotten as books became more readily available to the masses. Mechanical typesetting equipment and a great variety of new—and mostly vulgar—typefaces in the nineteenth century were partly to blame. Near the turn of the century, one man in England, William Morris, fighting the trend, revived the earlier roman types and brought hand craftsmanship back into vogue. But only a few books were affected. W. A. Dwiggins in 1920 observed that "All books of the present day are badly made. . . . The book publishing industry has depraved the taste of the public."

But design was returning to books. In England, men like Eric Gill, and in America, men like Daniel Berkeley Updike, Bruce Rogers, Will Bradley, Merle Armitage, and Thomas Maitland Cleland, restored bookmaking to the high art it once had been. Dwiggins himself became a design consultant to Alfred A. Knopf, a publisher who then and now has produced some of America's finest books, from the standpoint both of content and design. Adrian Wilson calls Knopf "perhaps the greatest influence on the making of books in America after World War I." From 1926 to 1956 Dwiggins designed an average of ten books a year for the publisher. "His salty typography and ornament were additional hallmarks of the Knopf firm, the assurance of an inviting page and pleasurable reading."[1] Others who designed for Knopf were Warren Chappell, Herbert Bayer, Rudolf Ruzicka, and George Salter.

These designers combined classic roman faces with appropriate decorative borders. In the meanwhile in Germany the Bauhaus, before Hitler moved in and shut it down, developed a revolutionary concept in graphic design: "Form follows function." Gone were the flourishes. In their place: a stark, highly organized, geometric look. It was a look that, applied to books, had a beauty that seemed particularly appropriate to the times.

Still, to most publishers of popular books, design was not much of a consideration. In more expensive books, design played a role, but often it looked as if it were an afterthought, something tacked on just before the book went to press. For many books, no one designer took charge. "If the carpenter still determined our architecture, what would our buildings be like?" asked the book designer Ralph E. Eckerstrom in 1953.

With the coming of television, with increased competition from other media, with a growing appreciation of visual beauty even among the less sophisticated book buyers, this changed. Textbooks, especially, took on a more exciting look both outside and in. One reason textbook publishers were willing to devote extra effort to design was that mass adoptions of these books were often dependent on their appearance. Futhermore, the average textbook enjoyed greater total sales than the average tradebook, so more could be spent in anticipation of sales.

Some of the best design was found in the product of the university presses. Feeling less pressure than commercial publishers felt to show a profit, they could afford to devote a larger percentage of their budgets to the design and printing of their books.

Does design spur the sale of a book? Probably not, admits Marshall Lee, a book design and production specialist. But poor design can hurt sales. "The general public's reaction to book design is, in most cases, subconscious," he writes. "Except where the visual aspect is spectacular, the nonprofessional browser is aware of only a general sense of pleasure or satisfaction in the presence of a well-designed book and a vague feeling of irritation when confronted by a badly designed one."[2]

1. Adrian Wilson, *The Design of Books*, Reinhold Publishing Corporation, New York, 1967, p. 23.
2. Marshall Lee, *Bookmaking: The Illustrated Guide to Design and Production*, R. R. Bowker Co., New York, 1965, p. 13.

Who does the design?

Only the large houses, those publishing more than 100 books a year, seem willing to employ full-time art directors and designers. Some houses don't even have production departments, turning that job over instead to independent shops and studios.

Some houses—Alfred A. Knopf is one—use the same designer or group of designers to develop a "house style," making books from that house easily recognizable.

The typical book designer, though, is a free-lancer who works for a number of houses. He may design a book for as little as $100. For a jacket, a designer sometimes gets even less. The book publishing industry is not noted for its lush commissions to free-lancers. But there is a satisfaction in this work, designers tell themselves, that can't be had in the much higher paid area of advertising or even in the slightly higher paid field of magazine journalism.

The designer's approach

There are two basic approaches to book design (and this is true, really, of all graphic design). One is the *transparent* approach (Marshall Lee's term), where the design does not intrude. The designer makes reading as effortless as possible.

The other is the *mood* approach, in which the designer sets a stage for the reader. His choice of typefaces and illustrations amplifies what is in the text. In some cases, they call attention to themselves. Obviously, this second approach is the more

A spread from Robert L. Tyler's Rebels of the Woods: The I.W.W. in the Pacific Northwest. *Designer Douglas Lynch chose a condensed sans serif type for his chapter headings to give them the feel of newspaper headlines. Note his use of a vertical axis and short, heavy horizontal rule. (Reproduced with the permission of University of Oregon Books.)*

spectacular, perhaps even the more desirable. But it has to be good. The designer has to know what he's doing.

The first approach is safer. The second approach—more fun.

When dealing with mood, the designer takes into account not only the subject matter but also the nature of the audience. Certain typefaces, he knows, are more appropriate for children than for adults (although, ironically, it is the child, whose eyes see best, who gets the larger, bolder faces). The kind of picture used depends to a large extent on the kind of reader the book seeks to reach.

Some of the best design in publishing—certainly some of the best art—can be found in children's books. That children may not appreciate all this—may miss some of it—is beside the point. It is the adult, after all, who decides which children's book to buy.

The designer is particularly concerned about unity for his book. He achieves unity by sticking to the same typeface throughout, preferably for both titles and text; using the same "sink" for the beginning of each chapter; placing the page numbers and running heads at the same spot on each page; and establishing a standard copy area and sticking to it throughout the book. He should insist that the printer honor his placements and measurements. He asks for perfect backup. This means a reader (if he has nothing better to do) should be able to stick a pin through the printed book at either bottom corner of the copy block on an opening page and have the copy blocks on all other pages line up perfectly with the hole.

Production and the book designer

On magazines the art director turns over the more routine chores to a production editor who follows through on fitting type, ordering halftones, and doing pasteups. In book publishing, the art director—let's call him the designer—plays a more subservient role. Often a production editor hires the designer and supervises his work.

The production editor, along with the editor himself, imposes upon the designer a number of limitations: a proposed number of pages for the printed book, some art that will have to be included, a budget. The designer goes to work from there.

If he's good, and if the editors have confidence in him, he can argue successfully for changes. Sometimes the designer is in on planning of the book. In a few cases, the book is designed first and the text then written to fit, or the design evolves as the book is written. A few books—juveniles and art books—are written, designed, and even illustrated by the same person.

In the course of his work the designer soon becomes an expert in production, if he wasn't one to begin with. Especially he learns how to cut costs—without lowering the quality of the book. He finds, for instance, that he can produce clean, simple pages and in the process cut typesetting and composition costs. By confining color and art to certain signatures, by slightly altering page size, by omitting head and tailbands (they pretty a book a bit but add nothing to the strength of the binding), by having process color reproductions tipped on rather than printed on the signatures, by avoiding multiple widths of the text, by changing from letterpress to offset and from hot type to cold type—by doing many of these things he finds he can save his publisher money and still produce a handsome book.

Ernst Reichl of Ernst Reichl Associates has observed that a book designer more than pays for himself in that "the charge for design, measured against the plant cost (composition and plates) of a book, is extremely small; and a well-planned book costs so much less to produce than an unplanned one. . . . [The designer's] most obvious value is that of a safeguard against unpleasant surprises."

The time needed for putting a book through production varies from as little as three weeks, for "instant" paperbacks based on news or special events, to six months, for complicated picture books. Of course, for the author, the time lag is more; because before the production department gets the job, the manuscript has to be accepted, approved, and copyread— processes that can take more time than production takes.

The look of the book

So far as the designer is concerned, the book represents a problem with several possible solutions. Ideally he tries them all, then chooses the solution that seems to work best, bearing in mind the theme of the book, the nature of the book's audience, and the method by which the book will be sold.

If the book is to sell mainly in bookstores, it should have an attractive jacket, a thick or hefty appearance, and, if possible, lots of pictures. If it is a gift book, it should look large and expensive, even if it isn't. If it is a mail order book, it should be printed on lightweight paper, to save postage costs. If it is designed primarily for library sales, it should have a strong binding. If it is a textbook for elementary and high school use, it should have lots of color.

In choosing typefaces and illustrations the designer should avoid satisfying his own taste at the expense of what the author's approach calls for. The design should be appropriate to the book.

In every case, the designer reads the manuscript rather carefully before starting his design. He must stay within his budget, but at the early stages he can forget the budget and come up

with the ideal solution even though it is beyond what the budget can support. He can then modify the design to fit the
budget.

The lineup of book pages

Once in a while a designer gets a book like Stephen Schneck's
The Night Clerk (Grove Press, 1965) to design. That book
started right out on page 9, in the middle of a sentence. People
who bought the book thought they had defective copies. The
publisher had to send a notice around to booksellers assuring
them the book was meant to be that way.

The usual book is a little more logically planned. In fact, the
lineup of pages stays pretty much the same, book after book.

Here's the lineup of pages for a nonfiction book:

"Half" title (this page goes back to the time when books
were sold without covers; the real title page was thus protected).

Advertising card (list of the author's previous works or of
other books in the series).

Title.

Copyright notice and catalog number.

Dedication.

Acknowledgments (or they can follow the table of contents).

Preface or foreword (it's a preface if written by the author,
a foreword if written by someone else).

Table of contents.

List of illustrations.

Introduction (or it can follow the second "half" title).

Second "half" title.

Chapter 1.

Additional chapters.

Appendix.

Footnotes (if not incorporated into the text).

Bibliography (or it can follow the glossary).

Glossary.

Index.

Colophon (a paragraph or two giving design and production
details about the book).

This list does not take into account blank pages in the front
and back of the book. Nor does it show whether these are left-
or right-hand pages. Customarily, main pages, like the title
pages, are given right-hand placement.

Up through the second "half" title page, the numbering system used is small roman. From chapter 1 (or from the introduction, if it follows the second "half" title page) the numbering
is arabic.

How far to go

The designer does not design all the book's pages. That would be repetitious; most of the pages are essentially the same. He designs only the opening and strategic pages and sets basic standards for the others.

Among the pages he designs are the title, table of contents, a chapter opening, and two facing pages inside a chapter (to show how running heads, subheads, and page numbering will look).

The designer also provides the printer with a specification sheet on which he lists or describes the following:

1. trim size of pages,
2. size of margins,
3. size of copy area,
4. size and style of type and amount of leading,
5. amount of paragraph indentation,
6. handling of long quotes (set in different type or size? narrower width? centered or flush left or flush right?),
7. handling of footnotes,
8. size and placement of page numbers (folios),
9. handling of chapter titles, subheads, running heads, and initial letters,
10. amount of drop between chapter titles and beginnings of chapters,
11. handling of front matter, including title page and table of contents,
12. handling of back matter, including bibliography and index.

The printer goes ahead and sets some sample pages according to the designer's specifications to enable the designer to check them to make sure all instructions are understood, and that his design works. He can change his mind better at this point than after the entire book is set. The setting of the front matter of the book is deferred until last.

The necessary steps

The designer starts with a carbon copy of the manuscript. The first order of business is to "cast off"—count the number of words or, better, the number of characters in the manuscript and, using standard copyfitting techniques, determine how many pages of print the characters will occupy. The longer the manuscript, the more likely he is to choose a small typeface, but he does not go smaller than 10 point, unless he chooses to set the book in narrow columns. If the manuscript is short, he may use a larger face and more leading than usual, and he may choose a high-bulk paper to give extra thickness to the book. Whenever possible, he arranges the book so that the final number of pages, including front and back matter and blank pages, comes to a multiple of 32.

After the editor approves the designer's type selection and sample page layouts, the original manuscript, now copyread, goes to the printer or typographer for setting. When proofs are ready, the designer gets one set to use to prepare a dummy of the book. The extra number of pages remains somewhat flexible as he wrestles with fitting problems. He may have to increase or decrease some of his spacing in order to come out even on signatures. He may find it necessary to add or subtract a signature.

The designer prepares his dummy by cutting and pasting the proofs roughly into place, along with copy prints of the art. That's as far as he carries the pasteup, unless the book is to be printed offset or gravure; then he or someone in production does a camera-ready pasteup, using reproduction proofs rather than galley proofs. The dummy serves as a guide, then, either for the printer, if the book is letterpress, or for the pasteup man, if it is offset or gravure.

What role does the author have in all this? It depends upon the publisher. Obviously, most publishers prefer that their writers stay out of the process once the manuscripts are copyread. But many send sample designs and trial pages to the author to get his okay before the book is finally put on the presses.

Book paper

As much as 25 percent of the retail price of a book goes to pay for production and printing. According to an estimate by Marshall Lee, one-fifth of that 25 percent goes for paper.

More so than other designers, the book designer must know the special qualities of papers. Where a magazine designer usually needs to make a choice only once, the book designer must make a choice for every job. These are the four basic kinds of paper used for book printing:

1. *antique stock.* There are many textures, finishes, and weights, but essentially these papers are soft, rough, and absorbent. They are especially good for books made up wholly of text matter; that they are nonglare makes them easy on the eyes. For quality books, the designer may choose an antique stock with deckle edges.

2. *plate or English-finish stock.* Essentially, these are antique papers that have been smoothed out, making possible sharper reproduction, especially for pictures. Paper used for the big magazines falls into this category.

3. *coated stock.* Simple polishing (calendering) may not suffice to give the paper a finish that is smooth and slick

enough. The designer, then, can choose a coated stock, smooth to the feel, rich looking, and highly desirable where maximum fidelity is desired in picture reproduction. But coated stock is expensive.

4. *offset stock.* The offset printing process needs special papers that will resist moisture. (Offset, you'll remember, makes use of plates that carry both moisture and ink.) Were the paper not treated, it would stretch, shrink, and curl. Offset papers come in a variety of textures and finishes, but the most common is the rather smooth, severely white stock used for so many company magazines and for books that carry numerous halftones.

In addition to these basic papers the designer should familiarize himself with the special papers, including kraft, available for end sheets.

Doubleday once brought out a book, *The Sleeping Partner,* in a great variety of papers, a different one for each 32-page signature, causing William Jovanovich, president of Harcourt, Brace & World (now Harcourt Brace Jovanovich) to remark: "This is, no doubt, a way to clear out one's inventory in the name of Art."

Book page sizes

These days books come in a greater variety of sizes than ever, but the most common trim sizes still are 5⅜"x8", 5½"x8¼", and 6⅛"x9¼". Mass paperbacks come usually in 4⅛"x 6⅜" or 4⅛"x7" sizes. As in magazine publishing, there is a trend toward the square format, especially for volumes dealing with the fine arts.

As for all printing, the designer should check with his printer on paper sizes available and choose a page size that can be cut with a minimum of waste.

Establishing the margins

It may not seem that way, but the nontype area of a book—the white space—accounts for close to 50 percent of the total area. For art books and highly designed books, white space may account for as much as 75 percent of the total area.

Where he puts this white space counts heavily in the designer's thinking. For his all-type pages, he concentrates white space on the outside edges of his spreads, but not in equal-width bands.

The idea is to arrange the copy on facing pages so that the pages will read as a unit. For the typical book the designer establishes margins that tend to push the copy area of the two pages together. Book margins are like magazine margins. The narrowest margin on each page is at the gutter (but the combined space at the gutter is usually wider than other margins). The margin increases at the top, increases more at the outside edge, and increases most at the bottom. The designer is careful to keep the margin at the gutter wide enough (never less than ⅝" for books in the 6"x9" range) so that the type does not merge into the gutter when the book is bound. When he runs a headline or title across the gutter, he leaves a little extra space at the gutter to take care of space lost in the binding.

Book typography

Typesetting may be done by one firm, photoengraving by another, printing by another, binding by another. It is the job of the book designer, working with the publisher's production department, to combine the various parts of the book into a unified whole.

By far his most critical decisions will be made over matters of typography. Hot type or cold type? Which faces? Which sizes? How much leading? What about placement and spacing? His decisions on type hinge upon his decisions regarding other production matters.

His showplace pages are the title page and the pages with chapter openings.

The trend is toward a two-page title spread. Why should the left-hand page be blank and the right-hand page be crowded with all the information that makes up a title page? The title, or elements of the title page, cross the gutter to unify the two pages. The effect is dramatic. It seems to say: "This book is important."

Type for the chapter headings usually matches the type for the title pages. The headings seldom go over 18 or 24 points, and often they are smaller. Small-size type displayed with plenty of white space has just as much impact as large-size type that is crowded.

Text type in books ranges from 8 points to 12 points, depending upon the width of the column, the length of the book, the face used (some faces have larger x-heights than others), the amount of leading between lines, and the age level of the reader.

The usual practice is to begin the opening paragraph flush left. Paragraph indentation starts with the second paragraph. The first paragraph is not indented because (1) the flush left arrangement looks more like a beginning and (2) the chapter title already serves as an arresting agent; an additional arresting agent—indentation—would be redundant. It is often the case that the paragraphs that follow subheads are not indented either.

At one time in book publishing it was popular—for some kinds of books it still is popular—to start first paragraphs of chapters with initial letters. Initial letters are usually larger than the type used for the chapter headings. The type style for the initials and for the headings should be the same.

For nonfiction books, and especially for textbooks, subheads are important. They help the reader organize the material as he reads. They also break up large areas of gray type into convenient takes.

Subheads are best when kept close to the size of the body type. Sometimes they are in bold face, sometimes in all caps, sometimes in italics. They should be accompanied by some extra white space (both above and below) to make them stand out.

The author of a book supplies subheads with his manuscript and usually establishes the level of importance for each. Subheads seldom have more than four levels of importance. The fewer the levels the better.

The designer determines the type size for each level. He often chooses to keep subheads all in the same size type, centering those of the first-level, running the second-level ones flush left, and indenting those of the third level. The fourth-level ones go in italics.

Sometimes the designer runs subheads at the side of rather than inside the text.

Book art

In the well-designed book the style of the art complements the style of typography. Boldface types; powerful art. Graceful types; fanciful art.

One style of art that made an impact on book design in the late 1800s and early 1900s was Art Nouveau. It was then as it is now in its revival a revolt against the classical style. Japanese in origin, it is traceable nevertheless to Aubrey Beardsley in England, its most notable exponent. More decorative than functional, Art Nouveau is a style marked more by pattern than outline, although its outline, too, is remarkable in its grace and precision.

An Art Nouveau painter who saw a close relationship between art and typography in books was Maurice Denis. He said: "A book ought to be a work of decoration and not a neutral vehicle for transmitting a text." He added: "For each emotion, each thought, there exists a plastic equivalent and a corresponding beauty."[3]

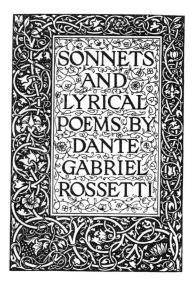

A title page designed by England's William Morris in 1894. Morris was influenced by the books of incunabula.

3. Quoted by John Lewis, *The Twentieth Century Book: Its Illustration and Design*, Reinhold Publishing Corporation, New York, 1967, p. 9.

Another art movement that influenced book design was German Expressionism with its rugged woodcut techniques. Such art when used in books invariably called for a heavy sans serif type face.

Impressionism, Surrealism, Pop Art—all the various art movements have had their influence on book illustration. And with today's printing techniques the designer is free to call in artists who work in any technique or any medium. Still, the predominant art form for books seems to be the line drawing done in the manner of Frederic Remington, Charles Dana Gibson, Howard Pyle, A. B. Frost, E. W. Kemble, and Rockwell Kent. One reason is that such art is the easiest to reproduce under any printing conditions.

In works of nonfiction, the photographer seems to have preempted the assignments from the illustrator, but perhaps not to the same degree as in newspaper and magazine publishing.

To give photographs and illustrations the display they need, the designer either bleeds them or places them next to white space. He does not crowd them up against copy blocks.

Where art occupies all or most of a page, he leaves off the page number and the running heads, because these tend to detract from the art. If he feels the paper used is not opaque enough, he may decide to leave blank the sheet backing the printed art.

As in magazine design, he usually sets the captions in a face different from the body copy. He lines the captions up with the edges of the pictures or with edges inside the pictures. The pictures and captions should look as if they belong together.

The binding

Books come in four kinds of bindings:

1. *Sewn binding.* For this kind of binding signatures are placed next to each other. They are not nested, as for saddle-stitched magazines. Open up a book and look at the binding from the top or bottom, and you can see how the signatures fit together.

Two kinds of sewing are available: (a) Smythe sewing, in which the sewing is done through the gutter of each signature and then across the back; and (b) side sewing (less common), in which the thread goes through the entire book about ⅛" from the back. A side-sewn book does not lie flat when opened. But the binding is sturdy. Libraries, when they find it necessary to rebind a book, frequently use side sewing.

2. *Stapled binding.* The staples can go in through the spine, if signatures are nested; or they can go in through the side. Such binding is reserved for low-budget books.

3. *Adhesive binding.* Sometimes called "perfect binding,"

A Will Bradley-designed page of 1896. Bradley was one of the American book designers influenced by William Morris.

this system brings together loose pages rather than signatures. The binding is accomplished by applying glue across the back. Cheap, mass audience paperbacks use this kind of binding. Unfortunately, the pages have a tendency to separate when subject to constant use.

4. *Mechanical binding.* The most common mechanical binding is *spiral binding*, in which loose pages are held together by a wire that spirals along a series of punched holes. The covers of such a book can be heavy paper, cardboard, or boards covered with paper. Pages can be torn out easily. With some mechanical bindings, new pages can be inserted. Mechanical binding is used for books with short press runs—books written for technical- or practical-minded audiences.

The first three binding processes—the main binding processes—can be used for paperback as well as hardbound books. Most hardbound books, however, come with sewn binding since it permits a book to lie flat when it is opened.

Designing the cover for a paperback is not unlike designing the jacket for a hard-cover book. Here are the front cover, back cover, and spine for The Tales of Rabbi Nachman *by Martin Buber (Discus Books, New York: Barbara Bertoli, art director). The publisher evidently feels that the name of the author, "one of the great thinkers of our time," is more important than the name of the book. Note that the designer has arranged his type and illustration on the front cover into a sort of an upside-down L, leaving one big area in white. The type and illustration form one unit. The original is in black, grayed red, and light olive.*

The cover

With the kind of binding decided, the designer of a hardbound book turns his attention to the cover.

The designer must decide whether he wants the boards of the cover to be wrapped fully in cloth, partially in cloth and partially in paper, or fully in paper. If the boards are to be wrapped in cloth, should the cloth be all of the same color and texture? Or should the designer seek a two-tone effect? And what color or colors should he use?

He must further decide whether the cover should be printed by offset or silk screen. Or should it be die stamped?

For many books the cover consists merely of wrapped boards with the name of the book, author, and publisher printed or stamped on the spine. But even that small amount of type should be coordinated with the other elements of the book.

The type used can be printed on the cover material before it is wrapped around the boards or stamped on afterwards.

For their cover material publishers once used animal skins —vellum or leather—but now they use cloth, vinyl, or paper. Cloth gained popularity as book cover material in the latter part of the nineteenth century. The cloth used today is often a cotton impregnated or coated with plastic. Paper became popular during World War II when cloth was scarce. The paper most commonly used is kraft.

The cloth, vinyl, or paper is wrapped around binder's board (found in most textbooks), chip board (found in cheaper books), pasted board (found in most trade books), or red board (found in limp books meant to be carried around in pockets).

To keep the top edges of the book's pages from soiling, the designer may decide to have them stained. He can choose a color that complements the endpapers.

Endpapers in hardbacks serve more of an aesthetic than structural purpose. Their main function is to hide folded cloth and stitching. Endpapers often are nothing more than tan kraft paper, but increasingly they have taken on color and even art.

For *sets* of books, hardbound as well as paperback, publishers often supply *slipcases*, which unite and encase the books, leaving only their spines exposed.

The cover for a *paperback* book represents a special challenge to the designer in that it is both a jacket and a cover. Because paperback sales are so dependent on impulse buying, paperback cover art must be particularly compelling. Like the jacket for a hardbound book, the cover for a paperback is as much an exercise in advertising design as in book design.

The jacket

Once he knows for sure how many pages the book will take, the designer asks for a bound dummy, with pages blank, so he can get the feel of the book and so the jacket designer can properly fit the jacket.

Books didn't always come with jackets. The introduction of modern distribution methods required that books be protected, and the idea of the "dust" jacket was born. At first the jacket was nothing more than a plain wrapper. It did not become a display piece until after World War I. Then it helped sell the book as well as protect it.

Publishers run off more jackets than are needed to cover their books; they use the extra copies for promotion and as replacements for jackets worn and torn in shipping and handling.

The quality paperbacks of the 1950s with their well-designed covers upgraded the design of jackets for hardbound books. But in 1965 David Dempsey, writing in *Saturday Review*, said the dust jacket was "still a poor relation" in the book publishing industry. He observed that only a small group of design studios did jackets; Paul Bacon, Push Pin Studios, Chammayeff & Geismar, and Janet Halverson among them.

The best-designed jackets, he observed, were to be found on first novels. The jackets for best sellers were less imaginative because they had to carry in large type both the name of the author and the title. That didn't leave much room for experimentation.

The typical jacket features the name of the book and the name of the author on the front; a picture of the author on the back; and a description of the book and biographical information about the author on the inside flaps. The names of the book, author (often last name only), and publisher run from left to right at the top of the spine, if the book is thick enough; if the book is too thin, the names run in a single sideways line, from top to bottom for books published in America, from bottom to top for books published in Great Britain.

A jacket should emphasize a single idea, reflect the mood or character of the book, and lure the reader inside. Sometimes the name of the author is featured most prominently, sometimes the name of the book.

A question of ethics comes in when the designer gives undue play to a popular earlier work of the author, perhaps deceiving the reader into thinking that is the work he is buying. Ethics also become involved when the designer uses an illustration that promises other than what the book actually delivers.

What we are talking about here, really, is advertising. That is what a jacket is: a piece of advertising. For that reason the designer of the book itself often has nothing to do with the design of the jacket. In purpose, it is design of a different order.

For one of his zany books Alexander King once got his publisher to wrap each copy with two jackets, an inner one, staid and conservative, and an outer one featuring one of his somewhat vulgar paintings. Tongue-in-cheek, he invited any reader who was easily offended to dispose of the outside jacket.

Alfred A. Knopf brought out Edward Luttwak's *Coup d'Etat* with jackets in two different color combinations: half the copies had one jacket, half the other. Booksellers were encouraged to make what in effect was a two-tone display of the books to help sell them.

Grove Press, for a novel called *Commander Amanda*, produced three different jackets, all designed by Kuhlman Associates. Sets were sent to booksellers; they were invited to pick the one they wanted on copies they would be selling. This involved booksellers in the book's production and presumably made them more interested in the book.

The designer may find that, except for the author's portrait, he doesn't need art for the jacket. Type alone, artfully arranged, or calligraphy, along with some color bands, perhaps, could do the job.

Most jackets come in black plus a second color. The black is for the author's portrait on the back. To save costs, some publishers run their jackets in a single color on a colored stock.

The paper used is coated or varnished only on the side on which the printing is done. The side next to the book itself is rough-finished so the jacket will cling to the book.

Janet Halverson's jacket for Joan Didion's novel about "an emotional drifter" who has played her various roles "to the sound of one hand clapping." In black, magenta, orange, and yellow. (Reprinted by permission of Janet Halverson and Farrar, Straus & Giroux, Inc.)

First things first

All of these considerations add to the reader's enjoyment of a book, but they are as nothing compared to the Big Three contributions the designer can make:

1. Picking a paper that does not bounce the light back into the reader's eyes.

2. Picking a typeface big enough so he can read without squinting.

3. Printing the text of the book far enough in from the gutter so he does not have to fight the binding to keep the book open.

Yearbooks

As a print medium, yearbooks fall somewhere in between magazines and books. Because they are permanently bound and because they serve both historical and reference purposes, they have many qualities of the book. But because they are issued periodically, they also fit the magazine category. Increasingly, they have taken on the look of the magazine.

Many kinds of organizations issue yearbooks, but schools and colleges make the most notable use of this medium. While interest in yearbooks may be waning in the large state universities, it continues strong in the smaller colleges, and especially in high schools, where students identify more with each other and their institutions. Most junior high schools and many elementary schools publish yearbooks, too.

The yearbook's main offering is the photograph: the informal shot, the group shot, the mug shot. Over the years as visual sophistication has increased, editors have given more attention to the informal shot, less to the group and mug shots. But they ignore the latter at the peril of decreased sales. Yearbooking these days turns out to be a constant battle between the editor's and designer's urge to be creative and the reader's desire to have an album of portraits he can file away for later perusal. There is room for experimental typography and design in the front of each book, of course, but the real challenge to the designer is to work out a readable, orderly, and attractive display of the routine lineup of same-size pictures in the back.

To arrange the large, dramatic, informal pictures in the front of the book, the typical yearbook designer draws inspiration from the picture magazines, especially *Life*. The look there is modular. The mood is one of excitement.

Often the designer works with some central theme chosen by the editor or his staff. The photographs, art, and copy are produced and selected to buttress the theme, sometimes unfortunately at the expense of readability. The better yearbooks, if they do adopt themes, work them in subtly. Editors of the top books realize that a theme is often a crutch, that design by itself can do much or more than a theme to unify a book.

Publication designers have a tendency to imitate one another; yearbook designers carry imitation to an extreme. Because most of the designers are inexperienced and unsure of themselves, they gather all the yearbooks from other schools they can get their hands on and study and borrow liberally from them. It is a sort of blind-leading-the-halt operation. If

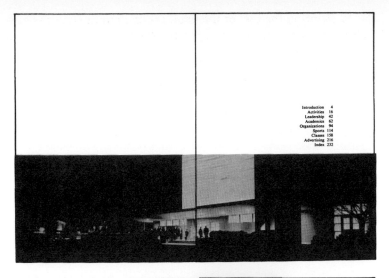

*High school yearbooks, long a
repository of examples of what
not to do in graphic design, have
in recent years become much
more design conscious. This is
the title page spread and a
spread from the introduction to
the* Eugenean, 1968, *award-win-
ning yearbook of South Eugene
High School, Eugene, Oreg.*

not that, they engage in wild typographic experiments that
succeed only in making the text difficult to read and the pictures hard to identify.

So the tendency to imitate the major magazines, when it
does occur, is encouraged by yearbook advisers and judges
of organizations that rate yearbooks.

The most common ailments in yearbooks, from the standpoint of design, are these:

1. "Clutterphobia." This comes about when the designer
is afraid to discard anything. "We used two pictures of the fall
term dance; we better use two from the winter term dance,
too." Or: "Here are fifteen pictures of the class play, and

they're all so *good!*" This condition can be cleared up when the designer adopts a policy of no more than two or three pictures per page. Mug shots, of course, are an exception.

2. "Myriad fever." "The printer has thirty-four typefaces; let's use one of each."

3. "Differentitis." The designer desperately wants his book to look different from last year's, so he distorts type, cuts pictures into strange shapes, and otherwise creates chaos on his pages. "There! They didn't do *that* last year!"

A summary

Art directors for yearbooks—and for other publications as well—resort to contortions in design when they forget the lesson that is central to this book: *content is more important than form.* The medium is *not*—or should not be—the message.

Readers do not buy publications to admire the versatility of their art directors. They buy publications so that they can be informed; they buy them for guidance; they buy them to relax with.

What they expect—what they must have—are headings and columns of type arranged for effortless assimilation, with large, clear pictures unencumbered by visual scars and typographic clutter.

What art directors must do, then, more than anything else, is make their publications useful to their readers. Design should help readers; it should not get in their way.

This is not to say that art directors should shy away from imaginative approaches. Far from it. It takes imagination— more of it—to truly organize the pages of a publication than merely to decorate them.

Suggested further reading

BAILEY, HERBERT S., JR., *The Art and Science of Book Publishing*, Harper & Row, Publishers, New York, 1970.

BENNETT, PAUL A., *Books and Printing: A Treasury for Typophiles*, Forum Books, World Publishing Co., Cleveland, 1963.

BLAND, DAVID, *A History of Book Illustration*, University of California Press, Berkeley, 1969. (Second Edition)

BREWER, FRANCES J., ed., *Essays on Book Illustration*, Verlag Gebr. Mann, Berlin, 1963.

COLBY, JEAN POINDEXTER, *Writing, Illustrating and Editing Children's Books*, Hastings House, Publishers, New York, 1966.

DAL, ERIK, *Scandinavian Bookmaking in the Twentieth Century*, University of Illinois Press, Urbana, 1968.

DAY, KENNETH, ed., *Book Typography 1810–1965: In Europe and the United States of America*, University of Chicago Press, Chicago, 1966.

GRANNIS, CHANDLER B., *What Happens in Book Publishing?* Columbia University Press, New York, 1967. (Second Edition)

HANSON, GLENN, *The Now Look in the Yearbook*, National Scholastic Press Association, Minneapolis, Minn., 1971.

HARROP, DOROTHY, *Modern Book Production*, Archon Books & Clive Bingley, Hamden, Conn., 1968.

JENNETT, SEAN, *The Making of Books*, Frederick A. Praeger, Inc., New York, 1967.

KLEMIN, DIANA, *The Art of Art for Children's Books*, Clarkson N. Potter, Inc., Publisher, New York, 1966.

———, *The Illustrated Book: Its Art and Craft*, Clarkson N. Potter, Inc., New York, 1970.

LEE, MARSHALL, *Bookmaking: The Illustrated Guide to Design and Production*, R. R. Bowker Company, New York, 1965.

LEE, MARSHALL, ed., *The Trial of 6 Designers: Designs for Kafka's The Trial by George Salter, P. J. Conkwright, Merle Armitage, Carle Zahn, Joseph Blumenthal, Marshall Lee*, Hammermill Paper Company, Lock Haven, Penna., 1968.

LEVARIE, NORMA, *The Art & History of Books*, James H. Heineman, Inc., New York, 1968.

LEWIS, JOHN, *The Twentieth Century Book: Its Illustration and Design*, Reinhold Publishing Corporation, New York, 1967.

MADISON, CHARLES A., *Book Publishing in America*, McGraw-Hill Book Co., New York, 1966.

SALTER, STEFAN, *From Cover to Cover: The Occasional Papers of a Book Designer*, Prentice-Hall, Englewood Cliffs, N.J., 1970.

SMITH, DATUS C., JR., *A Guide to Book-Publishing*, R. R. Bowker Company, New York, 1966.

WEIDEMANN, KURT, *Book Jackets & Record Covers: An International Survey*, Frederick A. Praeger, Inc., New York, 1969.

WILLIAMSON, HUGH, *Methods of Book Design*, Oxford University Press, New York, 1966. (Second Edition)

WILSON, ADRIAN, *The Design of Books*, Reinhold Publishing Corporation, New York, 1967.

Glossary

Terminology in journalism and art varies from publication to publication and from region to region. This glossary gives meanings of terms as the author uses them in the text and in his lectures.

abstract art   simplified art; art reduced to fundamental parts; art that makes its point with great subtlety. Opposite of realistic or representational art.

agate type   5½-point type.

airbrush   tool that uses compressed air to shoot a spray of water-color pigment on photographs or artwork. Used for retouching.

all caps   all-capital letters.

antique paper   rough finish, high-quality paper.

art   all pictorial matter in a publication: photographs, illustrations, cartoons, charts and graphs, etc.

Art Deco   the look of the 1920s and 1930s: simple line forms, geometric shapes, pastel colors, rainbow motifs.

art director   person in charge of all visual aspects of a publication, including typography.

art editor   see *art director*.

axis   imaginary line used to align visual elements and relate them.

back of the book   section of a magazine following the main articles and stories and consisting of continuations of articles and stories, ads, and filler material.

balance   stability in design; condition in which the various elements on a page or spread are at rest.

bank   see *deck*.

banner   main headline running across the top of a newspaper page.

bar chart   art that shows statistics in bars of various lengths.

Bauhaus   school of design in Germany (1919–1933). It championed a highly ordered, functional style in architecture and applied arts.

Ben Day   process by which engraver or printer adds pattern or tone to a line reproduction.

Bible paper   thin but opaque paper.

binding   that part of a magazine or book that holds the pages together.

bird's-eye view   view from above.

blackletter   close-fitting, bold, angular type that originated in Germany. Also known as *Old English* and *text*.

bleed   a picture printed to the edge of a sheet. Use also as a verb.

blind embossing   embossing without printing.

blueline   see *Vandyke*.

blurb   follow-up title for a magazine article, longer than the main title and in smaller type. Also, a title displayed on the cover. Also, copy on a book jacket.

blowup   enlargement. *Blow up* when used as a verb.

body copy   column or page of type of a relatively small size.

body type   type 12 points in size or smaller.

boldface type   black type.

bond paper   crisp paper used for business stationery, often with rag content.

book   bound publication of 48 pages or more, usually with a stiff or heavy cover. Some magazine editors call their publications *books*.

book paper   paper other than newsprint used in the printing of books and magazines. Includes many grades and finishes.

box   design element composed usually of 4 rules, with type or art inside.

brownline   see *Vandyke*.

by-line   the author's name set in type, usually over his story or article.

calender   to polish, as in the making of paper.

calligraphy   beautiful handwriting.

camera-ready copy   a pasteup ready to be photographed by the platemaker.

Camp   art so bad it's good.

caption   legend accompanying a photograph; newspapers use *cutlines*.

caricature   drawing of a person that exaggerates or distorts his features.

cartoon   humorous drawing, done usually in pen or brush and ink, or in washes.

cast off   estimate the amount of copy in a book. In magazines, it's *copyfit*.

center fold   center spread that opens out for two more pages.

center spread   two facing pages at the center of a magazine or newspaper.

character   any letter, number, punctuation mark, or space in printed matter.

circulation   number of copies sold or distributed.

cliché   something used too often, hence boring and no longer effective.

clip book   pages of stock art usually on slick paper, ready for photographing by the platemaker.

clip sheet   see *clip book*.

cold type   type composed by typewriter, paper pasteup, or photographic means.

collage   piece of art made by pasting various elements together.

colophon   paragraph or paragraphs of information about a book's design and typography, carried at the end of the book.

color separation   negative made from full-color art for use in making one of the plates.

column   section of a book's or magazine's text that runs from top to bottom of the page. Also, regular editorial feature in a newspaper or magazine, usually with a by-line.

column inch   area that is one column wide by one inch deep.

column rule   thin line separating columns of type.

combination cut   printing plate made from both a line and halftone negative.

comic strip   comic drawing or cartoon that appears in a newspaper on a regular basis as a series of panels.

commercial art   art prepared for editorial or advertising purposes, for any of the media.

comp   short for *comprehensive layout*.

compositor   craftsman who sets type.

comprehensive layout   layout finished to look almost as the printed piece will look.

condensed type   type series with narrow characters.

continuous tone art   photograph or painting or any piece of art in which tones merge gradually into one another. Requires halftone reproduction.

contrast   quality in design that permits one element to stand out clearly from others.

copy   article, story, or other written material either before or after it is set in type.

copy area   see *type page*.

copyedit   see *copyread*.

copyfit   estimate how much space copy will take when it is set in type.

copyread   check the manuscript to correct errors made by the writer or reporter.

copyright   protection available to the owner of a manuscript, piece of art, or publication, preventing others from making unfair use of it or profiting from it at the expense of the owner.

copywriting   writing copy for advertisements.

cover stock   heavy or thick paper used as covers for magazines or paperback books.

credit line   the photographer's name set in type, usually right next to his picture.

crop   cut away unwanted areas in a piece of art, usually by putting marks in the margins.

cut   art in plate form, ready to print. For the letterpress process.

cutlines   see *caption*.

deck   portion of a headline, consisting of lines set in the same size and style type.

deckle edge   ragged, feathery edge available in some of the quality paper stocks.

design   organization; plan and arrangement of visual elements. A broader term than *layout*. Use also as a verb.

designer   person who designs pages or spreads.

die-cut   hole or other cutout punched into heavy paper.

display type   type larger than 12-point, used for titles and headlines.

double truck   newspaper terminology for *spread*.

downstyle   style characterized by the use of lowercase letters wherever possible.

drop   see *sink*.

dropout halftone   see *highlight halftone*.

drybrush   rendering in which partially inked brush is pulled across rough-textured paper.

dummy   the pages of a magazine in its planning stage, often unbound, with features and pictures crudely sketched or roughly pasted into place.

duotone halftone printed in two inks, one dark (usually black), one lighter (any color).

duplicator machine that reproduces a limited number of copies of a publication. Large press runs require regular printing presses.

dust jacket see *jacket*.

ear paragraph, line, or box on either side of a newspaper's nameplate.

edit change, manage, or supervise for publication. Also, as a noun, short for *editorial*.

editing the process by which manuscripts and art are procured and made ready for publication.

edition part of the press run for a particular *issue* of a publication.

editorial short essay, usually unsigned, stating the stand of the publication on some current event or issue. Also used to designate the non-business side of a publication.

editorial cartoon single-panel cartoon of opinion found on the editorial page of a newspaper.

element copy, title or headline, art, rule or box, border, spot of color—anything to be printed on a page or spread.

em width of capital M in any typesize.

emboss print an image on paper and stamp it, too, so that it rises above the surface of the paper.

en width of capital N in any typesize.

endpapers sheets that help connect the inside front and back covers to the book proper.

English finish smooth finish. English-finish papers are widely used by magazines.

expanded type type series with wider-than-normal characters.

face style or variation of type.

family subdivision of a type race.

feature any story, article, editorial, column, or work of art in a publication. Also used as a verb: play up.

filler short paragraph or story used to fill a hole at the bottom of a column of type.

fine art art created primarily for aesthetic rather than commercial purposes.

fixative clear solution sprayed onto a drawing to keep it from smearing.

flag see *logo*.

flat color see *spot color*.

FlexForm ad newspaper ad in other than the usual square or rectangle shape.

flop change the facing of a picture. If a subject faces left in the original, he will face right in the printed version. Not a synonym for *reverse*.

flow chart art showing a manufacturing process.

flush-left aligned at the left-hand margin.

flush-left-and-right aligned at both the left- and right-hand margins.

flush-right aligned at the right-hand margin.

folio page number. Also, a sheet of paper folded once.

font complete set of type of a particular face and size.

foreshorten exaggerate the perspective.

format size, shape, and appearance of a publication.

formula editorial mix of a publication.

foundry type hand-set metal type.

fourth cover back cover of a magazine.

four-color   red, yellow, blue, and black used to produce effect of full color.

free-lancer   artist, photographer, designer, or writer called in to do an occasional job for a publication.

gag cartoon   humorous drawing, usually in a single panel, with caption, if there is one, set in type below.

galley   tray on which type is assembled and proofed.

galley proof   long sheet of paper containing a first printing from a tray of type.

gatefold   magazine cover that opens out to two additional pages.

gingerbread design   design with an overabundance of swirls and flourishes; cluttered design.

glossy print   photograph with shiny finish.

gothic   term applied in the past to various typefaces that have challenged the traditional. Currently, modern sans serifs.

graphic design   design of printed material.

graph   see *bar chart, line chart,* and *pie chart.* Also, short for *paragraph.*

gravure   method of printing from incised plate. For magazines, a rotary press is involved, hence *rotogravure.*

grid   carefully spaced vertical and horizontal lines that define areas in a layout; a plan for designing pages.

gutter   separation of two facing pages.

hairline   very thin rule or line.

halftone reproduction   process by which the printer gets the effect of continuous tone, as when he reproduces a photograph. It's done with dots.

hand lettering   lettering done with pen or brush.

head   short for *headline.*

headband   piece of rolled, striped cloth used at the top of the binding to give a finished look to the book.

heading   headline or title. Also, the standing title for a regular column or section in a publication.

headline   display type over a story, article, or editorial in a newspaper.

headline schedule   chart of different headline sizes and arrangements used by a newspaper.

hed   short for *head,* which is short for *heading* or *headline.* Mostly a newspaper term.

high Camp   see *Camp.*

highlight halftone   halftone in which some parts have been dropped out to show the white of the paper.

horizontal look   lines of type, rules, and art are arranged to make the page or spread look wide rather than deep.

hot type   type made from metal.

house ad   advertisement promoting the publication in which it appears.

house organ   publication of an organization or business released regularly for public relations reasons.

house style   style that is peculiar to a publisher or that remains the same from issue to issue or publication to publication.

illustration   drawing or painting.

illustration board   cardboard or heavy paperboard made for artists, available in various weights and finishes to take various art mediums.

incunabula   books printed before 1501.

index   alphabetical listing of important words and names in a book or magazine, accompanied by page numbers. Found in the back of the publication. The table of contents is found in the front.

India ink   drawing ink.

India paper   see *Bible paper*.

initial   first letter of a word at the beginning of an article or paragraph, set in display size to make it stand out.

intaglio   see *gravure*.

interabang   combination exclamation mark and question mark.

Intertype   linecasting machine similar to Linotype.

issue   all copies of a publication for a particular date. An issue may consist of several *editions*.

italic type   type that slants to the right.

jacket   paper cover that wraps around a book.

jump   continue on another page.

justify   align the type so it forms an even line on the right and the left.

keyline drawing   drawing done partly in outline to use in making plates for spot color printing.

kicker   short headline run above main headline, usually underscored.

kraft paper   heavy, rough, tough paper, usually tan in color.

lay out   put visual elements into a pleasing and readable arrangement.

layout   noun form of *lay out*.

lead   (pronounced *ledd*) put extra space between lines of type.

leading   extra space between lines of type.

legibility   quality in type that makes it easy for the reader to recognize individual letters.

letterpress   method of printing from a raised surface. The original and still widely used printing process.

letterspace   put extra space between letters.

letterspacing   extra space between letters.

libel   published defamatory statement or art that injures a person's reputation.

ligature   two or more characters on a single piece of type that join or overlap.

line art   in its original form, art without continuous tone, done in black ink on white paper. Also, such art after it is reproduced through *line reproduction*.

linecasting machine   see *Linotype* and *Intertype*.

line chart   art that shows trends in statistics through a line that rises or falls on a grid.

line conversion   continuous tone art that has been changed to line art.

line reproduction   process by which printer reproduces black-and-white drawing.

Linotype   linecasting machine that produces type for letterpress printing or type from which reproduction proofs can be pulled.

lithography   process of making prints from grease drawing on stone. See also *offset lithography*.

logo   short for *logotype*. The name of the publication as run on the cover and sometimes on the title or editorial page. On a newspaper it is called the *flag* or *nameplate*.

lowercase   small letters (as opposed to capital letters).

Ludlow   machine that casts lines of display-size letters from matrices that have been assembled by hand.

magazine   publication of eight pages or more, usually bound, that is issued at least twice a year. Also, storage unit for mats for linecasting machine.

mass media   units of communication: newspapers, magazines, television and radio stations, books, etc.

masthead   paragraph of information about the publication. It is run on an inside page, under the table of contents, for a magazine, and on the editorial page for a newspaper.

mat   short for *matrix*. Cardboard mold of plate, from which a copy can be made. Also, brass mold from which type can be cast.

matrix   see *mat*.

matte finish   dull finish.

measure   width of a line or column of type.

mechanical   see *camera-ready copy*.

mechanical spacing   non-adjusted spacing between letters; the opposite of *optical spacing*.

media   see *mass media*.

medium   singular for *media*. Also, paint, ink, or marking substance used in drawing or painting. In this context, the plural of medium is *mediums*.

modular design   highly ordered design, marked by regularity in spacing.

moiré   undesirable wavy or checkered pattern resulting when a halftone print is photographed through another screen.

Monotype   composing machine that casts individual letters. Used for quality composition.

montage   combination of photographs or drawings into a single unit.

mortise   a cut made into a picture to make room for type or another picture. Use also as a verb.

mug shot   portrait.

Multilith   duplicating or printing process similar to offset lithography, but on a small scale.

nameplate   see *logo*.

"new journalism"   journalism characterized by a highly personal, subjective style.

news hole   non-advertising space in a newspaper.

newsprint   low-quality paper lacking permanence, used for printing newspapers.

offset lithography   method of printing from flat surface, based on principle that grease and water don't mix. Commercial adaptation of *lithography*.

offset paper   book paper made especially for offset presses.

Old English   see *blackletter*.

Op Art   geometric art that capitalizes on optical illusions.

op-ed   short for "opposite the editorial page." The page across from the editorial page.

optical center   a point slightly above and to the left of the geometric center.

optical spacing   spacing in typesetting that takes into account the peculiarities of the letters, resulting in a more even look.

optical weight   the visual impact a given element makes on the reader.

organization chart   art that shows how various people or departments relate to each other.

overlay   sheet of transparent plastic placed over a drawing. The overlay contains art or type of its own for a plate that will be coordinated with the original plate.

page   one side of a sheet of paper.

page proof   proof of a page to be printed letterpress.

paginate   to number pages.

painting   illustration made with oil, acrylic, tempera, casein, or water color paints. Requires halftone reproduction; if color is to be retained, it requires process color plates.

paper stock   paper.

pastel colors   soft, weak colors.

pastel drawing   drawing made with color chalks.

pasteup   see *camera-ready copy.*

paste up   verb form for *pasteup.*

pencil drawing   drawing made with lead or graphite pencil. Usually requires halftone reproduction.

perspective   quality in a photograph or illustration that creates the illusion of distance.

photo essay   series of photographs that make a single point.

photocomposition   composition produced by photographic means.

photoengraving   cut or plate made for letterpress printing.

photojournalism   photography used in the mass media to report news, express opinion, or entertain.

photolettering   display type produced photographically.

pic   short for *picture.*

pica   12 points, or one-sixth of an inch.

pictograph   a chart or graph in picture form.

picture   photograph, drawing, or painting.

pie chart   art that shows statistics—usually percentages—as wedges in a pie or circle.

pix   plural for *pic.*

plate   piece of metal from which printing is done. See also *cut.*

point   unit of measurement for type; there are 72 points to an inch.

Pop Art   fine art inspired by comic strips and packages. See also *Camp.*

Pre-print   ad in a sort of wallpaper design printed in rotogravure in another plant for insertion in a letterpress newspaper.

press run   total number of copies printed during one printing.

printer   craftsman who makes up the forms or operates the presses.

printing   the act of duplicating pages and binding them into copies of publications.

process color   the effect of full color achieved through use of color separation plates; way to reproduce color photographs, paintings, and transparencies.

production   process that readies manuscripts and art for the printer. Can also include the typesetting and printing.

proofread   check galley and page proofs against the original copy to correct any mistakes the compositor made.

proportion   size relationship of one part of the design to the other parts.

psychedelic art   highly decorative art characterized by blobs of improbable colors, swirls, and contorted type and lettering.

publication   product of the printing press.

publishing   act of producing literature and journalism and making them available to the public.

race   major category of typefaces.

ragged left   aligned at the right but staggered at the left.

ragged right   aligned at the left but staggered at the right.

readability quality in type that makes it easy for the reader to move easily from word to word and line to line. In a broader sense, it is the quality in writing and design that makes it easy for the reader to understand the journalist.

readership number of readers of a publication. Larger than the *circulation*.

ream 500 sheets of printing paper.

register condition in printing in which various printing plates, properly adjusted, print exactly where they are supposed to print. Use also as a verb.

relief raised printing surface.

render execute, as in making a drawing.

repro short for *reproduction proof*.

reproduction a copy.

reproduction proof a carefully printed proof made from a galley, ready to paste down so it can be photographed.

retouch strengthen or change a photograph or negative through use of art techniques.

reverse white letters in a gray, black, or color area. Opposite of *surprint*. Mistakenly used for *flop*. Use also as a verb.

roman type type designed with thick and thin strokes and serifs. Some printers refer to any type that is standing upright (as opposed to type that slants) as "roman."

rotogravure see *gravure*.

rough in cartooning, the first crude sketch presented to an editor to convey the gag or editorial idea.

rough layout crude sketch, showing where type and art are to go.

rout cut away.

rule thin line used either horizontally or vertically to separate lines of display type or columns of copy.

run-in let the words follow naturally, in paragraph form.

running head heading that repeats itself, page after page.

saddle stitch binding made through the spine of a collection of nested signatures.

sans serif type typeface with strokes of equal or near-equal thicknesses and without serifs.

scale quality in a photograph or illustration that shows size relationships.

schlock vulgar, heavy, tasteless.

scratchboard drawing drawing made by scratching knife across a previously inked surface.

script type that looks like handwriting.

screen the concentration of dots used in the halftone process. The more dots, the finer the screen.

second color one color in addition to black or the basic color.

second cover inside front cover.

sequence series of related elements or pages arranged in logical order.

series subdivision of a type family.

serif small finishing stroke of a roman letter found at its terminals.

set solid set type without leading.

sidebar short story related to major story and run nearby.

side stitch stitch through side of publication while it is in closed position.

signature all the pages printed on both sides of a single sheet. The sheet is folded down to page size and trimmed. Signatures usually come in multiples of 16 pages. A magazine or book is usually made up of several signatures.

silhouette   art subject with background removed.

sink   distance from top of page to where chapter begins.

sinkage   see *sink*.

slab serif type   type designed with even-thickness strokes and heavy serifs. Sometimes called "square serif" type.

slick magazine   magazine printed on slick or glossy paper. Sometimes called simply "slick."

slug   line of type from linecasting machine. Also, 6-point spacing material.

slug line   significant word or phrase that identifies story. Found usually on galley proofs.

small caps   short for *small capitals*. Capital letters smaller than regular capital letters in that point size.

sort   what a printer calls a piece of type.

SpectaColor   ad printed in rotogravure in another plant for later insertion in a newspaper. Unlike a Pre-print ad, a SpectaColor ad has clearly defined margins.

spine   back cover of a book or magazine, where front and back covers join.

spot color   solid color used usually for accent. Less expensive, less involved than *process color*.

spot illustration   drawing that stands by itself, unrelated to the text, used as a filler or for decorative purposes.

spread   facing pages in a magazine.

stereotype   plate made from mat that in turn was made from photoengraving or type.

stock   paper or other material on which image is printed.

stock art   art created for general use and stored until ordered for a particular job.

straight matter   text that is uninterrupted by headings, tables, etc.

style   distinct and consistent approach to art or design.

subhead   short headline inside article or story. Also *subhed*.

surprint   black letters over gray area, as over a photograph. Opposite of *reverse*. Use also as verb.

swash caps   capital letters in some typefaces with extra flourishes in their strokes, usually in the italic versions.

swatch   color sample.

swipe file   artist's or designer's library of examples done by other artists, used for inspiration.

Swiss design   design characterized by clean, simple lines and shapes, highly ordered, with lots of white space; based on a grid system.

symmetric balance   balance achieved by equal weights and matching placement on either side of an imaginary center line.

table   list of names, titles, etc.

tabloid   newspaper with pages half the usual size.

tailband   piece of rolled, striped cloth used at the bottom of the binding to give a finished look to the book.

technique   way of achieving style or effect.

text   see *body copy*.

text type   see *blackletter*.

third cover   inside back cover.

thumbnail   very rough sketch in miniature.

tint   weaker version of tone or color.

tint block   panel of color or tone in which something else may be printed.

title   what goes over a story or article in a magazine. On a newspaper, the term is *headline*.

tombstone heads   same size and style headlines, side by side.

tone   the darkness of the art or type.

trade magazine   magazine published for persons in a trade, business, or profession.

transparency   in photography, a color positive on film rather than paper.

type   printed letters and characters. Also, the metal pieces from which the printing is done.

typeface   particular style or design of type.

type page   that part of the page in which type is printed, inside the margins. Sometimes called "copy area."

type specimens   samples of various typefaces available.

typo   typographic error made by the compositor.

typography   the type in a publication. Also, the art of designing and using type.

unity   design principle that holds that all elements should be related.

upper case   capital letters.

Vandyke   photographic proof from a negative of a page to be printed by the offset process. Sometimes called *brownline* or *blueline.*

Velox   photoprint with halftone dot pattern in place of continuous tone, ready for line reproduction.

vignette   oval-shaped halftone in which background fades away gradually all around.

visual   having to do with the eye.

visualization   the process by which an artist or designer changes an idea or concept into visual or pictorial form.

wash drawing   ink drawing shaded with black-and-white water color. Requires halftone reproduction.

white space   space on a page not occupied by type, pictures, or other elements.

widow   line of type less than the full width of the column.

woodcut   engraving cut in wood. Also, the impression made by such a plate.

worm's-eye view   view from low vantage point.

x-height   height of lowercase *x* in any typeface.

Zip-A-Tone   transparent sheet on which is printed a pattern of dots or lines. Fastened over part of line drawing, it gives the illusion of tone. See also *Ben Day.*

Index

The text and titles for this book
were set in Palatino,
a typeface designed by Hermann Zapf
and named after the sixteenth-century Italian calligrapher,
Giambattista Palatino.
Page numbers were set in Helvetica Bold.

The book was designed by the author.
In charge of production
was Ruth Richard.
The cameraman was Gerald Gourley.